THE SHAAR PRESS

THE JUDAICA IMPRINT
FOR THOUGHTFUL PEOPLE

The Gross Family Edition

תורת חיים

Wisdom for Living

Rabbi Noach Weinberg זצ"ל
on the Parashah

Adapted by

Rabbis Nechemia and **Yitzchak Coopersmith**

The Rabbi Noach Weinberg Legacy Series

Published by **SHAAR PRESS**
Distributed by MESORAH PUBLICATIONS, LTD.
4401 Second Avenue / Brooklyn, N.Y 11232 / (718) 921-9000

Distributed in Israel by SIFRIATI / A. GITLER
Moshav Magshimim / Israel

Distributed in Europe by LEHMANNS
Unit E, Viking Business Park, Rolling Mill Road / Jarrow, Tyne and Wear, NE32 3DP/ England

Distributed in Australia and New Zealand by GOLDS WORLD OF JUDAICA
3-13 William Street / Balaclava, Melbourne 3183 / Victoria Australia

Distributed in South Africa by KOLLEL BOOKSHOP
Northfield Centre / 17 Northfield Avenue / Glenhazel 2192, Johannesburg, South Africa

ISBN 10:1-4226-1578-2 / ISBN 13: 978-1-4226-1578-2

Printed in the United States of America
Custom bound by Sefercraft, Inc. / 4401 Second Avenue / Brooklyn N.Y. 11232

It is our privilege to dedicate
this sefer in honor of
the Bar Mitzvah of our eldest grandson

Shlomo Elimelech Gross
שלמה אלימלך נ״י

We had the *zechus* of hosting Rav Noach Weinberg, zt"l for many Shabbosos in our home. Over the years we discovered the secret to Rav Noach's drive and success: he truly loved every Jew!

The pain he felt over what was happening to *Klal Yisrael* was palpable, and changed our lives. He had a burning desire to save the Jewish people and mobilize an army of concerned Jews to feel that pain and reach out to their brothers and sisters.

Rav Noach would often say, "There is no end to what Jews would do to try and save their fellow Jews from the Nazis. We must be jolted into similar action today when we see millions of our brethren assimilating."

Eli, our dear grandson, you embody Rav Noach's trait of loving your fellow Jew. May Hashem enable you to continue along this path, and may your parents and the entire family continue to see much nachas from you.

Love
Zeidy Isaac and Bobby Edie Gross

APPROBATION

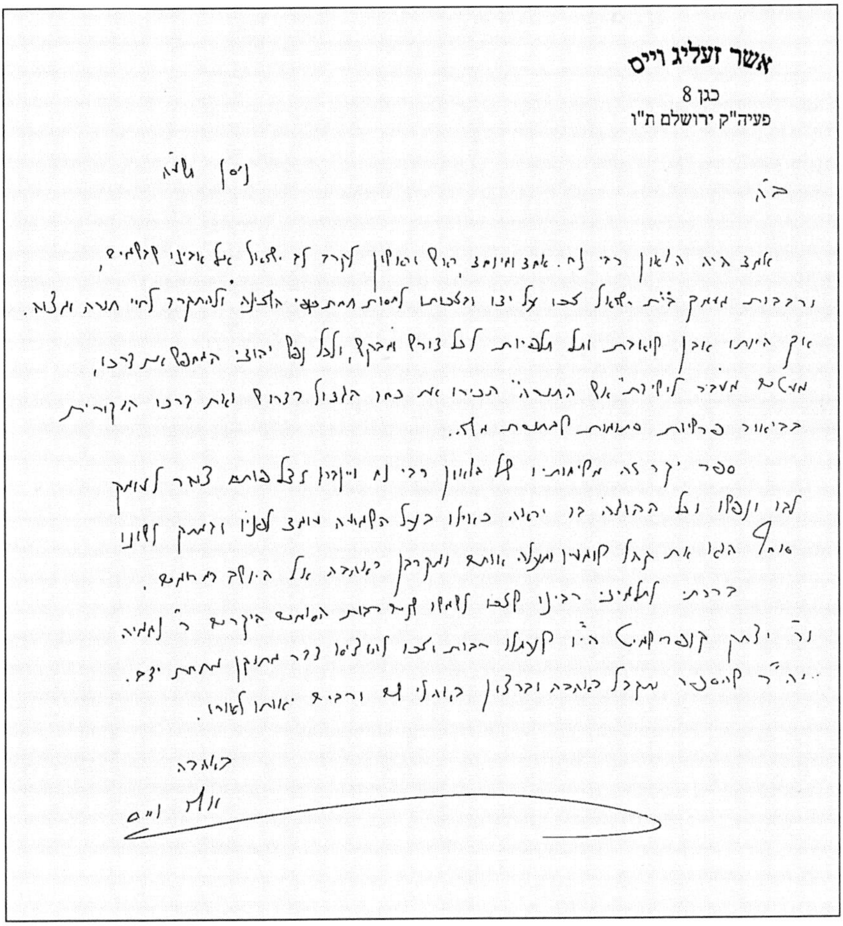
אשר זעליג וייס
כגן 8
פעיה"ק ירושלם ת"ו

HaGaon Rav Noach Weinberg was one of a kind. He was the trailblazer in bringing the Jewish people closer to their Father in Heaven.

Through Rav Weinberg's efforts, tens of thousands of Jews from around the world merited to bask in the glory of Hashem and to live a life of Torah and mitzvos.

He was a magnet and a leading figure for all those seeking truth and for every Jewish soul looking to find its way.

Few people outside of Aish HaTorah were exposed to the greatness of Rav Noach's educational methodologies and creative approaches to explaining difficult sections of Toras Moshe.

This valuable book of HaGaon Rav Noach Weinberg's discourses opens a window into the depth of his heart and soul. Anyone who studies it will feel as if Rav Noach himself is standing before him and with the sweetness of his words will be drawn closer to the One Who sits on high.

I offer my blessing to Rabbis Nechemia and Yitzchak Coopersmith, dedicated students of Rabbi Weinberg who merited to study under him for many years, who have invested much effort to produce this fine work.

May it be His will that this book be widely accepted with love and goodwill in the tents of Torah and that many walk in its light.

With love,
Asher Weiss

APPROBATION

תפארת גדליה

From the Desk of

RABBI AHRON LOPIANSKY

Rosh HaYeshiva

בס״ד

YGW When chancing upon a living person, we are struck twice. First, we notice the living person himself: the color in his face, the sparkle in his eyes, the spring in his step and the aura and glow that a living body possesses. But at second glance we are filled with much greater awe, realizing that this life force is not an innate characteristic of the flesh and blood, but something descending from without, and fusing so naturally with man that for a moment we had felt that the life force was the body itself!

Rav Noach zt"l was perhaps that very model of life itself. When you came into his presence, you felt that he was the totality of life: his warmth embraced you, his passion shook you to your core; and his joy and optimism lit up your soul. At second glance, you realized that this life force of his was the Torah that he carried in his mind and heart, and pumped him with a never-ending Divine Breath. For people who had never seen or heard Torah before, he showed them that "yes, there is an instruction manual" written by the Creator Himself. But he also had a message for those who were already following closely the manual's instruction; people who had the details right, but did not know what is it that the manual is guiding them to construct. Dispirited, they were attempting to build a body with no life force. And to these, his message was "Torah is life itself." If you are doing it correctly, then you too will flame with the energy of Torah. But if you are an apathetic shell, then you may have connected the pieces correctly — but you have not plugged in the electric cord!

Rav Noach's Torah was infused with life. You felt that he was right on in understanding the Torah, and right on in understanding life. I urge people to watch a video of him to catch some of that incredible life force that the written word cannot convey. Yet, despite the limitations of writing, the authors of this compilation have done a remarkable job of bringing together some of his most important teachings. They have made it clear and lucid without straying from the original intent. As you learn Rav Noach's Torah, keep in mind that it is being taught by someone who lived these words to their fullest; and when he spoke, he infused you with some of his own powerful life force. His words were not intended to entertain or satisfy intellectual curiosity; they were spoken in order to teach a way of life, for those so desperately seeking it.

Ahron Shraga Lopiansky

YESHIVA OF GREATER WASHINGTON - TIFERES GEDALIAH
1216 ARCOLA AVENUE, SILVER SPRING, MD 20902 ▪ 301·649·7077 ▪ WWW.YESHIVA.EDU

Table of Contents

ספר בראשית
Sefer Bereishis

*S*efer Shemos
ספר שמות

*S*efer Vayikra
ספר ויקרא

‮ספר במדבר‬
Sefer Bamidbar

ספר דברים
*S*efer Devarim

Preface

By Rabbi Yehuda Weinberg

"Many waters cannot extinguish the fire of love" (*Shir HaShirim* 8:7).

When my father, Rav Noach Weinberg zt"l, learned Torah, especially the Chumash, it was with the joy and passion of reading a love letter from Hashem.

The Sea of Torah is vast, but the source of it all, he would always remind us, is the Five Books of Torah. My beloved father drew an ocean of wisdom from every line of the Chumash. He would constantly remind us that the Torah is not a history book; it is a *Toras Chaim*, a treasure trove of wisdom for living. For my father, this was not just a statement; it was his all-encompassing way of life. The deep-seated satisfaction and delight he derived from learning and teaching *Toras Chaim* was "like a person who finds a great treasure" (*Tehillim* 119:162). He thirsted to share his prized riches with everyone, since nothing could be more precious than learning the Almighty's wisdom.

Every word of Torah is full of life and wisdom. My father's artistry was the ability to discover these lofty concepts and bring them down to earth in an interesting and exciting manner. He used the Chumash to bring the most distant Jews closer to Torah, following David Hamelech's prescription, "The Torah of Hashem is perfect, restoring the soul" (ibid 19:8). This was my father's life mission. He knew there is nothing more effective than Hashem's words to rejuvenate the soul, and he understood that the best way to reach the Jewish people was to connect them to the beauty, relevance, and wisdom of Torah, which contains everything we need to succeed in life.

One of my fondest memories as a child is seeing my father sitting for hours Shabbos afternoon learning Chumash, extracting endless wisdom like a person pumping water from a well. This is also the last memory I have of my father. The evening before he passed away, I came by to say goodnight. He was sick and very frail, but his mind was as strong as ever. I walked in and there he was, learning from his Chumash, using yet another opportunity to connect to Hashem and His Torah.

In my opinion, the revolution that my father started in the field of *kiruv* was in the merit of the special connection he had to *Toras Chaim*. It was the wisdom of Torah that forged his vibrant relationship with God, which led to the burning love and concern he felt for every single Jew. With every fiber of his being, my father undertook the responsibility to bring this precious *Toras Chaim* to every Jew. He felt the *tzaar haShechinah*, the pain and sadness of our Father in Heaven Who yearns to bring back and hold close each of His wayward children.

My father's students were like his own children, and he encouraged all of them to share their Torah wisdom. The book you have before you is the culmination of the great love my father had for Hashem, and the great love he had for his students. It has been prepared by his *talmidim*, who faithfully edited and adapted his *shiurim*. I am sure he is deriving enormous *nachas* in *Shamayim* seeing this book, which is based on his *shmuessen* and classes, made accessible to the wider public. Without a doubt his *neshamah* is having an *aliyah* through the learning of this *sefer*.

Yehuda ben HaRav Yisrael Noach Weinberg

Introduction

As *talmidim* in Yeshivas Aish HaTorah, the highlight of the week for us — as well as for all the students in the various programs, from the drop-in beginners' program to the *semichah* program — was 7:10 on Thursday night, when our Rosh Yeshivah, HaGaon HaRav Noach Weinberg zt"l, would give his *shmuess* on the *parashah*. The *beis midrash* was packed and the anticipation hung in the air as we waited eagerly to hear the penetrating insights of Rav Noach, our rebbi.

Rav Noach was a genius at uncovering the Torah's timeless wisdom and demonstrating how it addressed the issues of the day, with piercing clarity and relevance. He was a master orator and a riveting storyteller: humorous, down to earth, and totally accessible, while at the same time fiercely passionate and intense. Sometimes, he shook us to the core. He challenged and provoked us, pushing us to think for ourselves and embrace the formidable responsibilities that the Torah placed upon us. Rav Noach was a towering figure who took personal responsibility for bringing every Jew back to Hashem and His Torah. He lived with the constant awareness of Hashem and he burned with a love for *every* Jew.

Rav Noach's approach to *kiruv* was what he called *Toras Chaim*, wisdom for living. By showing Jews from all backgrounds the relevance and depth of Jewish wisdom, he made Torah irresistible to the unaffiliated. And he built Aish HaTorah from a small yeshivah consisting of five students into a groundbreaking, international outreach organization.

To many, Rav Noach is synonymous with Aish HaTorah. For nearly 40 years, Rav Noach toiled endlessly to nurture and build the yeshivah that he founded into a movement that would inspire a spiritual renaissance within the Jewish people. Standing at the forefront of the fight against assimilation and apathy, Rav Noach's profound belief in each and every Jew's spiritual potential inspired his students to heed his call and join his cause. Today, Aish-trained rabbis and rebbetzins continue Rav Noach's legacy. In the more than 20 Aish branches on five continents, Rav Noach's Torah and vision live on, inspiring a new generation of Jews to the true meaning of a Torah life.

While preparing this book based on Rav Noach's *shmuessen* and classes for publication, we tried our best to retain his unique voice and remain as faithful as we could to the transcripts of his talks, which form the basis of this book. The reader will notice several major themes running through the book that touch on the core principles of Rav Weinberg's worldview: responsibility as the key to greatness, living with *yiras Shamayim* and feeling the reality of Hashem's love, actualizing man's awesome potential through using the power of our free will, the primacy of Torah, and the depth of our responsibility to the Jewish people and to perfecting the world.

Many people were instrumental in the creation of this book. First and foremost we thank Allen Isaac Gross and his wife Edie, personal friends and supporters of Rav Noach and Aish HaTorah, for dedicating the book. Thank you to Rabbi Boruch Rabinowitz and Rabbi Hershel Lutch for helping shepherd this project to completion. To Rabbi Aaron Dayan, who took great care over the years to tape Rav Noach's *shiurim*. To Rabbi Jamie Cowland, who laid the initial groundwork by overseeing the transcription process, and to Avi Noam Taub, who did a masterful job at transcribing the tapes.

We thank Rabbi Shraga Simmons and Rabbi Chaim Willis for their contribution to some of the essays, and Rabbi Yehuda Weinberg for his support. We are grateful to Rabbi Pinchas Waldman who was always available for us, and managed unfailingly to unearth the specific sources we needed. We also thank him for taking the time to review the entire manuscript. We would like to thank the professional staff at ArtScroll Publications, especially Mrs. Malky Heimowitz, who did an excellent job editing the manuscript and offering insightful comments.

We would like to express our great *hakaras hatov* to Rebbetzin Denah Weinberg. Without her steadfast support and commitment, Aish HaTorah would never have started, nor would it have flourished to become the international organization it is today. Hashem should bless her with longevity, good health, and much *nachas* from all of her biological and spiritual descendants.

We thank our wives and families for their ongoing support and encouragement for everything we do, including this book.

And above all we thank *HaKadosh Baruch Hu* for giving us the great privilege of being part of Aish HaTorah and enabling us to reach out to the Jewish people with the wisdom that Rav Weinberg, our beloved rebbi, imparted to us.

The publication of this book coincided with the petira of our beloved mother, Mrs. Myrtle Coopersmith, *a"h*. She and our father, Dr. Harvey Coopersmith יבלחט"א were married for almost 63 years, and together they instilled wtihin us and our siblings the Jewish values of responsibility, humility and *chessed*. Our mother was a very dynamic woman who dedicated her life to her extended family and to the Jewish people. We are grateful that we were able to give her a copy of this book just before she passed away, giving her great *nachas*. May the learning from this *sefer* be a *iluyi neshama* for Mahtel Blima bas Tavi Yitzchak.

Nechemia Coopersmith and Yitzchak Coopersmith

ספר בראשית
Sefer Bereishis

Experience without Torah is enticing, like the fruit on the Tree of Knowledge of Good and Evil, but ultimately it is a death trap.

פרשת בראשית
arashas Bereishis:
Eating in the Garden

וַיַּצְמַח ה' אֱלֹהִים מִן הָאֲדָמָה כָּל עֵץ נֶחְמָד לְמַרְאֶה וְטוֹב לְמַאֲכָל וְעֵץ הַחַיִּים בְּתוֹךְ הַגָּן וְעֵץ הַדַּעַת טוֹב וָרָע . . . וַיְצַו ה' אֱלֹהִים עַל הָאָדָם לֵאמֹר מִכֹּל עֵץ הַגָּן אָכֹל תֹּאכֵל: וּמֵעֵץ הַדַּעַת טוֹב וָרַע לֹא תֹאכַל מִמֶּנּוּ כִּי בְּיוֹם אֲכָלְךָ מִמֶּנּוּ מוֹת תָּמוּת . . . וַתֵּרֶא הָאִשָּׁה כִּי טוֹב הָעֵץ לְמַאֲכָל וְכִי תַאֲוָה הוּא לָעֵינַיִם וְנֶחְמָד הָעֵץ לְהַשְׂכִּיל . . .

And Hashem God caused to sprout from the ground every tree that was pleasing to the sight and good for food; also the Tree of Life in the midst of the garden, and the Tree of Knowledge of Good and Bad…. And Hashem God commanded Adam, saying, "Of every tree of the garden you may freely eat; but of the Tree of Knowledge of Good and Evil, you must not eat thereof; for on the day you eat of it, you shall surely die… And the woman perceived that the tree was good for eating and that it was a delight to the eyes, and that the tree was desirable as a means to wisdom… (Bereishis 2:9, 16-17; 3:6).

The Almighty created an absolutely gorgeous garden filled with "every tree that was pleasing to the sight and good for food." Right in the center of this garden He placed this unbelievably desirable tree called the Tree of Knowledge of Good and Evil, and He warned Adam, "Watch out! You can't eat from this tree! Yes, it looks incredibly delicious and mouthwatering, but if you eat from it, you will die."

Now, would you place an exquisite table of delectable delights in front of your children, placing the most appetizing dish of all right in the middle, and then lace that dish with poison and tell them, "Watch out for that one! Although it is extremely desirable, it will kill you"? Why did Hashem bait Adam and Chavah in such a seemingly cruel way and place a deadly booby trap in front of them?

Living Forever

The key to unlocking this mystery is to consider what would have happened if Adam had eaten from the Tree of Life before eating from the Tree of Knowledge of Good and Evil. We can derive the answer from Hashem's reaction after Adam mistakenly ate from the Tree of Knowledge first. The Torah says that Hashem drove Adam out of the garden to ensure that he would not eat from the Tree of Life and live forever. Even after Adam ate from the Tree of Knowledge and became mortal, the Tree of Life could have offset his eventual death and enabled him to live forever.

Imagine how different this story would have been if Adam had eaten from the Tree of Life first. He would have become eternal, and immune to the danger of the Tree of Knowledge of Good and Evil.

Hashem was not dangling a booby trap in front of Adam, for Adam could have eaten from the delicious Tree of Knowledge, as long as he ate from the Tree of Life first. In fact, Hashem commanded him to eat from *all* the trees — including the Tree of Life — when He said, "Of every tree of the garden you may freely eat." Adam's mistake was the order in which he ate from these two trees.

Wisdom vs. Experience

What is the Torah teaching us here? What does the Tree of Life represent, and what is represented by the Tree of Knowledge of

Good and Evil? And lastly, what is the mistake that Adam made that we need to watch out for in our own lives?

The Tree of Life represents the Torah: "It is a Tree of Life to those who grasp it" (*Mishlei* 3:18). The Torah is the ultimate repository of wisdom; it teaches us how to live meaningfully in every single facet of life. It is the Almighty's blueprint of creation, from which all existence flows. It is the defining source of ethics and morality, the instruction manual (*Toras Chaim*) on how to use this world to understand our purpose, reach our potential, and forge a meaningful connection with our Creator.

What is the Tree of Knowledge of Good and Evil, and why is it problematic? This tree represents the knowledge that comes from life experience. It is the desire to go see the world and taste all its fruits, and through the process of trial and error try to discover what is good, what is destructive, and what is the proper path in life. It is the thrill of traveling across the country with no map or destination, open to whatever comes your way.

But growing through the method of experience entails running into obstacles, falling down, and getting bruised along the way. Mistakes will certainly happen, sometimes serious ones, but we hope we will eventually figure things out. This is the underlying attitude of the person who chooses to learn about life from the school of hard knocks instead of first learning Torah.

Experience without Torah is enticing, like the fruit on the Tree of Knowledge of Good and Evil, but ultimately it is a death trap. Diving into the vast, alluring arena of life blindfolded inevitably leaves a path of destruction in its wake: broken hearts and homes, shattered dreams, cynicism, confusion, and alienation.

Potential *baalei teshuvah* experience a burning conflict when wrestling with the decision to drop what they are doing — whether it is traveling across Europe and the Middle East or enjoying themselves in college — and come to yeshivah to learn Torah. Essentially, they are choosing between the Tree of Knowledge and the Tree of Life.

The Torah is teaching us a crucial life lesson: before indulging in the myriad experiences, we must first learn Torah, life's instruction manual, to understand the ethical principles that govern existence and the proper parameters for engaging in this world. Once these definitions and concepts are clear, we can eat from the Tree of Knowledge of Good and Evil, because we already know how to use the world as a vehicle to connect to Hashem and reach our potential.

Experience life! We are not meant to live in an ivory tower. But we must first gain the necessary wisdom on how to live life so that we can avoid the pitfalls and not be destroyed in the process.

> *No one plans on getting divorced, but the fact is that just over 50 percent of all marriages will end in divorce.*

For example, everyone wants to get married, and no one plans on getting divorced, but the fact is that just over 50 percent of all marriages will end in divorce. Don't wing it. Learn Torah's wisdom on marriage and then get married.

Hashem wants us to get the most out of life. And to do that you've got to know what you are living for. Ask a student: Why are you going to college? I've got to get a degree. Why do you need a degree? I've got to get a job. Why do you need a job? I've got to make money. Why do you need money? I've got to buy food. Why do you need food? I've got to eat. Why do you need to eat? I've got to live. Why do you need to live? I've got to go to college. . .

> *Hashem wants us to get the most out of life. And to do that you've got to know what you are living for.*

You need to know the answer to life's most important question: what are you living for? The answer is in the Torah. First eat from the Tree of Life. Then apply your learning and experience the breathtaking beauty and meaning life has to offer.

When we are unified, respecting
each other and genuinely listening
to each other, nothing can stop us.

פרשת נח

arashas Noach:
The Power of Unity

כִּי אֶרְאֶה שָׁמֶיךָ מַעֲשֵׂי אֶצְבְּעֹתֶיךָ יָרֵחַ וְכוֹכָבִים אֲשֶׁר כּוֹנָנְתָּה: מָה
אֱנוֹשׁ כִּי תִזְכְּרֶנּוּ וּבֶן אָדָם כִּי תִפְקְדֶנּוּ: וַתְּחַסְּרֵהוּ מְּעַט מֵאֱלֹהִים
וְכָבוֹד וְהָדָר תְּעַטְּרֵהוּ:

When I behold Your heavens, the work of Your fingers,
the moon and the stars that You have set in place,
[I think,] "What is man that You should remember him,
and the son of man that You should be mindful of him?"
Yet You have made him but slightly less than God, and
crowned him with honor and splendor
(Tehillim 8:4-6).

Looking up at the cosmos, at the specks of light that seem to stretch onward forever into the millions of galaxies light-years away, we are struck with an overwhelming sense of awe. We get a taste of the Infinite power of the Creator of the universe and in contrast feel so infinitesimally small. "What is man that You should remember him?" David Hamelech proclaims.

And then he explains, "You have made him but slightly less than God." Human beings have incredible power! We can almost match the Almighty.

What is this enormous power that makes us "but slightly less than God"? In this week's *parashah* the Torah reveals our secret power, a power so strong that mankind realized that it gave them the ability to wage battle against the *Ribbono Shel Olam* Himself.

How can this be? Who would be crazy enough to fight with the Creator of the universe?

Sounds ludicrous, but this is exactly what the builders of the Tower of Bavel did.

Fighting Against the Almighty

The whole world was united as one nation, with one language and one purpose, as the *passuk* says, "The whole earth was of one language and of common purpose (*devarim achadim*)" (*Bereishis* 11:1). Rashi explains that the words "*devarim achadim*" mean "one plan." "Hashem has no right to take the upper regions for Himself," they reasoned. "Let us ascend to the heavens and wage war against Him."

They plan on building a tower and invading the heavens to fight the Almighty. What are their chances? It's ridiculous.

But listen to Hashem's response: "Behold, they are one people with one language for all, and this they begin to do! And now, it will not be withheld from them" (ibid. 11:6). The Almighty Himself testifies in the Torah that as long as they are united, nothing will stop them from attaining their goal, even though their undertaking is diametrically opposed to Hashem's purpose.

In order to thwart their rebellion, Hashem sowed seeds of dissension among them. "Come, let us descend and there confuse their language, that they should not understand one another's language" (ibid. 11:7). By changing their language, He made it difficult for them to communicate with each other, and that caused their unity to implode. Once they were at odds with each other, Hashem was able to disperse them. "And Hashem dispersed them from there over the face of the whole earth, and they stopped building the city" (ibid. 11:7-8).

How Great Is Peace

The Midrash (*Sifri, Nasso* 42) describes the incredible power of unity: "How great is peace, for even if Israel worships idolatry, if there is peace among them, the Omnipresent, so to speak, cannot overcome them since there is peace among them."

The generation of the Tower of Bavel was far worse than the generation of the Flood, because they actually went to war against Hashem! Despite that, Hashem did not wipe them out, since they had one crucial redeeming quality: They were unified, with one purpose and one language, working in complete harmony to achieve their mission. Humanity came together. And as long as they were united, they were unstoppable.

Hashem said, "I cannot punish them since they are united. Nonetheless, I cannot let them succeed with their attack, so I will undermine their unity and scatter them."

The Torah is teaching us the astonishing power of unity. When we are unified, respecting each other and genuinely listening to each other, nothing can stop us. There is an exponential power that is unleashed when we come together.

The Torah says, "Five of you will pursue one hundred, and one hundred of you will pursue ten thousand; and your enemies will fall by the sword before you" (*Vayikra* 26:8). But the math seems wrong. If five will chase one hundred, one hundred should chase two thousand. The Midrash says that the Torah is teaching us that "There is no comparison between a few who fulfill the Torah and a multitude who fulfill the Torah" (*Toras Kohanim* 26:10). When we are unified, our power is exponentially greater.

*I*f you want to be in awe, Hashem says, look at mankind.

It is this power of unity that David Hamelech referred to when he wrote, "Yet You have made him but slightly less than God, and crowned him with honor and splendor." If you want to be in awe, Hashem says, look at mankind. When they are unified, nothing can stop them. Humanity tapped into this incredible power, but they misdirected it, using it against Hashem's plan.

Unleash the Power

The Jewish people's ultimate purpose is "to perfect the world through the Almighty's sovereignty." We are a "kingdom of priests, a holy nation" (*Shemos* 19:6), but do we know it? Does the entire Jewish people know it? There's no unity because we have forgotten our purpose, and as a result, we become preoccupied with our own egocentric goals, thinking only about ourselves and forgetting about the *klal*, the nation.

Through our Torah we have taught the world the pillars of morality: monotheism, love your neighbor, justice for all, one nation will not lift their sword against another.

The Jewish people civilized humanity. Through our Torah we have taught the world the pillars of morality: monotheism, love your neighbor, justice for all, one nation will not lift their sword against another. Just imagine what we could accomplish if we would respect each other and genuinely listen to each other! We would change the world.

We are living in precarious times. With genuine unity, we can become "but slightly less than God," and then nothing can stop us. We can unleash the power that the Almighty gave us to bring Torah to His people and clarity to mankind. The world is counting on us.

There are many people who are willing to give up their life for a cause. But there are very few heroes who dedicate their entire lives to the cause for which they are willing to die.

פרשת לך לך

arashas Lech Lecha:
The Challenge of Independence

he word "Torah" literally means instruction; in our daily prayers we refer to it as a *Toras Chaim*, instructions for living. Hashem is our Father in Heaven Who created us and only wants our good. He wants to give us pleasure, and through the Torah He teaches us how to live and get the most out of life. So when we learn Torah, we always have to ask ourselves: What is it that the Almighty is trying to teach me?

The Mishnah tells us that Avraham Avinu withstood 10 tests. But why did the Almighty have to test him? Didn't He know who Avraham was?

The test was not for Hashem's sake; every test was precisely calibrated to help Avraham grow. That's what all tests are about. Every test you'll ever have in your life, every challenge, is sent by the Almighty to help you grow. Let's carefully examine Avraham's first test and see what it teaches us.

The Torah says: "Hashem said to Avram, 'Go for yourself from your land, from your birthplace, and from your father's house to the land that I will show you. And I will make of you a great nation; I will bless you, and make your name great, and you shall be a blessing'" (*Bereishis* 12:1-2).

What is the test? Is it really so impressive that Avraham left his home? Every year thousands of people move to Israel — or elsewhere, for that matter. Furthermore, if the Almighty would speak to you and tell you to leave the United States to go to Israel, wouldn't you drop everything and go? Even if you would already be living in Israel and Hashem would tell you to go to China, isn't it obvious that you would go? It's the Almighty telling you to go! So what's the big deal here? Why is this considered one of the 10 tests Avraham had to go through?

Out of Order

Let's focus on the words of the Torah to find the answer. We find something very strange in the *passuk*. "Hashem said to Avram, 'Go for yourself from your land, from your birthplace, and from your father's house to the land that I will show you.'" This is similar to saying: "Leave the United States, leave New York City, and leave 314 East 4th Street to go someplace." Is this how you would phrase the command to leave?

If you left the United States, haven't you already left New York City? And if you left New York City, haven't you already left your father's house on East 4th Street? The *passuk* is not written in a logical order, and it seems redundant. First you leave your father's house, then the city you live in, and then your country! So why does Hashem reverse the order?

*V*alues and beliefs come from three primary sources: your society, your social group, and your home.

It must be that Hashem is not describing a physical departure. Rather, He is giving Avraham the more difficult challenge of leaving behind the spiritual impact these places have on him. From that perspective, the order now seems perfectly logical; it's going from the lesser sphere of influence (his country) to the most intense one (his home).

The Torah is teaching us that values and beliefs come from three primary sources: your society (land), your social group (birthplace), and your home.

The Three Spheres of Influence

To forge a relationship with Hashem, you first need to leave the influence of your general society; your beliefs can't be just an accident of birth. You've got to become fiercely independent and learn to think for yourself. You have to leave behind the false ideas you've absorbed from the society you are submerged in: whether it's the secular, western civilization of America, or the polytheistic society that Avraham was raised in.

The next step is to leave your birthplace. This is more difficult. It means leaving behind the values you absorbed from your immediate society, your school, the media that surrounds you. Whom do your friends respect? How do they define success? That no longer determines whom *you* respect and how *you* define success.

And lastly, you have to leave behind the impact of your father's house. That doesn't mean to abandon your parents and sever contact with them. It means to leave behind the identity they gave you, the limitations they may have placed on you, and the expectations that may not have been in your best interest. Examine them. Be independent. *Lech Lecha* means go for *yourself*, discover who you really are and what you really believe in. Don't compromise your aspirations and clarity of what is right.

By understanding Hashem's test of Avraham as the challenge of attaining independence, we can appreciate why this is indeed a serious test. It wasn't just a matter of physically leaving a country. The Almighty was telling Avraham to completely rethink all of his values and the way he viewed the world and himself, to become fully independent. That is no small undertaking.

Why No Mention of Ur Kasdim?

There is another question concerning Avraham's first test. According to the Midrash (*Bereishis Rabbah* 38:13), before Hashem appeared to Avraham and told him to leave his country, Avraham smashed his father's idols and began to teach people about monotheism. Nimrod, the king of Shinar, perceived this as a threat, and he gave Avraham an ultimatum: bow down to idols or be thrown into a fiery furnace.

What would you have done? You could save your life by bowing down to the idols. After all, it's just an external action; in your heart you know it's nonsense.

But Avraham understood, even before the Torah was given, that the obligation of *Kiddush Hashem* (sanctifying Hashem's Name) requires one to give up his life rather than commit any of the three cardinal transgressions: idol worship, murder, and illicit relations (*Pesachim* 25a). The prohibition against idolatry includes even outward acts of worship to an idol you don't believe in.

Avraham refused to bow down, and was thrown into the fire. He expected to die, knowing that one may not depend on miracles. But the Almighty performed a miracle and he walked out of the fiery furnace alive.

This was an incredible act of *mesirus nefesh* (self-sacrifice). Avraham was willing to die for what he knew was right. Yet the Torah doesn't mention a word about this story. Why not? Isn't this test far greater than the first test of leaving Ur Kasdim mentioned at the beginning of this *parashah*?

Dying for a Cause vs. Living for a Cause

There's no question that Avraham's willingness to die rather than to bow down to idols was a sign of tremendous commitment. But which is harder: to die for a cause or to live for a cause?

Many people are willing to give up their life in order to do the right thing. In 1967, when Israel's existence was threatened, Jews came out of the woodwork to volunteer and fight, risking their very lives. Even today, if you were ordered to kill one hundred children or be killed, would you kill them or choose to die instead?

We all understand that there are values and beliefs that are more important than life itself.

But does the recognition that a cause is important enough to die for automatically spur you to dedicate your life to that cause? If you care about the Jewish people so much that you're willing to die for them, does that mean you're willing to drop everything and dedicate your life to living for them?

Being *moser nefesh*, giving up your life for Hashem, is a great act, but it is still only a one-time choice. It is far more difficult to undertake the constant struggle of living every single moment, day in and day out, according to what the Almighty asks of us.

There are many people who are willing to give up their life for a cause (often false ones, like jihad). But there are very few heroes who dedicate their entire lives to the cause for which they are willing to die.

_D_ying for a cause is not what the Torah wants to emphasize. The ideal is to _live_ for a cause.

Avraham's willingness to die in the furnace _al Kiddush Hashem_ isn't mentioned in the Torah or included in the list of 10 tests because dying for a cause is not what the Torah wants to emphasize. The ideal is to _live_ for a cause. The test of Lech Lecha was a greater challenge than the ordeal of Ur Kasdim because it demanded that Avraham become independent and totally dedicate his life to Hashem. This is the first test of every Jew, and it was Avraham's first step toward becoming the father of the Jewish people.

The Torah's paradigm of chessed
is an exchange that in the end did
not even benefit the recipients.

פרשת וירא
arashas Vayeira:
Building Through Kindness

וַיֵּרָא אֵלָיו ה׳ בְּאֵלֹנֵי מַמְרֵא וְהוּא יֹשֵׁב פֶּתַח הָאֹהֶל כְּחֹם הַיּוֹם:
וַיִּשָּׂא עֵינָיו וַיַּרְא וְהִנֵּה שְׁלֹשָׁה אֲנָשִׁים נִצָּבִים עָלָיו וַיַּרְא וַיָּרָץ
לִקְרָאתָם מִפֶּתַח הָאֹהֶל וַיִּשְׁתַּחוּ אָרְצָה:

*Hashem appeared to him in the plains of Mamre while he
was sitting at the entrance of the tent in the heat of the
day. He lifted his eyes and saw: And behold! Three men
were standing over him. He perceived, so he ran toward
them from the entrance of the tent, and bowed toward the
ground (Bereishis 18:1-2).*

Picture the scene. Avraham is having a prophetic experience,
communicating directly with the *Ribbono Shel Olam* Himself.
He then sees three guests and says to Hashem, "Pardon me,
Almighty, I have to go take care of my guests. I'll be right back."

Why does Avraham take leave of the *Shechinah* (Divine Presence),
in the midst of experiencing the transcendental, to entertain three
nomadic strangers? Imagine that you are hosting the *gadol hador*,
the leading rabbi of our generation, and while having a private face-

to-face talk with him, you see three strangers passing by. Would you tell the great rabbi, "I'll be back in 45 minutes, I need to go whip up dinner for these guests"?

Amazingly, the Talmud (*Shabbos* 127a) teaches us that Avraham was actually correct in what he did, for "*hachnassas orchim* (welcoming guests) is greater than experiencing the *Shechinah*."

Being Like God

How do we understand what the Talmud is saying? If the Creator of the universe, the infinite, all-powerful Source of existence, would appear to you, even an atheist would tell you not to budge! There can be no greater experience than communing with the Divine. So how can *hachnassas orchim* possibly trump that?

The answer is clear: Greater than talking to Hashem is emulating Him. The most powerful way to understand and connect to Hashem is by becoming like Him. "*Ma hu chanun verachum, af attah heyeh chanun verachum* — just as Hashem is merciful and compassionate, so, too, you should be merciful and compassionate" (*Shabbos* 133b). The Almighty is infinite and perfect, which means there is nothing He needs. He does not gain anything from our keeping the mitzvos. His creation of the universe is a perfect act of altruism; it is 100 percent *chessed*, aimed at giving us the deepest pleasure and meaning attainable simply because He loves us.

If you want to understand the Almighty's love for you, then you have to become like Him, and one of the essential ways to emulate Him is by doing *chessed* and loving other human beings. Becoming a giver is really the only way to understand Who Hashem is and what life is all about.

If you want to really appreciate the Almighty, then undertake to be like Him and take care of as many people as you can. Even if you're sick, try to give another human being pleasure. Work at it, make it your priority — and by doing so you will understand just a little bit more what existence is all about.

If you do not change yourself by inculcating Hashem's attributes, you will never fully understand Hashem. He will remain an abstraction. By way of illustration, one of the criteria for appointing a judge to a Sanhedrin, a Jewish court that can judge capital offenses, is that the candidate must be a father. Rambam explains that this is necessary "in order to ensure that he will be merciful" (*Hilchos Sanhedrin* 2:3). He may be the greatest *talmid chacham* in the world, but if he does not have children he cannot sit in judgment, because he cannot fully grasp the reality of Hashem's compassion for His children. He can be a prophet who communes with the Almighty, but he cannot judge a capital crime. To truly have compassion you must be a father; likewise, to fully understand Hashem you must become like Him.

Just Do It

The Torah goes into great detail when describing Avraham's *chessed:*

> "Let some water be brought and wash your feet, and recline beneath the tree. I will fetch a morsel of bread that you may sustain yourselves..." So Avraham hastened to the tent to Sarah, and said, "Hurry! Three se'ahs of meal, fine flour! Knead and make cakes!" Then Avraham ran to the cattle, took a calf, tender and good, and gave it to the youth, who hurried to prepare it. He took cream and milk and the calf that he had prepared, and placed these before them; he stood over them beneath the tree, and they ate. (*Bereishis* 18:4-8).

Every detail here teaches us an important insight about kindness. First, you need to run to do *chessed*. Don't procrastinate, don't kvetch about it. Run and joyfully embrace the opportunity to give to another human being.

Avraham offered the wayfarers bread and water, but when he sprang into action he prepared them a lavish meal. "*Emor me'at ve'aseh harbeh* — say little and do a lot" (*Pirkei Avos* 1:15). Talk is cheap. Momentarily it may create the appearance that you are doing something, but in the end you are just a bluffer, and everyone will know it. The sign that someone is serious about doing good is that he says little and does a lot. Don't grandstand. Don't promise a lot. Just get the job done.

Don't grandstand. Don't promise a lot. Just get the job done.

The Power of Kindness

The Midrash asks, "Who was the person who did *chessed* to those who did not need it? It was Avraham Avinu, who gave to the ministering angels" (*Vayikra Rabbah* 34:8). Amazingly, the Torah's paradigm of *chessed* is an exchange that in the end did not even benefit the recipients. Angels don't eat bread! They don't even eat tongue with mustard. Avraham's kindness didn't do them a bit of good.

Yet the Talmud (*Bava Metzia* 86b) describes the incredible reward Avraham received for doing this kindness:

> Rav Yehudah said in the name of Rav: Whatever Avraham did for the ministering angels himself, the Holy One, blessed is He, likewise did for his children Himself. But whatever Avraham did through an agent, the Holy One, blessed is He, likewise did for his children through an agent. "Then Avraham ran to the cattle," corresponds to, "A wind went forth from Hashem and blew quail from the sea and spread them over the camp." "And [Avraham] took cream and milk," corresponds to, "Behold, I will rain down for you food from heaven." "And [Avraham] stood over them beneath the tree and they ate," corresponds to, "Behold, I shall stand before you by the rock." "And Avraham walked with them to escort them," corresponds to, "Hashem went before them by day in a pillar of cloud to lead them on the way."
>
> [The above are all examples of actions that were taken directly by Avraham or the Holy One, blessed is He. The following two verses describe actions taken through an agent:]
>
> "Let some water be brought," corresponds to, "And you [Moshe] shall strike the rock, and water will come from it and the people will drink."

The Jewish people had water to drink for 40 years in the desert because Avraham gave the three guests some water. All of Avraham's descendants miraculously ate manna from heaven for 40 years in the desert because Avraham gave the three travelers milk. The Jewish people were surrounded by Clouds of Glory for 40 years in the desert because Avraham escorted his guests.

Look at the incredible impact of *every* act of *chessed* Avraham did. His actions affected the entire Jewish nation that descended from him, even though in reality he did not give the angels anything.

Chazal make the following *kal v'chomer* (*a fortiori* argument): "If the Holy One, blessed is He, rewards the children of a person who does *chessed* to someone who doesn't benefit from that *chessed*, then all the more will He reward the person who does *chessed* to someone who does benefit from his *chessed*" (*Vayikra Rabbah* 34:8).

Avraham's *chessed* yielded no real benefit, yet look at its impact! Now imagine the reward Hashem will give to your children and grandchildren as a result of your doing something to tangibly help a fellow Jew. Chazal are teaching us that your reward will be even greater than Avraham's!

The Talmud makes an additional point. Avraham told a messenger to get the water; he delegated. So the Almighty also delegated, and instead of giving water to the Jewish people directly, He gave it through the rock that was hit by Moshe. But Hashem gave *Bnei Yisrael* the manna directly because Avraham fetched the milk himself.

Chazal are telling us that how you do a *chessed* makes a tremendous difference. In the desert, the Jewish people could have had water pouring down to them straight from the Almighty, and that would have made it a totally different experience. Water that comes directly from Hashem is very different from water that comes from a rock; just as the bread that came directly from Hashem was not just regular bread, but rather manna. And the shelter they enjoyed in the desert was not just protection from the sun, but rather an experience of being enveloped by the Shechinah, the presence of God.

It is an altogether different act of kindness when you do it yourself.

The world is built through kindness. And so are we.

Whatever *chessed* you do, whether it is direct or through an intermediary, the impact and reward are mindboggling. "*Olam chessed yibaneh* — the world is built through kindness" (*Tehillim* 89:2). And so are we.

Chessed is the Almighty's trademark. Seize the opportunities to do *chessed* for others. You will become like God Himself.

One decision to reach out and help, one act, can leave your imprint forever.

פרשת חיי שרה
arashas Chayei Sarah:
Making History

His beloved wife Sarah has just died, and after eulogizing her, Avraham wants to give her a fitting burial. But first he has to contend with the children of Cheis, the Hittites, and the greedy, manipulative Ephron, in order to acquire a suitable burial plot.

If you look at the entire *perek* carefully, you will see that one group of people is mentioned repeatedly:

*Avraham rose up from the presence of his dead, and spoke to the **children of Cheis**...*

*And the **children of Cheis** answered Avraham...*

*Then Avraham rose up and bowed down to the members of the council, to the **children of Cheis**. . .*

*Now, Ephron was sitting in the midst of the **children of Cheis**, and Ephron the Hittite responded to Avraham in the hearing of the **children of Cheis**...*

*And Avraham weighed out to Ephron the price that he had mentioned in the hearing of the **children of Cheis**...*

> And Ephron's field...was confirmed as Avraham's as a purchase in the view of the **children of Cheis**...
>
> Thus, the field with the cave that was in it was confirmed as Avraham's as an estate for a burial site, from the **children of Cheis**.
>
> The field that Avraham had bought from the **children of Cheis**, there Avraham was buried, and Sarah his wife
>
> *(23:3-20; 25:10).*

The Torah is very exact; there are no extra letters or words. The repetition of the words *bnei Cheis,* the children of Cheis, is striking: they are mentioned nine times here in Parashas Chayei Sarah, and once later on in Parashas Vayechi (49:32). We know who the people in this story are. Why repeat their names ten times?

We know who the people in this story are. Why repeat their names ten times?

The Midrash explains: "Rabbi Elazar said: How much ink is spilled, and how many quills are broken, in order to write 'the children of Cheis'! Ten times [the Torah] writes, 'the children of Cheis, the children of Cheis.' These ten mentions correspond to the Ten Commandments, in order to teach you that whoever assists in the business dealings of a righteous person, it is considered as though he has fulfilled the Ten Commandments" (*Bereishis Rabbah* 58:8).

Bnei Cheis are not just recorded once for posterity in the Torah: they are written ten times! Just think how much ink has been used in writing those ten phrases over the course of 3,300 years in the world's top best-selling book. Why the repetition?

One Act Can Define Your Life

The Midrash is pointing out that one act can make history. The Hittites were a fierce nation whom everyone feared (the name "Cheis" comes from the Hebrew word for "fear"[1]). Despite their

1. According to the *Igra D'Kallah* (*Chayei Sarah* 28:20), by the author of *Bnei Yissachar*, Rav Elimelech Shapiro.

barbaric nature, the children of Cheis helped Avraham Avinu acquire Me'aras Hamachpelah from Ephron. They did one good deed: they helped a *tzaddik*, someone they recognized as a "*Nesi Elokim*," a prince of God. On account of this single action, they are considered to have fulfilled the Ten Commandments. What does that mean? It signifies that they made their life worth living.

Through one deed, a person can impact the world in a way that justifies his existence and makes him worthy of being remembered for all of eternity. He can make his mark in history.

Imagine seeing a toddler fall into a swimming pool. You jump in, fully clothed, and rescue the child. Your clothing is soaked, your cell phone is ruined, and yet you feel, *Wow, I just saved this kid's life.*

*T*he fact that you did something heroic does not mean you can now stop living, or that you have attained greatness.

The fact that you did something heroic does not mean you can now stop living, or that you have attained greatness. There is always so much more to accomplish in life. Yet you recognize that you did something that will forever give meaning to your existence. Your act is worth remembering, and deserves to be recorded for posterity.

Reaching Out

We all have opportunities every single day to add immeasurable meaning to our lives and the lives of those around us. But to access them we have to be alert. We may not even realize at the time just how consequential a single act could be. To illustrate, here is one true story. Eric Coopersmith was 19 years old, volunteering at Kibbutz Shaar Ha'amakim in Israel. During a visit to Jerusalem he stumbled across Aish HaTorah, where he met Ephraim Shore, a fellow Canadian who had been learning in the yeshivah for several months. Eric enjoyed his conversation with Ephraim and began to think that perhaps there is more to Judaism than what he was exposed to in Hebrew school. He told Ephraim that he would come back to visit in a month or so, but right now he had to complete his stint as a volunteer at the kibbutz.

Back at the kibbutz, Eric shared his impressions of Aish with his non-Jewish roommate. This roommate was a turned-off Roman Catholic, and he convinced Eric that the rabbis were snake-oil salesmen and that religion was empty. Eric subsequently decided to forget about spending any time at Aish and go directly back to Europe after he finished at the kibbutz.

Several weeks later, during *bein hazmanim*, Ephraim was on a bus heading north. Looking out the window, he suddenly saw a sign for Kibbutz Shaar Ha'amakim. *Hey, isn't that the kibbutz where that guy Eric is?* Ephraim said to himself.

He quickly pressed the stop button and got off the bus. He tracked Eric down at the kibbutz and re-convinced him that it would be worthwhile to come back to Aish HaTorah to check out the wisdom of Judaism before continuing his year of travel in Europe.

To make a long story short, a few weeks later Eric returned to Aish HaTorah, where he eventually became a rabbi and one of the rosh yeshivah's closest confidants, responsible for developing many of Aish HaTorah's most successful and influential programs worldwide.

Ephraim could easily have stayed on the bus, which is what most of us probably would have done. After all, he had only met Eric once, for a few hours. But instead he seized the opportunity to reach out, not knowing the impact his actions would eventually have on the Jewish people.

Leave Your Imprint

History is being made every day, and each one of us has the opportunity to leave our imprint for eternity. How? Every person can make the effort to reach out to a fellow Jew. You can change the course of someone's life and make your mark on history — and you never know when the person you touch will himself become an impetus to making history.

One decision to reach out and help, one act, can leave your imprint forever and add immeasurable meaning to your life and the lives of your family. The opportunities surround us. Take that one step today and make your mark for posterity.

*Yitzchak had a strategy. He
wanted Yaakov and Eisav to form
a partnership that would combine
their inherent strengths to perfect
the world.*

פרשת תולדות
arashas Toldos:
Don't Give Up on Your Brother

I n this week's *parashah* we have the enigmatic story of the struggle
between Yaakov and Eisav over acquiring the blessings from their
aged father, Yitzchak. Yitzchak sets the drama in motion by sum-
moning Eisav and telling him to prepare to receive his blessing.

> *"See, now, I have aged; I know not the day of my death.
> Now sharpen, if you please, your gear — your sword and
> your bow — and go out to the field and hunt game for me.
> Then make me delicacies such as I love and bring them to
> me and I will eat, so that my soul may bless you before I
> die" (Bereishis 27: 2-4).*

What was Yitzchak thinking? How is it possible that Yitzchak did
not recognize the extent of Eisav's depravity, and wanted to bless him?

Eisav's Destiny

It is a mistake to think that Yitzchak Avinu was a blind old man,
somewhat out of touch with reality, who was easily deceived by

Eisav. Yitzchak understood full well how depraved Eisav was — but he also clearly saw his enormous potential and the pivotal role he could play in enabling the Jewish people to accomplish their mission.

It is a mistake to think that Yitzchak Avinu was a blind old man, somewhat out of touch with reality, who was easily deceived by Eisav.

The Torah describes how Eisav looked when he was born: "The first one emerged ruddy (*admoni*), entirely like a hairy mantle; so they named him Eisav" (ibid. 25:25). Rashi explains that the fact that Eisav was "*admoni*" was a sign that he would have the propensity to shed blood (*Bereishis Rabbah* 63:8). Does this mean Eisav was destined to become a murderer?

The word "*admoni*" is used in only one other place in Tanach, and that is in describing the young David, whom the prophet Shmuel meets for the first time. "He [David] was ruddy (*admoni*), with fair eyes and a pleasing appearance. Hashem then said, 'Arise and anoint him, for this is he!'" (*I Shmuel* 16:12). How can the same word be used to describe the essence of the evil Eisav and the righteous David Hamelech?

David indeed had the propensity to shed blood, like Eisav. But unlike Eisav, he took that innate inclination and channeled it toward good by battling the enemies of the Jewish people and defending Hashem's honor.

All traits can be used for good or evil. Eisav was not compelled to become a murderer; he could have used his inborn traits to accomplish great things.

Partnership

Yitzchak had a strategy. He wanted Yaakov and Eisav to form a partnership that would combine their inherent strengths to perfect the world. Yaakov would lead the spiritual realm while Eisav would rule the material world, freeing Yaakov to focus on the loftier mission of spreading Hashem's word to humanity.

Yitzchak never intended to give Eisav the "*birkas Avraham,*" the spiritual blessing that represents the transfer of the covenant originally forged between Avraham and Hashem, and the inheritance of the Land of Israel. Yaakov was always the intended recipient of this far more important blessing, which Yitzchak gave him at the end of the *parashah*, when he knew that he was blessing Yaakov. "May He grant you the blessing of Avraham to you and to your offspring with you, that you may possess the land of your sojourns, which God gave to Avraham" (*Bereishis* 28:4).

The blessing that Yitzchak intended to give Eisav — which Yaakov received after he dressed up as Eisav — was for material abundance and political domination. "And may Hashem give you of the dew of the heavens and of the fatness of the earth, and abundant grain and wine. Peoples will serve you, and regimes will prostrate themselves to you; be a lord to your kinsmen, and your mother's sons will prostrate themselves to you..." (ibid. 27:28, 29).

The Seforno (ibid. 27:29) explains why Yitzchak deemed this blessing appropriate for Eisav, and what his intention was in telling Eisav that he would rule over his brother. He thought it would be best for Yaakov to remain in Eretz Yisrael and not be burdened with the responsibilities of the physical world. Yaakov could then focus all of his efforts on Torah, while Eisav, working toward the same objective, would rule the *gashmiyus* aspect, the material world.

Yitzchak was correct in his assessment of Eisav's potential and the impact that the combined abilities of Yaakov and Eisav could have on the world. His mistake was in strategy. He realized Eisav was immoral, but he thought that if Yaakov would just reach out to him he would be able to set him on a righteous path. Yitzchak thought that forging a partnership between his two sons would force Yaakov to influence Eisav. But Rivkah realized that this strategy was terribly mistaken, because empowering Eisav before he did *teshuvah* would remove his greatest impetus to change. Once Eisav would have this power, he would never be motivated to face his demons and improve.

Eisav's Tears

Yaakov's potential to reach out to Eisav and turn him around sheds light on another curious statement of Chazal. The *Zohar* (*Shemos* 12b) says that the prolonged exile of the Jewish people is because of the tears Eisav shed upon discovering that Yitzchak blessed Yaakov. "And Eisav said to his father, 'Have you but one blessing, Father? Bless me too, Father!' And Eisav raised his voice and wept" (*Bereishis* 27:38). The redemption will come, the *Zohar* says, when our tears (of repentance) will override the tears of Eisav.

Why should the Jewish people have lost the *Beis HaMikdash* and gone through a lengthy, brutal exile due to Eisav's tears? Eisav was evil, and did not deserve the blessing Yitzchak intended to give him. So why were Yaakov and his descendants punished for the poor choices Eisav made that caused him to be undeserving of the blessings?

The Torah's answer is that it was not entirely Eisav's fault. Ultimately, the Jewish people share the blame for Eisav's conduct, because Yaakov should have reached out to his brother. Had he done so, he would have succeeded in bringing him back to Hashem.

We find the same point made in Parashas Vayishlach, with regard to Yaakov's preparations for meeting his feared brother Eisav: "But he got up that night and took his two wives, his two handmaids, and his eleven sons and crossed the ford of the Yabbok" (ibid. 32:23).

Ultimately, the Jewish people share the blame for Eisav's conduct, because Yaakov should have reached out to his brother.

Rashi comments: "And where was Dinah? [Yaakov] put her into a chest and closed it over her, so Eisav would not set his eyes upon her. Yaakov was punished for withholding his daughter Dinah from his brother, for [had Dinah married him] she might have returned him to virtuous conduct. So she fell into the hands of Shechem."

Yitzchak's vision of his two sons working in tandem — with Yaakov ruling the spiritual realm and Eisav ruling the physical realm — was indeed correct. And Yaakov is faulted for not doing what he could have to prompt Eisav's *teshuvah*. Imagine the punishment for not doing all we can to reach out to our Jewish brothers and sisters who are innocent victims of assimilation and ignorance.

*Yes, Lavan, Hashem blessed you
because of me. But Hashem isn't
the only One you need to thank.*

פרשת ויצא

arashas Vayeitzei:
Thanks, But No Thanks

I n this week's *parashah* we meet Lavan Ha'arami, the coldhearted
swindler who repeatedly deceives Yaakov. He tricks Yaakov into
marrying Leah instead of Rachel and, as Rashi explains (*Bereishis*
31:7), he then tries to cheat Yaakov by changing the terms of their
agreement more than 100 times.

And then the despicable Lavan says something so completely out
of character, you can't help but stop in your tracks and take notice.

Yaakov has completed the 14 years of work that he committed
to do for Lavan in exchange for marrying his daughters Rachel and
Leah, and now he wants to return to Israel. Lavan is not happy to
see Yaakov go, however: "But Lavan said to him, 'If I have found
favor in your eyes! I have learned by divination that Hashem has
blessed me on account of you'" (ibid. 30:27).

Lavan is telling Yaakov, "I figured out the secret to my wealth —
Hashem blessed me because of you. Now, of course I don't want
you to work for nothing, so let's cut a deal and figure out a way for
you to continue working for me." What is so striking is that Lavan
says that Hashem, the transcendental, eternal Source of existence,
is the One Who blessed him on account of Yaakov. Does this appre-

ciation of Hashem sound like the Lavan we know? Why has he suddenly become so pious?

We understand that Lavan wants to manipulate Yaakov to continue working for him, but that does not explain his admission that Hashem is behind his success. Recognizing Hashem as the Source of all your blessings is no easy task! That is why the Hebrew word for thanks, *todah*, comes from the root "to admit," because saying thank you means we are admitting we have a debt of gratitude that must be repaid. None of us likes to owe anything to others. We have a tendency to minimize our debt of gratitude and thereby lessen the extent to which we are beholden to others and Hashem.

If we Jews, who say *Shema Yisrael* and *Modim Anachnu Lach* every day, have a tough time admitting that the Almighty has blessed us, how can a self-absorbed swindler like Lavan explicitly recognize that Hashem is the Source of all his blessings and wealth?

It's All a Sham

One person understood Lavan's true intentions, and that was Yaakov Avinu. Look at Yaakov's response to Lavan's acknowledgment of Hashem:

> But he [Yaakov] said to him, "You know how I served you
> and what your livestock were with me. For the little that you
> had before I came has expanded substantially as Hashem
> has blessed you with my coming; and now, when will I also
> do something for my own house?" (ibid. 30:29-30).

Yaakov is confronting Lavan and telling him, "I see right through your verbiage and lies. Yes, Hashem blessed you because of me. That's true, Lavan. But Hashem isn't the only One you need to thank. You cannot ignore the fact that I worked hard for your sheep. I was the one who took care of your livestock and increased the size of your flock. You owe me as well. And if you cannot recognize your debt of gratitude to me, then don't talk to me about how much the Almighty did for you."

Yaakov has Lavan's number. He understands that *hakaras hatov*, gratitude, begins with appreciating the debt you have toward humans. If you cannot admit to that more concrete debt of gratitude, then you cannot truly recognize your more ephemeral debt of gratitude to Hashem. It's all a sham.

Pharaoh vs. Moshe

Pharaoh exhibited a profound lack of gratitude, as the Torah says, "A new king arose over Egypt who did not know of Yosef" (*Shemos* 1:8). Pharaoh was an ingrate of the highest order, because he did not recognize all that Yosef had done to save Egyptian society from starvation. This lack of gratitude made it possible for him to oppress the Jewish people, and inevitably led him to deny Hashem. As the Midrash says, "Today Pharaoh does not know of Yosef; tomorrow he says, 'I do not know Hashem'" (*Tanchuma, Shemos* 5).

It is much easier to be real with another human being than it is to be real with Hashem, because Hashem cannot be perceived on a sensory level. Therefore, if you want to genuinely appreciate all the Almighty does for you, you first have to appreciate everything your parents have done for you. They are more concrete, and their giving is more real and far more tangible. First recognize your debt of gratitude to them, and then you will be able to appreciate what the Almighty has done for you and continues to do for you. The opposite is also true. If you cannot admit that you were helped by a human being, in the end you will certainly have a tough time admitting that you were helped by Hashem.

If you want to genuinely appreciate all the Almighty does for you, you first have to appreciate everything your parents have done for you.

Moshe's behavior was the opposite of Pharaoh's; he excelled in his ability to be grateful. Moshe not only appreciated the kindness he received from others, he was also careful to show his gratitude even to inanimate objects. As the Midrash says in explaining why Aharon, and not Moshe, was the one who brought the plagues of blood and frogs, "Since the Nile protected Moshe when he was cast into it, it therefore was not hit by him, neither with blood nor with frogs, but was hit by Aharon" (Rashi on *Shemos* 7:19, based on *Tanchuma, Va'eira* 14).

Pay Your Debts

Lavan Ha'arami is willing to recognize Hashem's existence and even admit that the Almighty Himself is involved in the affairs of man and has personally blessed him, as long as he does not have to admit that he owes Yaakov anything. That is why Lavan suddenly uses the word Hashem, which he never mentions again in the Torah.

Unless we are willing to recognize our debt of gratitude to our fellow man — whether it is to our parents, our friends, our teachers, or to anyone else who tries to help us — and to appreciate that the effort alone creates a debt of gratitude, then we are not truly *makir tov*, we do not recognize the good done to us. As a result, we will not be able to appreciate what the Almighty has given us, either. In the end, we may even say, "I do not know Hashem. I did all this myself. It was my hard work, my intelligence, my commitment, that brought this about. I don't owe Hashem anything."

We do not like to recognize the good that people do for us, for we think being beholden to them impinges on our independence.

We bristle against the idea that we are indebted to others. We do not like to recognize the good that people do for us, for we think being beholden to them impinges on our independence. But we are deceiving ourselves, just as Lavan did. Real independence means having the inner strength and humility to appreciate the gifts we have received from the people in our lives. Doing so is the only way to truly appreciate the gifts we have received from the Almighty as well.

We can discover where we are falling short by examining the strengths of the enemies that the Almighty has empowered against us.

פרשת וישלח

*P*arashas Vayishlach:
Encounters with the Enemy

Thirty-six years after fleeing from the murderous Eisav, Yaakov Avinu returns to Eretz Yisrael. While traveling, he gets word that Eisav is coming to meet him with an army of 400 men. "Yaakov became very frightened, and it distressed him" (*Bereishis* 32:8).

Why was Yaakov afraid? When he fled from Eisav many years ago, Hashem promised him that he would protect him: "Behold, I am with you; I will guard you wherever you go, and I will return you to this soil; for I will not forsake you until I will have done what I have spoken about you" (ibid. 28:15). Hashem certainly keeps His promises, so what was Yaakov worried about?

Yaakov was concerned that he no longer merited Hashem's protection. As Rashi says (ibid. 32:11), "My merits have diminished because of the kindnesses and the truth that You have done to me. Therefore, I fear lest I have become sullied with sin since the time that You promised me, and it will cause me to be delivered into the hand of Eisav."

What specific transgressions prompted Yaakov's self-doubt? The Midrash gives us the answer:

> Yaakov said, "All these years Eisav dwelt in the Land of Israel. Perhaps you will say that he will attack me on the strength of having dwelled in the Land. Furthermore, all these years Eisav remained and honored his parents. Perhaps he will attack me on the strength of having honored his father and mother" (Bereishis Rabbah 76:2).

Yaakov was afraid because Eisav excelled in two mitzvos in which Yaakov was weak. Namely, *yishuv Eretz Yisrael*, dwelling in the Land of Israel, and *kibbud av v'eim*, honoring parents. Since Yaakov lived outside of Israel for 36 years and was away from his parents during that time, he was deficient in those two mitzvos. He was vulnerable to attack by Eisav, because Eisav had merits in the areas where he was weak.

That Eisav was strong precisely in the areas where Yaakov was deficient was no accident. Hashem used Yaakov's enemy as a means to get his attention and spur him to do *teshuvah*. If we are not internally motivated to grow spiritually and improve the weak areas of our *avodas Hashem*, then Hashem may deploy our enemy's strength to reveal the exact areas we need to grow in and give us an external push to confront our weaknesses.

As a nation today, we can discover where we are falling short by examining the strengths of the enemies that the Almighty has empowered against us. In contemporary times we have two primary enemies that we need to contend with: Christianity and Islam. Each one embodies a strength that Hashem is using to point out where we need to improve.

Each year, the Christian world spends billions of dollars and hundreds of thousands of man hours missionizing Jews and other non-Christians across the globe. They are driven by the understanding that if you know you have the truth, you are morally obligated to expend huge resources and effort to reach out to those who are ignorant and unenlightened. Though misguided in who they worship, they realize that truth is not only for the individual; the Almighty wants His truth spread to the world.

In a perverse manner, the Muslims exemplify the trait of self-sacrifice. They operate according to the principle that if you know you have the truth, you must be prepared to do everything in your power to bring that truth to the world, even if it means making the ultimate sacrifice and giving up your life for your beliefs. There are eternal truths that are worth dying for.

The Almighty is talking to the Jewish people through our two primary enemies. It behooves us to take to heart each of these lessons: to strengthen our efforts in reaching out to the rest of the Jewish people, and to be willing to sacrifice everything to fulfill Hashem's will.

Preparing to Meet the Enemy

Yaakov implements three different strategies in preparation for his fateful confrontation with Eisav.

First, hoping to bribe Eisav, he sends messengers with an enormous gift consisting of waves of livestock and servants. "I have acquired oxen and donkeys, flocks, servants, and maidservants and I am sending to tell my lord to find favor in your eyes" (*Bereishis* 32:6).[2]

Next, Yaakov prepares to do battle with Eisav in case his gifts do not appease him. "He divided the people with him, and the flocks, cattle, and camels, into two camps. For he said, 'If Eisav comes to the one camp and strikes it down, then the remaining camp shall survive'" (ibid. 8-9). On the words, "then the remaining camp shall survive," Rashi explains: "against [Eisav's] will, for I will wage war with him."

Yaakov's third and final preparation is to pray to Hashem to save him. "Then Yaakov said, 'God of my father Avraham and God of my father Yitzchak... Rescue me, please, from the hand of my brother, from the hand of Eisav, for I fear him...'" (ibid. 10-12).

The order of Yaakov's three-pronged defense strategy is obviously not random. Why, then, did he leave prayer for last? We know that the Jew's primary weapon is prayer: "*Hakol kol Yaakov* — the voice is the voice of Yaakov" (ibid. 27:22). Shouldn't praying

2. See Ramban on *Bereishis* 32:6.

to Hashem to save him be the first and most significant act of preparation?

Gifts and Guns

The Torah is teaching us several important lessons through the steps that Yaakov took and their specific order.

Yaakov first sends gifts to Eisav, because if a confrontation can be avoided through bribery, that is the best possible outcome at the least cost. If a few gifts can buy peace and avoid bloodshed, that is certainly the preferred route.

But a gift alone is a very dangerous strategy. A bribe is effective only if the enemy knows that beneath the velvet cover lies an iron fist. Eisav needs to know that if appeasement fails, Yaakov is fully committed to waging war and doing whatever it takes to protect his family.

Gifts that are not backed up by a clear readiness for confrontation become a statement of capitulation that breeds contempt, not peace. The enemy smells weakness, and his appetite is only whetted.

This is one of the reasons why the Oslo accords were such a dismal failure. Our Arab enemies realized that the nation of Israel was tired of war. The Israeli government was offering concessions without the readiness to go to war, if need be. As a result, land for peace brought only conflict and escalation. The Arab leaders viewed our concessions as capitulation, and as a result they were emboldened to harden their stance and attack Israel.

Prayer: Escape or Responsibility

Yaakov Avinu's decision to make prayer his third and final act of preparation teaches us a crucial lesson about the interplay between prayer and taking responsibility.

Prayer is only appropriate once we have undertaken as much responsibility as we possibly can. In the absence of assuming responsibility, we can cloak ourselves in self-righteousness and use prayer as an escape from our obligations. This is antithetical to what Hashem wants from us.

Imagine stumbling across a butterfly as it struggles to break out of its cocoon. You look in wonder at the metamorphosis that is occurring right before your eyes, and out of compassion, you tear open the cocoon to help the poor butterfly go free. You think you are doing a kindness for the emerging butterfly, but in fact you are harming it irrevocably. Hashem arranged it that the butterfly needs to exert its muscles by breaking out of its cocoon, because through this effort it gains the strength to flap its wings and fly.

The Almighty wants us to exert our muscles, to put in the necessary effort and learn what it means to be responsible. Turning to prayer as a quick fix that sidesteps responsibility runs counter to Hashem's overall purpose in this world because it robs us of the opportunity to emulate Him by utilizing our free will.

> *The Almighty wants us to exert our muscles, to put in the necessary effort and learn what it means to be responsible.*

Prayer reminds us that, ultimately, everything comes from the Almighty. But it is not appropriate until we have done our part and demonstrated to Hashem that we are acting responsibly and doing all that is in our power. That is why Yaakov Avinu prays only after he has completed the other two steps of preparation, and why we need to ensure that we are doing our utmost in being responsible before relying on prayer to save us.

*When you take responsibility for
the world, you become master of
the world.*

פרשת וישב

Parashas Vayeishev:
Defining Greatness

וַיֵּשֶׁב יַעֲקֹב בְּאֶרֶץ מְגוּרֵי אָבִיו בְּאֶרֶץ כְּנָעַן:

*Yaakov settled in the land of his father's sojournings, in
the land of Canaan (Bereishis 37:1).*

*After Yaakov sought to dwell in tranquility, the troubles
of Yosef sprang upon him. The righteous seek to dwell
in tranquility. Said the Holy One, blessed is He, "What
is prepared for the righteous in the World to Come is
not sufficient for them, but they seek [also] to dwell in
tranquility in this world!" (Rashi on Bereishis 37:2).*

Yaakov Avinu wanted some peace. After a difficult life — confrontation and struggle with Eisav and his angel, dealings with the dishonest Lavan, and the defilement of his daughter Dinah in Shechem, to name just a few — surely it was reasonable to desire a period of tranquility. But Hashem answers, "*Olam Haba* is not enough? You want peace in this world, too? No way!" And Hashem brings upon him the misfortunate of Yosef's disappearance for twenty-two years.

What was Yaakov's mistake? He certainly did not want to retire and spend his waning days golfing in Florida. He wanted to live *b'shalvah*, in tranquility, so he could learn Torah without distractions and interruptions. He wanted to grow closer to Hashem without stress or conflict. In short, he wanted a piece of *Olam Haba* in *Olam Hazeh*. What was wrong with that?

Since Hashem's reprimands always come to focus our attention on what we are doing wrong, we can discern Yaakov's mistake by working backward and examining his punishment. Yaakov's desire for tranquility caused Yosef to be taken away. After Yaakov's sons showed him Yosef's torn, bloodstained coat, Yaakov assumed that Yosef was dead, and he became inconsolable: "He refused to comfort himself, and said: 'For I will go down to the grave [*avel she'olah*] mourning for my son'" (ibid. 37:35).

Based on the word "*she'olah*," grave — which can also mean Gehinnom, purgatory — the Midrash teaches us that Yaakov thought Yosef's apparent death was a sign from Hashem that he needs to journey through Gehinnom, since he had a tradition that he would be assured a place in the World to Come if all twelve of his sons would remain alive in his lifetime (*Tanchuma, Vayigash* 9; see also *Midrash Shocher Tov, Vayigash* 44:29).

What did Yaakov Avinu really want? He wanted to feel that he accomplished his mission. He fathered the 12 tribes, the *Shivtei Kah*, and built the foundations of the Jewish people. To him, tranquility was knowing that his job was completed and that he could now focus exclusively on learning Torah. But Hashem replied, "You are not done until this world is transformed back into Gan Eden. You cannot live in peace when the world is filled with idol worshipers and is in such moral decay and turmoil. Your job is not at all done. It only ends once you leave this world and receive your reward in *Olam Haba*."

Responsibility and Leadership

Let us contrast this lesson about Yaakov Avinu with the next few *pesukim* that introduce us to Yosef.

> *These are the chronicles of Yaakov: Yosef, at the age of seventeen years, was a shepherd with his brothers by the flock, but he was a youth with the sons of Bilhah and the*

sons of Zilpah, his father's wives; and Yosef would bring
evil reports about them to their father. Now Yisrael loved
Yosef more than all his sons since he was a child of his old
age, and he made him a fine woolen tunic. His brothers
saw that it was he whom their father loved most of all his
brothers so they hated him; and they could not speak to
him peaceably. Yosef dreamt a dream, which he told to his
brothers, and they hated him even more (Bereishis 37:2-5).

Yosef has a prophetic dream that he is going to be a king over his brothers. What information does the Torah give us to shed light on why Yosef deserves to become king? In these few sentences the only action attributed to Yosef is that he brought evil reports to his father Yaakov regarding his brothers.

What was the evil report? Rashi tells us:

Any evil he saw in his brothers, the sons of Leah, he would
tell his father: 1) that they ate limbs from living animals, 2)
that they demeaned the sons of the handmaidens by calling
them slaves, and 3) that they were suspected of illicit
relationships.

Hashem punished him, measure for measure, for misjudging and speaking badly about his brothers. As Rashi says:

For these three reports he was punished: For [the report
that his brothers ate] limbs from living animals, "they
slaughtered a kid" (Bereishis 37:31) when they sold him,
and did not eat it alive. For the report that he related
about them that they called their brothers slaves, "Yosef
was sold as a slave" (Tehillim 105:17), and concerning
the illicit relationships that he related about them, "his
master's wife lifted her eyes" (Bereishis 39:7).

Hashem made it abundantly clear to Yosef that giving these reports was wrong. How, then, does this explain why Yosef should be king?

The Torah is teaching us a very important lesson: Yosef was trying to correct his brothers. In the end he was mistaken and was punished for his misplaced criticism, but his motivation was good; he wanted to help his brothers. He saw an issue and he took personal responsibility for it. That is what made him king. When you take responsibility for the world, you become master of the world. You are its caretaker.

If Jews in the world are trapped in Syria or Iran, can we live in peace? If Jews in Israel are being bombarded by rockets, forced to run for cover in bomb shelters, can we live in peace? If we care about the Almighty, can we rest if His children are estranged from Him? We cannot sit in peace when there is so much suffering.

Although he made a mistake in judgment, Yosef nonetheless took responsibility for his brothers, and by doing so he merited to become their leader.

The Clean-Up Man

The ascendancy of Yehoshua as the leader of the Jewish people is another example of how taking responsibility is the key to leadership. Although Yehoshua was 56 years old at the time of the giving of the Torah, he is nevertheless described as a *naar*, a lad: "Hashem would speak to Moshe face-to-face, as a man would speak with his fellow; then he would return to the camp. His servant, Yehoshua son of Nun, a lad, would not depart from within the Tent" (*Shemos* 33:11).

A *naar* is a youth, a lightweight, someone not very important. Why is Yehoshua described in this derogatory manner?

It was the Jewish people who described Yehoshua this way. They pointed a finger at him and said, "This guy is immature, he's a nobody." What did they have against Yehoshua? They thought he was unimportant because his primary role was in assisting Moshe. The Midrash says that the Jewish people learned Torah every day from Moshe, Aharon, and the *Zekeinim*. They would all come together in the tent to learn Torah, and go home at the end of the day to eat and discuss what they learned. After everyone was long gone, Yehoshua would stay behind to clean up, organize all the benches and chairs, and put away the *sefarim*. He wanted to make sure there would be no *bittul Torah*, no wasted time, the following morning. So the Jewish people viewed him as a maintenance man, the guy who cleans up because he has nothing else to contribute (*Yalkut Shimoni, Pinchas* 776).

They were wrong.

As Shlomo Hamelech said, "*Notzer te'einah yochal piryah* — the protector of a fig tree will eat its fruit" (*Mishlei* 27:18). The one who cares enough to take responsibility, without concern for his own standing, will be the next leader (based on *Tanchuma, Pinchas* 11).

> The Jewish people viewed Yehoshua as a maintenance man, the guy who cleans up because he has nothing else to contribute. They were wrong.

Imagine entering an exclusive art gallery where everything costs a fortune. Many wealthy, distinguished people are milling around, and it is impossible to discern who the owner is. Suddenly water starts gushing out of a broken pipe and a man quickly takes off his jacket, rolls up his sleeves, and starts fixing the pipe, getting soaked in the process. Now everyone knows who the owner is. He is the one who cares. He is the one who takes responsibility, rolls up his sleeves, and gets dirty fixing the pipe if that's what's needed.

Notzer te'einah yochal piryah, the protector of a fig tree will eat its fruit. The leader is the one who thinks about the needs of *Klal Yisrael*. He thinks about the tumult that will ensue the next morning when everyone returns to learn and the chairs are in disarray. Yehoshua was no lightweight. Serving Moshe and taking responsibility for the needs of *Klal Yisrael*, whatever they may be, is precisely what made him the next great leader of the Jewish people. "Hashem said to Moshe, 'Take to yourself Yehoshua son of Nun, a **man** in whom there is spirit, and lean your hand upon him'" (*Bamidbar* 27:18). The *naar*, the boy, became a man.

No Retreat

Yaakov Avinu wanted to sit *b'shalvah*, in tranquility, to learn Torah and grow. After dedicating himself to building the Jewish people, and all the suffering and conflict that it entailed, he yearned to climb to greater spiritual heights, unencumbered by the needs of the community, and finally focus on his own growth. Now, he thought, it was time for the 12 tribes of Israel to take the lead.

Hashem corrected him and showed him that as long as you are living in this world you cannot retreat from your responsibilities and focus only on self-perfection. "You are My partner," Hashem reproved him, "and I am suffering. My children still do not know Me; the job is not yet done. Your responsibility for the world ceases only once you enter *Olam Haba*." So Yaakov was punished with the disappearance of his son Yosef in order to teach him this lesson.

> As long as you are living in this world you cannot retreat from your responsibilities and focus only on self-perfection.

In contrast, Yosef was concerned for his brothers and took responsibility to correct them. Even though he was mistaken in his judgments, he merited to become a king because he took responsibility for them. Yehoshua, a descendant of Yosef, was concerned for *Am Yisrael* and as a result became the leader of *Klal Yisrael*.

We must ask ourselves: What responsibility can we undertake to help the Jewish people? We need to feel the *tzaar HaShechinah*, the pain Hashem feels, so to speak, over the assimilation and intermarriage of His children. When you truly care you will take responsibility. And when you take responsibility, you attain greatness and become a leader.

It is human nature to refuse to question the very axioms our worldview is based upon and become impervious to hearing an opposing message.

פרשת מקץ

Parashas Mikeitz: Getting the Message

Hashem is always sending us messages through His *Hashgachah Pratis*, His Divine Providence. But what do we need to do in order to understand His messages clearly? The saga of Yosef and his brothers gives us a critical insight regarding how to decipher Hashem's messages to us.

After Yosef's brothers falsely accused him of being a megalomaniac with fanciful dreams of ruling over them, they sold him into slavery. Yosef was separated from his beloved father for twenty-two years, and eventually became the viceroy in Egypt. There was famine in the land that forced his brothers to go down to Egypt to get food. Upon seeing them, Yosef devised a scheme to make them realize that they had misjudged him, and to cause them to do *teshuvah*.

Yosef's brothers were great men, the future progenitors of the Jewish people, who lived with a constant awareness of Hashem's presence in their lives. They knew that life is not a series of random events and that everything that happens is orchestrated by Hashem and contains a message.

But for some reason, no matter what events Hashem and Yosef conspired to bring upon his 10 brothers, they never fully got the message that Yosef's dreams were actually prophetic. It never occurred to them that they had completely misjudged him when they labeled him a usurper who was trying to push them out of the role of *Bnei Yisrael*, the children of Israel.

A Series of Partial Recognitions

Their first recognition that they had done something wrong is recorded in Parashas Vayeishev, when Yehudah was removed from power: "It was at that time that Yehudah went down from his brothers" (*Bereishis* 38:1). Rashi comments: "Why was this section placed here, where it interrupts the section dealing with Yosef? To teach us that [Yehudah's] brothers demoted him from his high position when they saw their father's pain. They said, 'You told us to sell him. Had you told us to return him, we would have obeyed you.'"

They did not recognize that it was wrong to sell Yosef; they realized only that they were wrong to cause their father such pain.

They did not recognize that it was wrong to sell Yosef; they realized only that they were wrong to cause their father such pain.

The second time they recognized that they had erred was when they went to Mitzrayim to purchase food, after Hashem brought a famine to the region. "So Yosef's brothers — ten of them — went down to buy grain" (ibid. 42:3). Why does the Torah refer to them as "Yosef's brothers" and not the sons of Yaakov? Rashi, based on the Midrash (*Bereishis Rabbah* 91:6), explains: "They regretted selling him and decided to behave toward him in a brotherly manner and to ransom him for whatever price would be demanded of them." Twenty-two years after selling Yosef, they took to heart Hashem's message in bringing a famine so that they should go find him and redeem him. The pain they had caused was too great, and now they wanted to correct their misdeed.

In Egypt, they were falsely accused of being spies. All ten brothers were placed in prison for three days until Yosef decided to detain only Shimon — the brother who actually threw Yosef into the pit — while the others headed back to Yaakov. Once again they realized that Hashem was sending them a message, and they asked themselves, "Why is this happening to us? What is the message?" The Torah says, "They then said to one another, 'Indeed we are guilty concerning our brother inasmuch as we saw his heartfelt anguish when he pleaded with us and we paid no heed; that is why this anguish has come upon us" (Bereishis 42:21). Nine of the brothers said it was their fault because they did not have mercy on their brother. They got part of the message. Reuven, the oldest brother, went even further and told them that they were wrong in their judgment about Yosef. But they still did not put all the pieces together; they did not realize that Yosef was standing before them.

After money was discovered in each of their sacks, they were again falsely accused of stealing. "Their hearts sank, and they turned trembling one to another, saying, 'What is this that God has done to us?'" (ibid. 42:28). They were afraid; they realized something was happening, but they still could not connect all the dots.

Then Yosef did something that only someone intimately familiar with the sons of Yaakov could have done: he sat them around the table according to their order of birth. "They were seated before him, the firstborn according to his seniority and the youngest according to his youth. The men looked at one another in astonishment" (ibid. 43:33). What are the odds of getting this order right? Who else could have known this information besides a member of Yaakov's family? How obvious can it get? But the brothers still did not dream that the viceroy in front of them was their brother Yosef!

And finally, Binyamin was framed with the viceroy's cup and taken captive. The brothers mistakenly assumed that he was guilty, but they did realize that they had to fight for him. Seeing their commitment to their brother, Yosef could no longer withhold his identity, and he finally revealed himself to them: "Ani Yosef — ha'od avi chai? I am Yosef — is my father still alive?"

Why Did They Not Get the Message?

The ten brothers were great men who continuously strove to understand the deeper meaning behind Hashem's Providence. Why did they not grasp what the Almighty was telling them? Why did they not realize that the viceroy was none other than Yosef?

Had they just asked themselves one question, it would have been impossible for them to miss the message. That question was: Is it possible that Yosef's dreams were really prophetic? Once they asked themselves that question, they would then have had to ask themselves: If the dreams were prophetic, and we were destined to bow down before Yosef, could it be that the man who somehow knew the order of our births, the man we bowed down to — just as Yosef's dream depicted — is actually Yosef? All the pieces would have suddenly clicked, and they would have realized how badly they misjudged Yosef twenty-two years earlier. They would have understood that the viceroy chose to leave Shimon behind bars since he was the one who cast Yosef into the pit and said to Levi, "Look! That dreamer is coming!" (ibid. 37:19). It would have explained all the false accusations leveled at them, as well as why they were being forced to defend Binyamin.

Had they at some point reconsidered their original judgment of Yosef and entertained the possibility that their assessment of him as a usurper was wrong, they would have immediately recognized him.

Their core mistake was their unwillingness to reevaluate their underlying assumptions. Once they made their judgment twenty-two years earlier, that judgment became sacrosanct. Their assessment became an immovable pillar of truth holding up an entire edifice of subsequent decisions. They were not prepared to dismantle this edifice by challenging the assumptions underpinning it, and that blinded them to what was patently obvious.

Reevaluate Your Assumptions

If Yosef's brothers fell into the trap of closed-mindedness, then we most certainly need to be on guard to prevent ourselves from being ensnared in tunnel vision. It is human nature to refuse to question the very axioms our worldview is based upon and to become impervious to hearing an opposing message.

There is an old joke about a small town that gets a flood warning. As soon as the storm begins, everyone in the town runs, except one man. A state trooper drives by in his jeep and says, "Buddy, get inside. A flood is coming!"

"It's O.K.," says the man. "I trust in God. He will save me." Shaking his head, the state trooper drives off.

A short while later, the man is standing in two feet of water, and a heavy-duty amphibian truck manned by the Coast Guard finds him. "Hey, come on aboard!" they shout. "The water is rising!"

"It's O.K.," he assures them. "I'm fine, I trust in God. He will save me."

The water creeps up to his second-floor window. There are no trucks around anymore, just emergency boats looking for stranded people. The skipper of one of these boats spots him and calls out, "Come on board!"

But the man stays put. "No thanks," he says. "I trust in God. He will save me."

The water rises to his roof, forcing him to scramble to the top of his chimney. A helicopter swoops by, dropping a rope. "Grab on to the rope and let's get out of here!" the pilot yells.

"No, no," the man says serenely. "My trust in God is complete. He will save me."

The helicopter flies away, and the water engulfs the man, drowning him. He goes to Heaven and complains to Hashem, "I trusted You! Why didn't You save me?"

"I kept sending messengers to save you!" Hashem replies. "I sent you a jeep, I sent you an amphibian truck, I sent you a boat, I sent you a helicopter. What more did you want Me to do?"

The man was trapped by his notions of what trusting in Hashem means. He never considered the possibility that the Almighty wanted him to grab onto the rope and put in his *hishtadlus*, his effort.

When was the last time you challenged your assumptions and truly questioned the basic underpinnings of your life? Ask yourself: Why do I learn Torah? What are my goals? Why am I learning Torah according to this *derech*, this approach? Should I consider a different approach? Why am I working as a professional? Should I dedicate my life to working for *Klal Yisrael*, the Jewish people? Should I curb back my efforts to advance my career and spend more time learning, or doing outreach, or with my family? Just how much money do I really need each year?

We would likely discover a number of startling insights if we would step out of our box and question our assumptions. It is not easy, but with courage, open-mindedness, and fierce objectivity, it is doable. But if we remain stuck in our thinking, then we can miss the obvious that is right under our nose.

At the very least, we should pray to Hashem to give us the clarity to understand His messages and uncover the faulty assumptions that may be hampering our ability to hear what He is saying.

Hashem is trying to get our attention. If we remain oblivious, that compels Him to send us louder wake-up calls.

Hashem is talking to us. He wants us to understand His messages. Sometimes they are very obvious, but we need to discover them ourselves. In the end the brothers did not get the message themselves, and Yosef had to reveal himself. Hashem is trying to get our attention. If we remain oblivious, that compels Him to send us louder wake-up calls. Let us embrace Hashem's Providence, reconsider our assumptions, and open ourselves up to seeing His guiding Hand and internalizing the messages He is transmitting to us.

*Hashem has the entire record of
our lives before Him, and when He
shows us what we were capable of
doing when we were motivated, we
will be left with no reply.*

פרשת ויגש

Parashas Vayigash:
Judgment Day

It is one of the most dramatic moments depicted in the Torah. Risking his life, Yehudah confronts the viceroy of Egypt, pleading that he be allowed to take the place of his imprisoned youngest brother Binyamin in order to spare his father the debilitating anguish of losing the last of Rachel's children.

Moved by Yehudah's dedication and self-sacrifice, Yosef can no longer continue to conceal his identity.

> *Now Yosef could not restrain himself in the presence of all
> who stood before him, so he called out, "Remove everyone
> from before me!" Thus no one remained with him when
> Yosef made himself known to his brothers. He cried in a
> loud voice. Egypt heard, and Pharaoh's household heard.
> And Yosef said to his brothers, "I am Yosef. Is my father
> still alive?" But his brothers could not answer him because
> they were left disconcerted before him (Bereishis 45:1-3).*

In an instant, everything changes. *"Ani Yosef* — I am Yosef": I am the one you sold into slavery, the one you thought was a dreamer trying to usurp power. Upon hearing those words, the brothers suddenly realize that everything they had thought about Yosef for the last twenty-two years was wrong. All the pieces come together, and they are rendered speechless in shock and embarrassment.

Chazal say that this experience will be replayed for each of us when we stand before Hashem and face our final judgment.

> Woe unto us on the Day of Judgment; woe unto us on the Day of Rebuke! Yosef was the youngest among the tribes [he was younger than all those who sold him], and yet they could not withstand his rebuke... *How much more so, when Hashem will come and reproach everyone according to what He is, will we not be able to tolerate this rebuke* (Bereishis Rabbah 93:10).

The Almighty is going to say to all of us, "I am Hashem," and in an instant we, too, will be rendered speechless. All of our excuses and false thinking (this problem is unsolvable; I can't handle it) and insidious complaints (Hashem isn't being fair; how can He do this to me?) will evaporate when we encounter the reality of Hashem.

There is an additional element to Yosef's rebuke. He asks his brothers, "Is my father still alive?" But Yosef certainly knows his father is still alive. After all, immediately afterward he says, "Hurry — go up to my father and say to him, 'So said your son Yosef: "Hashem has made me master of all Egypt. Come down to me; do not delay"'' (Bereishis 45:9). So why does Yosef ask if his father is still alive?

The *Beis HaLevi* (Bereishis 45:3) explains that this is part of Yosef's *tochachah,* his rebuke to his brothers. Yehudah has just made an impassioned plea, telling Yosef that he cannot take Binyamin because it will kill his father Yaakov. "Even if Binyamin is a thief," Yehudah argues, "you cannot do something that will cause so much pain and anguish to my father. Take me instead."

To which Yosef replies, "I am Yosef, is my father still alive?" In other words: Where was your concern for our father's pain when you sold me into slavery?

With these few words, Yosef is showing his brothers their moral failing. He does not preach; instead, he focuses their attention on how their own actions contradict their stated goal of sparing their father pain. And just as Yosef showed his brothers the inconsistency of their behavior, Hashem will show each one of us our inconsistencies and hypocrisy, and then all our rationalizations will come crashing down.

Eliyahu and the Fisherman

The Midrash (*Yalkut Shimoni, Nitzavim* 940) relates that Eliyahu Hanavi was once walking down the street, when he encountered a man who was a scoffer and a cynic. Eliyahu asked him, "What will you answer your Creator on the Day of Judgment?"

"I have the perfect answer," the cynic responded. "Hashem did not give me the requisite wisdom and understanding to learn His Torah and Talmud. I tried, but it just doesn't go into my head."

Eliyahu then asks him, "My son, how do you make a living? What is your occupation?"

"I am a fisherman."

"Fascinating," Eliyahu replied. "Would you mind telling me about your profession?"

The man explained to him all the intricacies involved in making nets, casting them, and raising them from the water. Eliyahu listened to his lengthy explanation and said, "Fantastic, you really know your business. Tell me, who gave you the understanding to do this?"

"Hashem," the fisherman answered.

"Hashem gave you the wisdom and understanding to fish," Eliyahu challenged him, "but He did not give you the wisdom and understanding to learn His Torah, about which it is written, '[The Torah] is very near to you — in your mouth and in your heart — to perform it' (*Devarim* 30:14)? If the Almighty gave you this intelligence to fish, then there is no question He gave you the intelligence to learn His Torah."

Recognizing the truth of Eliyahu's words, the fisherman let out a gasp and burst out crying.

Every last one of us walking the face of the earth uses a similar excuse: "If only Hashem had taught me how to learn, if only

Hashem would show me how to change the world, if only I knew how to change myself — but what can I do? Hashem did not give me those gifts."

And Hashem will answer, "Your own deeds testify against you." He will remind us of how we mastered reams of material for that biology course, memorized the periodic table and the lineups of baseball teams, aced the LSAT test, graduated from medical school.

Hashem has the entire record of our lives before Him, and when He shows us what we were capable of doing when we were motivated, we will be left with no reply. The truth will be staring us in the face: "Woe unto us on the Day of Judgment; woe unto us on the Day of Rebuke!"

Examine the Consequences

Looking to soothe the distraught fisherman, Eliyahu told him that this tendency to rationalize is part of the human condition; we all think we have the perfect excuse that will get us off the hook when we face Hashem. It behooves us to look into ourselves *now*, to get real and wake up from our slumber. Let's not wait until we enter *Olam Haba*, the Next World, when it is too late to change.

With no rationalizations to rely on, wouldn't we know Shas? Wouldn't we love our fellow Jew, regardless what color kippah he wears — or even if he wears no yarmulke at all?

> We have to find the tools to wake ourselves up — and that is the purpose of *tochachah*, rebuke.

We have to find the tools to wake ourselves up — and that is the purpose of *tochachah*, rebuke. This is the message Yosef is sending his brothers when he asks, "Is my father still alive?" He is telling them to look at the consequences of their actions: "You do not want to cause your father torment; you are ready to fight to the death over the taking of Binyamin. But did you examine the consequences of your actions when you tore me away from my father? *Is my father still alive?*"

It is easy to remain within the comfort zone of our thought patterns and behaviors and take the path of least resistance. But we must stop and look at the consequences, rather than allow ourselves to hurtle forward in the grip of our desire without thinking where we are really headed. Then, we stand a chance of not making a mistake.

Think of the consequences of not learning Torah in the maximal way you are capable of; think of the impact it will have on you and your family. Think of the consequences of turning a blind eye to the rampant assimilation and intermarriage that are ravaging our nation, and think of how each of us will be taken to task for not saving the brothers and sisters that were within our reach: in the office, on the block, or within our extended families.

Think of the consequences. We must live in reality, because one day Hashem is going to say to every single one of us, "*Ani Hashem* — I am the Almighty,*" and He will then show us how our own lives directly contradicted our excuses. He will show us that when we were committed to getting something done, for whatever reason, we bore the frustration, sought out solutions, and did not give up until we reached our goal. He will show us that if, G-d forbid, it was our sister marrying a non-Jew, or it was our son trapped in a cult or off the *derech*, we would turn the world upside down and do everything in our power to save them. So where were we when it was Hashem's child, our Jewish brother or sister?

The clock is ticking; we will not live forever. So let's stop making excuses.

Hashem is going to show us, as Yosef showed his brothers. But we can avoid this embarrassment by waking up now and considering the consequences of our actions. Hashem is Life itself, and He wants us to wake up and live. There is no need for guilt, for this struggle is part of the human condition. That does not exempt us from getting moving, however. The clock is ticking; we will not live forever. So let's stop making excuses, and instead embrace our responsibilities in every way we can.

Ephraim and Menashe built a
relationship of love and mutual respect
that left no room for any misjudgments
or resentments, even when the younger
was favored over the older.

פרשת ויחי

Parashas Vayechi:
Eradicating Baseless Hatred

Realizing that his father, Yaakov, is deathly ill, Yosef brings his sons Ephraim and Menashe to him for a blessing: "So [Yaakov] blessed them that day, saying, 'By you shall Israel bless saying: May God make you like Ephraim and like Menashe'" (*Bereishis* 48:20).

Throughout history, Jewish fathers have blessed their sons every Friday night at the Shabbos table to be like Ephraim and Menashe. Jewish daughters, on the other hand, are blessed to emulate the ways of our matriarchs, Sarah, Rivkah, Rachel, and Leah.

Blessing our daughters to be like the matriarchs, the greatest women in Jewish history, is quite understandable. But why don't we bless our sons to be like our patriarchs, Avraham, Yitzchak, and Yaakov? Why do we bless them to be specifically like Yosef's sons, Ephraim and Menashe?

No Resentment

The relationship of Ephraim and Menashe epitomizes the way brothers should love and trust each other. When Yaakov gave the younger brother Ephraim the favored blessing (represented by Yaakov's right hand), Menashe, the firstborn, could have protested and resented his brother for taking what was rightfully his.

Menashe understood that what matters most is not his position or status, but rather what is best for the Jewish people.

But Menashe said nothing. He understood that what matters most is not his position or status, but rather what is best for the Jewish people. If Yaakov saw that favoring Ephraim was what the Jewish people needed, then Menashe accepted that with a full heart.

We bless our sons to emulate Ephraim and Menashe because their relationship was without any trace of resentment. They are our role models.

Seeds of Hatred

In the beginning of Parashas Vayigash, Yosef rebuked his brothers powerfully when he revealed himself. The Torah says, "Now Yosef could not restrain himself in the presence of all those who stood before him, so he called out, 'Remove everyone from before me!' Thus no one remained with him when Yosef made himself known to his brothers… And Yosef said to his brothers, "I am Yosef. Is my father still alive?" But his brothers could not answer him because they were left disconcerted before him" (ibid. 45:1, 3).

After hearing Yehudah's impassioned plea that he be imprisoned in Binyamin's stead in order to save his father the crushing pain of losing Rachel's only remaining son, Yosef could no longer restrain himself and continue to mask his identity. This implies that if Yosef could have held back longer, he would have. Why was this not the right time to reveal himself? What was missing from the process Yosef had put his brothers through in order to prompt them to do *teshuvah*?

Yosef disclosed his identity before the brothers realized on their own that they had misjudged him entirely. This robbed them of the opportunity to perform the truest form of *teshuvah*, which is *teshuvah* that is prompted purely by an internal recognition of one's misdeed. Because Yosef told them who he was, their subsequent *teshuvah* was based on an external catalyst, and was therefore slightly deficient.

Yosef's modus operandi all along was to get his brothers to realize their mistake on their own. Had he restrained himself longer, they would have had the chance to discover their mistake and completely eradicate their tendency toward *sinas chinam*, baseless hatred, forever.

*T*he seeds of hatred remained, creating a defect in the spiritual DNA of the Jewish people that dramatically affected the course of Jewish history.

Since they did not do that, the seeds of hatred remained, creating a defect in the spiritual DNA of the Jewish people that dramatically affected the course of Jewish history. *Sinas chinam* became the Jewish people's cancerous growth.

History has unfortunately demonstrated the horrific results of this cancer. The Talmud (*Yoma* 9b) pinpointed *sinas chinam* as the cause of the destruction of the Second Temple and our 2000-year exile. It is also the source of the tremendous internal strife and disunity our nation experiences today.

Yosef almost succeeded in exterminating this fatal flaw, which had caused him so much pain. He did not manage to do so, however, because he was overcome by emotion and could no longer hold back from revealing himself to his brothers.

Yosef himself managed to raise two children who recognized the destructive consequences of baseless hatred. Ephraim and Menashe built a relationship of love and mutual respect that left no room for any misjudgments or resentments, even when the younger was favored over the older. That is why Ephraim and Menashe, and not our patriarchs, are the role models we bless our children to follow. They represent the ultimate antidote to the most profound weakness of the Jewish people, and serve as a hopeful reminder that *sinas chinam* can indeed be eradicated from our nation.

‏ספר שמות‎

Sefer Shemos

We will tear our clothes in mourning when His fury pours out and we will cry, "Where were we? We read the studies; we saw what was happening. What did we do about it?"

פרשת שמות

Parashas Shemos: With Fury Poured Out

וּבְנֵי יִשְׂרָאֵל פָּרוּ וַיִּשְׁרְצוּ וַיִּרְבּוּ וַיַּעַצְמוּ בִּמְאֹד מְאֹד וַתִּמָּלֵא הָאָרֶץ אֹתָם: וַיָּקָם מֶלֶךְ חָדָשׁ עַל מִצְרָיִם אֲשֶׁר לֹא יָדַע אֶת יוֹסֵף: וַיֹּאמֶר אֶל עַמּוֹ הִנֵּה עַם בְּנֵי יִשְׂרָאֵל רַב וְעָצוּם מִמֶּנּוּ: הָבָה נִתְחַכְּמָה לוֹ פֶּן יִרְבֶּה וְהָיָה כִּי תִקְרֶאנָה מִלְחָמָה וְנוֹסַף גַּם הוּא עַל שֹׂנְאֵינוּ וְנִלְחַם בָּנוּ וְעָלָה מִן הָאָרֶץ:

The Children of Israel were fruitful, teemed, increased, and became strong — very, very much so; and the land became filled with them. A new king arose over Egypt, who did not know of Yosef. He said to his people, "Behold! The people, the Children of Israel, are more numerous and stronger than we. Come, let us outsmart it lest it become numerous and it may be that if a war will occur, it, too, may join our enemies, and wage war against us and go up from the land" (Shemos 1:7-10).

W hen the nascent nation of Israel first came to Mitzrayim, they were treated as royalty. Yosef ruled the country and his brothers lived on the fattest part of the land, in Goshen, separated from the Egyptian masses. Then the Egyptians turned on them, brutally persecuting and enslaving them. What changed?

The Torah seems to say only that "a new king arose over Egypt who did not know of Yosef." He didn't remember Yosef because he didn't want to be indebted to him. And then this new king said, "The Jewish people are more numerous than us, more powerful than us. Let's outsmart them, because if they keep on multiplying they will become a fifth column. If there will be a war, they will side with our enemies and destroy us."

Why did Pharaoh turn on the Jews? What caused the Egyptians to suddenly hate us? What hint does the Torah give us to help us understand why this happened?

Assimilation and Anti-Semitism

The Torah's depiction of the rise of the new king who turned against the Jews is preceded by the verse, "The Children of Israel were fruitful, teemed, increased, and became strong — very, very much so; and the land became filled with them."

The Midrash (*Yalkut Shimoni* 1:7) explains: What does it mean that the land was full of them? After all, there were many more Egyptians than Jews. Rabbi Yochanan says that they filled the theaters and circuses, and this caused the immediate decree that the Jews must be separated from them.

> *he Jews in Egypt filled the theaters, they became baseball fans, they started making films in Hollywood. As a result, the Egyptians began to detest them.*

Citing the verse, "They betrayed Hashem, for they begot alien children" (*Hoshea* 5:7), the *Midrash Tanchuma* (*Shemos* 5) teaches that when Yosef died, the Jews stopped circumcising their children, saying, "We will become like the Egyptians."

The Jews in Egypt were assimilating. They filled the theaters, they became baseball fans, they started making films in Hollywood.

As a result, the Egyptians began to detest them, and sought to remove them from their midst. This was the first demonstration in Jewish history of the spiritual axiom built into the fabric of the universe: assimilation generates anti-Semitism.

How does this rule operate? The prophet Yechezkel describes the process, and we would do well to pay heed:

> As for what you say, "We will be like the nations, like the families of the lands, to worship wood and stone," as I live — the word of the Lord Hashem/Elokim — [I swear that] I will rule over you with a strong hand and with an outstretched arm and with outpoured wrath. I will take you out from the nations and gather you from the lands to which you were scattered, with a strong hand and with an outstretched arm and with outpoured wrath... I will make you pass under the rod and bring you into the bond of the covenant... then you will know that I am Hashem (*Yechezkel* 20:32-34, 37).

You want to assimilate? You think you can become part of the non-Jewish world and no one will bother you? Hashem says, "I will not let that happen. I will reign over you with fury poured out and take you out from among the nations."

The Almighty made a covenant with the Jewish people, and He promises that He will not let us assimilate. He guarantees that we will not get lost no matter how high the intermarriage rate. But what will stop the assimilation? Hashem unleashes the hatred of the non-Jews toward the Jews to keep them from assimilating. As Rav Chaim Volozhin famously said, "If the Jews don't make Kiddush, the non-Jews will make Havdalah." It will be terrible, it will be horrific, but it will save us from oblivion, and we will eventually thank Hashem for it.

Our Generation

Look at our generation: the ever-increasing rate of intermarriage, the millions of Jews who grow up unaffiliated or are raised in other religions, the large-scale abandonment of the path of our Torah. There is no question that Yechezkel is describing our generation. We are living it; we see the confusion engulfing our nation. And we can take some solace in knowing that Hashem will not let us get lost. But can we say that we are looking forward to the anger and the wrath that will pour out to wake us up? Do we want to hear "Death to the Jews" once again on the streets of Europe? To witness pogroms?

Who is responsible? Whom is Hashem warning through his prophet Yechezkel?

He certainly is not talking to Jake and Christine, the nice intermarried couple who have decide to raise their kids with both religions. Christine will remain a Catholic who will take the kids to church now and then, and Jake will take them to temple for the High Holy Days. They plan on celebrating both Chanukah and Christmas. During the spring they will have Easter egg hunts on the lawn and also a Passover Seder. If the kids want to remain Jewish, fine. If they will be Catholics, also fine. Hashem is not addressing Jake and Christine since they do not know any better.

He is talking to us, to the *bnei Torah* and *frum Yidden* who know Hashem exists, who know He gave us His holy Torah. He is talking to those of us who understand that we are losing millions of our brothers and sisters, that we are experiencing another *churban,* a spiritual holocaust. We are the only ones on earth who can hear Hashem's message. There is no one else. We are the ones who are responsible.

The prophet is warning us. We can either make a program, or *chas v'chalilah* there will be a pogrom.

Tear Your Hearts

The prophet says, "*Vekir'u levavchem ve'al bigdeicheim veshuvu el Hashem* — Rend your hearts and not your garments, and return to Hashem your God" (*Yoel* 2:13). Tear your hearts and do *teshuvah*, so you won't have to tear your clothes in mourning. Wake up! Shake yourself out of your apathy. Fix the root of the problem so that Hashem won't have to shake us up to get the message.

Hashem is talking to us. We need to take the message to heart. The Talmud teaches, "If one has a headache, it should appear in his eyes as if they placed him in chains [to stand on trial]" (*Shabbos*

32a). Don't wait for the calamity. If the writing is already on the wall, in the form of mounting anti-Semitism, you can anticipate the next harsher step if you do not wake up now and do *teshuvah*. It's going to get worse, because Hashem is not going to give up on us. Look at the consequences and channel that fear into action.

"I will rule over you with a strong hand and with an outstretched arm and with outpoured wrath." Hashem means business. He promises that He will not let the Jewish people disappear. We will tear our clothes in mourning when His fury pours out and we will cry, "Where were we? We read the studies; we saw what was happening. What did we do about it?" *Kir'u levavchem*, tear your hearts and wake up. *Ve'al bigdeichem*, do not tear your clothes, do not allow the looming catastrophe to happen. It is not enough to feel bad about the masses of Jews assimilating and intermarrying. We cannot remain complacent; we have to act.

> It is not enough to feel bad about the masses of Jews assimilating and intermarrying. We have to act.

We are responsible. We must mobilize and do what we can to reach our brethren and stem the tide of assimilation. Each and every one of us must think about what we can do. Every night before you go to sleep, spend 10 minutes thinking about what can be done.[1] Get involved; join the thousands of people getting practical training tools

---

1. Rabbi Weinberg left the following statement as part of his *tzavaah*, his last will and testament:

   To my children, my students, and to the contributors who in any way contributed to Aish HaTorah's cause,

   I instruct, implore, and advise each and every one of you to spend ten minutes every night to first focus on the terrible profanation of Hashem's Name in the fact that a majority of the Jewish people deny the validity of Judaism and our charge of being a light to the world.

   Secondly, to focus on the pain of our Creator, the subsequent pain of mankind, and to think what you can personally do about this problem.

   I instruct, implore, and advise all those who are thankful for what Aish HaTorah has done for them and those who respect my judgment, to do whatever they can to help Aish HaTorah fulfill its mission of bringing home to our Creator His children, wherever they may be.

from Project Inspire and reaching out to their non-religious neighbors, colleagues, and family members.

Baruch Hashem, *kiruv* has become more of a priority within the frum world over the last 40 years, and we are making a difference. But it is not enough. We have bought some time, but the storm clouds are growing. There is much to do. Hashem is waiting for us.

If you ever find yourself
questioning one of Hashem's
directives, worried that you are
going to look foolish, remember
Moshe and Aharon and the staff
that turned into a snake.

פרשת וארא

arashas Va'eira:
Element of Surprise

וַיֹּאמֶר ה' אֶל מֹשֶׁה וְאֶל אַהֲרֹן לֵאמֹר: כִּי יְדַבֵּר אֲלֵכֶם פַּרְעֹה
לֵאמֹר תְּנוּ לָכֶם מוֹפֵת וְאָמַרְתָּ אֶל אַהֲרֹן קַח אֶת מַטְּךָ וְהַשְׁלֵךְ
לִפְנֵי פַרְעֹה יְהִי לְתַנִּין: וַיָּבֹא מֹשֶׁה וְאַהֲרֹן אֶל פַּרְעֹה וַיַּעֲשׂוּ כֵן
כַּאֲשֶׁר צִוָּה ה' וַיַּשְׁלֵךְ אַהֲרֹן אֶת מַטֵּהוּ לִפְנֵי פַרְעֹה וְלִפְנֵי עֲבָדָיו
וַיְהִי לְתַנִּין:

Hashem said to Moshe and Aharon, saying, "When
Pharaoh speaks to you, saying, 'Provide a wonder for
yourselves,' you shall say to Aharon, 'Take your staff
and cast it down before Pharaoh — it will become a
snake.'" Moshe came with Aharon to Pharaoh and they
did so, as Hashem had commanded; Aharon cast down
his staff before Pharaoh and before his servants,
and it became a snake
(Shemos 7:8-10).

The epic battle of wills begins. Hashem tells Moshe and Aharon that Pharaoh is going to want to see a wonder, a miracle that verifies that God Almighty Himself in fact sent them. He wants to see something powerful, unique, and compelling. Hashem tells them the game plan — you're going to throw your staff down and it will turn into a snake — and the Torah says that they came to Pharaoh and they "did as Hashem commanded."

When the Torah says that they did as they were commanded, it is a statement of praise; "Look, they listened to Hashem!" But what was so impressive that warrants commending them? Hashem gives them a miracle to perform; wouldn't anyone do it? What's the big deal? Furthermore, the Torah praises their coming to Pharaoh. Strangely, it does not commend their actual performance of the miracle, which is written *after* this commendation. Isn't *that* what really deserves to be praised?

And what was the response to this miracle? Moshe and Aharon became the laughingstock of Egypt. Every Egyptian knew this simple parlor trick, even little children. As the Midrash says:

> Pharaoh started to laugh at [Moshe and Aharon] and said to them, "This is the sign of your God? Don't you know that all magic is in my domain?" He immediately summoned schoolchildren and they also [threw down their staff, which turned into a snake]. Then he called his wife who also did it... as did the magicians of Egypt and four- and five-year-old boys
>
> (Midrash Rabbah, Va'eira 9:6).

Pharaoh mocks them, saying that their little trick is like bringing coals to Newcastle. Imagine what Moshe and Aharon are thinking. Pharaoh is anxiously waiting to see what this God of the Jews is capable of doing, and this is the big miracle Hashem wants us to perform? Throw the stick and it will become a snake? Imagine if Hashem would tell you that He is sending you to MIT as a messenger of the Creator of the universe to show them that God indeed exists. When the team of professors asks you to perform a miracle to demonstrate God's power, Hashem instructs you to take out a safety match and strike it. Lo and behold: fire!

Are you prepared to go before the panel of professors and make a fool of yourself? "Safety matches? That's a good one! This guy is certifiably crazy."

In a nutshell, that was the plan Moshe and Aharon had going in to confront Pharaoh. All Hashem told them was to throw down the staff and it will turn into a snake. In their mind, that was the entire plan. They are standing in front of Pharaoh, who has called in everyone to take a look at these two fools.

This is why Hashem praises them for going to Pharaoh: "Moshe came with Aharon to Pharaoh and they did so, as Hashem had commanded." They knew they were entering the lion's den completely unarmed. Yet they did not question the Almighty and did exactly as He requested.

Caught Off Guard

Then Hashem turns the table on Pharaoh and his followers; the entire spectacle was a setup. "And the staff of Aharon swallowed their staffs" (*Shemos* 7:12). After the snakes reverted to staffs, wooden sticks all over the floor, Aharon's staff devoured their staffs. That one was not in the Egyptian repertoire of magic tricks. It was unquestionably a miracle.

> That one was not in the Egyptian repertoire of magic tricks. It was unquestionably a miracle.

"Pharaoh strengthened his heart and he did not heed them, as Hashem had spoken" (ibid. 7:13). Pharaoh had to strengthen his heart. That means he was scared out of his wits but he overcame his inner fear. The Midrash says he thought that if their staff could swallow up all those sticks, it could just as easily turn on his throne and wipe him out.

Hashem's orchestration was genius. If Moshe and Aharon would have come before Pharaoh and immediately played their hand, casting the staff down and swallowing up their sticks, the impact would have been far less. Pharaoh was waiting to see a miracle; he had steeled himself. He was ready for it and would not have had to harden his heart. He would have been impressed, but not scared.

And who would have heard of the miracle? Only Pharaoh and a few of his ministers would have seen it, and they would have made sure it remained a state secret. The Egyptian populace would never have known about it. What happens instead? Pharaoh calls in everyone: the schoolchildren, the wise men and magicians, his wife. It's on the front-page news! Everyone is in hysterics laughing at Moshe and Aharon.

The element of surprise is a key to an effective military strategy, as ancient Chinese general Sun Tzu writes in *The Art of War*, "Appear weak when you are strong, and strong when you are weak." So while everyone is laughing and their defenses are down, Hashem suddenly sends the entire Egyptian nation a chilling message that shocks them to their core: you are vulnerable, you can be devoured, and you are messing with the miraculous power of the God of the Jews. And Pharaoh and the Egyptians are shaken.

> The element of surprise is a key to an effective military strategy, as Sun Tzu writes in *The Art of War*, "Appear weak when you are strong, and strong when you are weak."

Hashem had an exact plan and wanted to make sure the entire people heard His message. So if you ever find yourself questioning one of Hashem's directives, worried that you are going to look foolish, remember Moshe and Aharon and the staff that turned into a snake. Hashem knows exactly what He is doing. At times we just need to be patient in order to see it.

*When you ask Hashem to judge
someone, you are judged first —
even if you are in the right.*

פרשת בא

arashas Bo:

The Last Plague

וַיֹּאמֶר ה׳ אֶל מֹשֶׁה עוֹד נֶגַע אֶחָד אָבִיא עַל פַּרְעֹה וְעַל מִצְרַיִם
אַחֲרֵי כֵן יְשַׁלַּח אֶתְכֶם מִזֶּה . . .

וַיְהִי בַּחֲצִי הַלַּיְלָה וַה׳ הִכָּה כָל בְּכוֹר בְּאֶרֶץ מִצְרַיִם מִבְּכֹר פַּרְעֹה
הַיֹּשֵׁב עַל כִּסְאוֹ עַד בְּכוֹר הַשְּׁבִי אֲשֶׁר בְּבֵית הַבּוֹר וְכֹל בְּכוֹר בְּהֵמָה:

*Hashem said to Moshe, "One more plague shall I bring
upon Pharaoh and upon Egypt; after that he shall send you
forth from here..."*

*It was at midnight that Hashem smote every firstborn in
the land of Egypt, from the firstborn of Pharaoh sitting on
his throne to the firstborn of the captive who was in the
dungeon, and every firstborn animal (Shemos 11:1, 12:29).*

Hashem tells Moshe, "This is it. I will strike down every firstborn
of the land of Egypt, from the firstborn of Pharaoh until the firstborn of the foreign captive that sits in jail." "*Kol bechor* — every firstborn" — implies that even if there was a tourist or temporary resident
from a different nation who was a firstborn or had a firstborn son, he

died as well (See Rashi, ibid. 12:29). And the Torah specifies that the firstborn of a prisoner of war was also killed in this final plague.

Rashi asks: Where is the fairness in killing the firstborn of a captive? Why should he die? He had nothing to do with enslaving the Jews. He was also one of the prisoners of Pharaoh.

Rashi gives two reasons, which means that both factors were necessary. One, these captives rejoiced at the suffering of the Jews. Two, so they would not say, "It was our gods who brought this punishment upon the Egyptians." So we can understand why the firstborn captives were killed as well. But Rashi does not include in his explanation why the firstborn of the temporary resident, the fellow from a foreign country who was living in Egypt, was killed. It seems that there was a different justification for killing him, even though he wasn't part of the government persecuting the Jews. What did he do wrong?

The answer is obvious, which is why Rashi did not bother to state it. You cannot be a tourist or a temporary resident in a country that is committing genocide. If you stay there, even if you are not actively involved, you are condoning the atrocity and are a part of it.

The captive in jail cannot get out. He is stuck there, so Rashi needs to explain the justification for killing his firstborn. But there is no need to explain why the temporary resident's firstborn is killed. How can he live in a country that is persecuting another nation? His silence means he is party to the crime.

> *There is no need to explain why the temporary resident's firstborn is killed. How can he live in a country that is persecuting another nation?*

There is no difference whether you're doing something actively or you're tacitly condoning it. As Edmund Burke famously said, "All that is necessary for the triumph of evil is that good men do nothing." According to intelligence services there are 1.2 billion Muslims in the world, of which 15-25 percent seek the destruction of the West. The remaining 75-85 percent of the Muslim population consists of peace-loving people, but that is irrelevant if they remain silent. It is the murderous radicals who drive the agenda, as Nazi Germany painfully testifies. When the majority is complacent, they are complicit to terror. They must take an active stance against violence.

Saving the Jewish Firstborn

If the Almighty was bringing a plague to kill the firstborn of the Egyptians, why did *Bnei Yisrael* have to take measures to ensure that *their* firstborn would not be killed?

> *Speak to the entire assembly of Israel, saying: On the tenth of this month they shall take for themselves — each man — a lamb or kid for each father's house... They shall take some of its blood and place it on the two doorposts and on the lintel of the houses in which they will eat it... The blood shall be a sign for you upon the houses where you are; when I shall see the blood and I shall pass over you; there shall not be a plague of destruction upon you when I strike in the land of Egypt*
> *(Shemos 12:3, 7, 13).*

Without the blood from the Korban Pesach on their doorposts, the firstborn of the Jews would have been killed as well. Why? The Jews were the ones being persecuted! Hashem was coming to save them. You need to have a reason to kill the firstborn of the captive; they enjoyed the persecution of the Jews or they would have said that their idols were the ones who did this. But the Jews were Hashem's people. They certainly did not enjoy their own persecution, and they knew it was Hashem doing all these miracles. So why did they have to put blood on their doorposts in order for the Almighty to skip over their homes and for them to remain unscathed by this plague? What did the Jews do wrong?

When you ask Hashem to judge someone, you are judged first — even if you are in the right. "Rav Chanan said: Whoever submits judgment to his fellow [to Heaven], he is punished [for his own sins] first" (*Bava Kamma* 93a). If you want justice served, you are asking Hashem to hold back his trait of mercy and stand in judgment. In that case, you need to be ready to bear the scrutiny of that justice, because Hashem will examine your actions first.

When you call out to Hashem and plead for mercy, you are appealing to His trait of kindness and forbearance. That becomes the reality of your relationship to Hashem. But when you say, "Hashem, look at what they are doing to me!" your relationship becomes one based on justice, and just as Hashem will judge your persecutor, so, too, He will judge you. If you fiercely criticize people for being wrong, then you believe that people's mistakes are their responsibility. That means you have accepted that your mistakes are your complete responsibility; otherwise you'd be a hypocrite.

Because justice was being meted out against the Jewish people's Egyptian oppressors, the Jews themselves were also subject to Hashem's judgment.

Like One Man with One Heart

This is an important lesson to take to heart. All too often we look at other people's mistakes with a fierce eye. We lack compassion and tolerance; we ignore the mitigating circumstances that help to explain why someone would make such a mistake. We refuse to see that deep down, others want to do the right thing and grow just as much as we do. They want to be kind. They want to share. They want to help. It's just that they're making a mistake; they're stuck in a box. Instead of understanding them, we condemn and create disunity, which weakens the foundation of our nation.

In the process, we also hurt ourselves, because by judging others, we are asking for judgment on ourselves. If you cannot tolerate someone else's mistake, the Almighty will not tolerate your mistake.

> *Our judgmentalism not only creates a barrier between ourselves and our brothers, it creates a barrier between us and Hashem.*

And our judgmentalism not only creates a barrier between ourselves and our brothers, it creates a barrier between us and Hashem, and drives away the *Shechinah*, the presence of the Almighty. This is the cause of our destruction.

At Sinai the Jewish people were united. "*Vayichan sham Yisrael neged hahar* — And Israel encamped there, opposite the mountain" (*Shemos* 19:2). The word "*vayichan* — encamped" is written in the singular; the nation became *ke'ish echad belev echad,* like one man with one purpose. When that happens, *HaKadosh Baruch Hu* leaves the heavens and communicates with us. That was Mount Sinai.

By uniting with other Jews, we can unleash the power of the Jewish people. But we have to overcome our cursed tendency to judge others and to be critical and intolerant. The genius of the Jewish people is within us, right here waiting to change the world. And we've seen glimpses of it, such as when much of the Jewish world united in 1948 to fulfill the dream of coming back to our land, to build our own nation. We saw it at the Siyum HaShas.

But we are divided by senseless hate, endless criticism, and constant infighting, which undermines our potential for greatness.

What is the answer? *Ke'ish echad belev echad,* like one man with one heart: to always keep in mind our ultimate purpose and vision, the unifying goal that brings us together "to perfect the universe under the Almighty's sovereignty."

When we keep focused on the bigger goal, we can rise above our pettiness and mean-spiritedness. We can learn to be forgiving and give the benefit of the doubt, to hold back our judgment and criticism. If we focus on our common vision, our power is unlimited, because we will have tapped into Hashem's unceasing energy and merited His presence. This will enable us to succeed far beyond our expectations and dreams.

Bedecked in their kippahs and shtreimels, Shmulik and Zelig conversed in Hebrew as they watched the Egyptian Olympics.

פרשת בשלח

arashas Beshalach:
The Merit to Leave Egypt

The Torah says, "The Children of Israel were armed (*chamushim*) when they went up from the land of Egypt" (*Shemos* 13:18).

Rashi explains, based on the Midrash, that the word "*chamushim*" means "divided by five (*chamishah*)." In other words, one out of five Jews left Egypt, while four-fifths died during the three days of darkness. Earlier, in Parashas Bo, on the verse, "And there was thick darkness over the entire land of Egypt for three days" (10:22), Rashi notes: "Because there were among the Jewish people of that generation wicked people who did not want to leave. They died during the three days of darkness, so that the Egyptians would not see their downfall and say, 'They too are being smitten like us.'"

This is an incredible statement. Four-fifths of the Jewish people wanted to stay in Egypt. Four-fifths of the Jewish people had assimilated so deeply that even though they understood that Hashem sent Moshe to take them out of Egypt, they preferred to stay in the land that oppressed them. This was after eight plagues that even Pharaoh and his advisers recognized were coming from the Almighty, as they stated, "*Etzba Elokim hi* — This is the finger of God."

Despised by the Egyptians, the vast majority of Jews nonetheless viewed themselves as part of the fabric of Egyptian culture. They were worshiping their idols, attending their theaters, visiting their museums — completely submerged in their culture.

It makes you pause and wonder: if Mashiach were to come today, how many of us in *chutz la'aretz* would pack our bags and leave our homes and businesses to come to Eretz Yisrael, even if we knew it was the Almighty telling us to come? Assimilation cuts very deep. It dulls the soul, seeps into our bones, and causes us to lose our bearings.

What was the merit of the one-fifth of the Jewish people who did leave Egypt? Chazal say that in the merit of three things our forefathers left Egypt: they did not change their clothes, their names, or their language. *Chochmas Adam* (89:1) explains:

> *Becoming close to [the nations] causes us to learn from their actions, as it is written, "But they mingled with the nations and learned their deeds" (Tehillim 106:35). Therefore, our Creator commands us to separate ourselves, as it is written, "And I have separated you from the peoples (Vayikra 20:27)."*
> [See also Vayikra Rabbah 32:5.]

The Jews in Egypt used their Hebrew names. They wore clothing that clearly identified them as Jews, perhaps a yarmulke or tzitzis. And they did not change their language; they spoke Hebrew. But they were completely assimilated, as Chazal say, "*Halalu ovdei avodah zarah vehalalu ovdai avodah zarah* — These [Egyptians] are idol-worshipers and these [Jews] are idol-worshipers" (*Zohar* 2, 170b). They were uncircumcised.

*T*he one-fifth that came out of Egypt was saved because they held onto their Jewish identity by the skin of their teeth.

"The land became filled with them" (*Shemos* 1:7): the persecution was triggered by the Jews becoming part of the nation, going to the theaters and circuses (see Shemos: With Fury Poured Out). Yet they did not change their names or their clothing, and they spoke Hebrew.

Chazal tells us that this was their saving grace. Eighty percent of the Jews died in Egypt. The one-fifth that came out was saved because they held onto their Jewish identity by the skin of their teeth. How could they have assimilated to such a degree but still kept their unique names, language, and clothing? What made them cling to that?

Rooting for Your Team

In 1977, during the height of the Cold War, when the Soviet Union was boycotting Israel, the Maccabi Tel Aviv basketball team was playing against CSKA Moscow, the team of the Red Army, in the European Cup semifinals. The Russians refused to play in Tel Aviv and they also refused to grant visas to Israelis to play in Moscow. In the end they compromised and played in a small town in Belgium. It was an emotionally charged game, infused with symbolic meaning.

While Israelis were glued to their television sets watching the pivotal game, Russian Jews in the Soviet Union who had never been to Israel and knew next to nothing about Judaism found themselves rooting for the Israeli team as well. They could not read *Aleph Beis*, but they identified with the Israeli team as being "our team."

Imagine Maccabi Tel Aviv playing against an American all-star team in Staples Center, or Israel's national soccer team playing in Brazil. Would the local Jews in these stadiums cheer for the opposing Israeli team in front of their friends and thousands of other spectators, or would they root for their home team? It's not so clear. But in the Soviet Union, where dissidents had to risk their lives to learn Torah and study Hebrew, Russian Jews proudly identified with the Israelis who represented their people, even though it was only in the context of a non-Jewish sporting event. (By the way, the Maccabi Tel Aviv team beat the heavily favored and mighty Soviets 91-79.)

Did they have the Jewish education to understand what it really means to be Jewish? No, but they knew they were Jewish, they knew that Jews had returned to their homeland and built a country against all odds, and they were proud of it. Most of them could not at that time articulate what exactly they were proud of, but holding on to that tenuous pride was their saving grace. Because they were proud to be Jews, they wanted to know what being a Jew really means. Their vestige of Jewish identity propelled them to learn Torah and speak Hebrew.

Chazal (*Zohar*, Parashas Yisro) tell us that *Bnei Yisrael* in Mitzrayim were on the forty-ninth level of *tumah*, on the verge of spiritual annihilation. The reason that one-fifth came out of Egypt was because even though they were totally assimilated, they were proud to identify themselves as Jews. They kept their names, their clothing, and their language. Bedecked in their kippahs and *shtreimels*, Shmulik and Zelig conversed in Hebrew as they watched the Egyptian Olympics.

Shevet Levi Was Not Enough

According to the Midrash, the Jews in Egypt were redeemed in the merit of not changing their names, their clothing, or their language. Why was this merit necessary? Throughout the Jewish people's stay in Egypt, the tribe of Levi spent their days immersed in Torah. They steadfastly observed the mitzvos they had been given, including *bris milah*. Shouldn't the merit accrued by the tribe of Levi have been enough to save the rest of the Jewish people?

The same question arises in connection to the Rambam's description of the history of idolatry and Avraham Avinu's revolutionary teaching of monotheism. The understanding of One God, as the Rambam explains, was about to be extinguished as the Jewish people languished in Egypt. He writes:

> When the Jews extended their stay in Egypt, however, they learned from the [Egyptians'] deeds and began worshiping the stars as they did, with the exception of the tribe of Levi, who clung to the mitzvos of the patriarchs, and never served false gods.
>
> Within a short time, the fundamental principle that Avraham had planted would have been uprooted, and the descendants of Yaakov would have returned to the errors of the world and their crookedness. Because of God's love for us, and to uphold the oath He made to Avraham, our patriarch, He brought forth Moshe, our teacher, the master of all prophets, and sent him [to redeem the Jews]. After Moshe, our teacher, prophesied, and God chose Israel as His inheritance, He crowned them with mitzvos and informed

them of the path to serve Him, [teaching them] the judgment prescribed for idol worship and all those who stray after it

(*Hilchos Avodah Zarah* 1:3).

The Rambam states that even though the tribe of Levi clung to the mitzvos and never served idols, the clarity of monotheism was about to be uprooted from the world, had the Jews not been redeemed right away.

It is clear from here that when Hashem judges the Jewish people He looks at the nation as a whole. It is not sufficient to have one distinct part of the *klal*, the nation, holding steadfast in their commitment to Torah and mitzvos. Even though the tribe of Levi was a bastion of Torah learning, they could not save the Jewish people in Egypt when the nation as a whole was on the brink of irreversible assimilation. It was the merit of the nation just barely clinging to their Jewish identity through their names, clothing, and language that redeemed them.

Even though the tribe of Levi was a bastion of Torah learning, they could not save the Jewish people in Egypt when the nation as a whole was on the brink of irreversible assimilation.

The *Olam HaTorah*, the vibrant Torah community, is the heart of our nation; without that life force we cannot survive. But all Jews are interconnected, forming parts of an integrated whole, and Hashem assesses the spiritual health of the entire Jewish people. No part can sever itself from the whole.

Never in Jewish history have there been more people learning Torah full time, but at the same time assimilation is wreaking havoc on our people. We are losing untold numbers of Jews. We cannot sanguinely take refuge in the teeming *batei medrashim* where, *baruch Hashem*, the *kol haTorah*, the sound of Torah learning, reverberates. Hashem is looking at the Jewish people as a whole and He sees millions of Jews, the vast majority of our people, on the brink of extinction.

Every Jewish *neshamah* is precious to the Almighty. Every intermarriage is a tragedy that hurts like parents losing a child. Hashem yearns to save His people. He is expecting us who appreciate

His Torah and mitzvos to reach out to our brothers and sisters. Otherwise we will become swept up, God forbid, in whatever measures Hashem deems necessary to straighten out His people. If the love for our fellow Jews burns strongly in our hearts, we can defeat the tide of assimilation. The Almighty, and all of humanity, is counting on us.

*We clung to our beliefs despite
unremitting persecution because we
were supremely confident that our
beliefs were true.*

פרשת יתרו

*P*arashas Yisro:
The First Mitzvah: Know Hashem

"I am Hashem, your God, Who has taken you out of the land of
Egypt, from the house of slavery" (*Shemos* 20:2).

The first of the *Aseres HaDibros*, the Ten Commandments, is
to know there is a God. It is also the first mitzvah in the Rambam's
listing of the 613 mitzvos. He explains:

> The foundation of all foundations and the pillar of wisdom is
> to know (*leida*) that there is a Primary Being Who brought
> into being all existence. All the beings of the heavens, the
> earth, and what is between them came into existence only
> from the truth of His being (*Sefer Mada, Hilchos Yesodei
> HaTorah* 1:1).

The Rambam specifically uses the verb "*leida*" — to know — in
explaining our obligation in this mitzvah. But whom is this mitzvah
addressing? Someone who does not believe in God does not believe
in a Commander, and without a Commander, there can be no
commandment. And someone who does believe in God is already
fulfilling the mitzvah. Therefore, this mitzvah seems to be either
irrelevant or redundant.

Our answer is predicated on the fact that one's belief in Hashem lies on a continuum of understanding. This mitzvah is speaking to the believer and it is telling him to deepen his belief in Hashem. A belief in God based only on the teachings of one's parents and teachers must be upgraded. Hashem wants a person to shake off his complacency regarding his belief in God and strengthen this fundamental conviction by independently verifying it.

This is accomplished by establishing a rational foundation to corroborate what you have been taught to believe and accept. Furthermore, by identifying your questions and doubts, and working on gathering the information you need to resolve them, you move your belief in Hashem further up the ladder of your convictions, bringing it to a higher level of knowledge. This is the ideal way to fulfill this mitzvah, as the *Sefer HaChinuch* explains (Mitzvah 25):

> And if one merits to climb the heights of wisdom, and his heart understands and his eyes see the clear-cut evidence that the belief he has believed is true and evident, there being no other possibility, then he is carrying out this mitzvah in the best way possible.

A Hierarchy of Convictions

The first step in upgrading your belief in God is to assess the current strength of your belief, by categorizing it into one of the following four levels of convictions:

1. Knowledge (*De'ah*)
   Knowledge is absolute clarity based on an overwhelming amount of evidence. For example, we all know we have 10 fingers, and no matter how hard someone tries to persuade us that we have 11 fingers, our conviction will remain unshakeable. This is the level of clarity we should ideally strive to achieve in our belief in Hashem, as outlined above by the *Sefer HaChinuch*.

2. Belief (*Emunah*)
   The second level of conviction is what we call *emunah*, belief. It, too, is based on evidence, but it lacks the full clarity of

knowledge. For example, you are willing to accept the check of a close friend without concern that it is going to bounce, even though you do not know the exact balance in your friend's account.

The gap between knowledge and belief can be caused either by a lack of evidence or by an unresolved question that undermines one's certainty.

Baseless Convictions

The next two categories of convictions lack any valid basis for belief.

3. Social Conditioning

Every person is raised with a certain set of beliefs, which varies from society to society. People brought up in India believe that cows are holy. Americans growing up in a liberal western society are likely to believe that there are no absolute truths. An Arab born and raised in Gaza is likely to believe that Jews are evil oppressors. Unless they examine the validity of their convictions, these people will remain nothing more than a product of their society, as their beliefs are merely an accident of birth.

It requires a concerted effort to independently think through your beliefs, and it is therefore much more comfortable to just go with the flow of your society and adopt their beliefs as your own.

4. Blind Faith (*Emunah Tefeilah*)

Blind faith is a conviction based on an emotional or physical desire for something to be true. This form of faith lacks any shred of evidence to substantiate its position. In fact, people who trust blindly are often willing to take a leap of faith that goes against the evidence contradicting their conviction. For example, a smoker might confidently state, "This cigarette won't harm me," despite knowing the overwhelming evidence that smoking is life threatening.

Use these four definitions to help you assess the current quality of your belief in Hashem. Once you have pinpointed where you are at, you can then begin to work on strengthening your belief by either filling in the gaps in your understanding or by seeking answers to the questions that weaken your confidence in Hashem's existence. Although this may be a bit uncomfortable, confronting your questions will ultimately strengthen your clarity and dispel your doubts, while disregarding your questions guarantees that your belief will never become rock solid.

> Confronting your questions will ultimately strengthen your clarity and dispel your doubts, while disregarding your questions guarantees that your belief will never become rock solid.

Who Is God?

A student at Aish HaTorah once challenged Rabbi Noach Weinberg with the following question. His sister was traveling with her friend through the American South. They had a terrible car accident, and her friend sustained painful burns all over her body. A born-again Christian came to speak to her in the hospital, and he told her that if she accepted their messiah as her savior, her terrible pain would end. The friend dismissed him and told him to leave.

The next day the Christian returned and again promised that her pain would end if she accepted their messiah. In a moment of weakness, she said that she accepted him as her savior, and sure enough, her pain immediately disappeared.

The student then asked Rabbi Weinberg, "If miracles are proof of the existence of God, doesn't this story serve as a proof for Christianity?"

Rabbi Weinberg replied with the following parable:

Imagine that the United Nations convenes an international conference on the existence of God. Leading philosophers and religious leaders from all over the world are in attendance.

In the middle of the discussions, a powerful-looking man walks up to the front podium and demands, "Silence!" The entire building suddenly lifts off the ground.

Everyone is in shock. The man then says, "Watch!" To the amazement of the entire group, the building begins flying all over Manhattan.

"Let's dive under the water now!" he says, and the UN building goes straight down into the ocean. People can see fish swimming by their window.

"Now let's fly into outer space!" The building heads straight up and lands on the moon.

After collecting moon rocks as souvenirs, the man steers the UN building back to earth, where it settles back down on its original foundation.

Everyone is speechless, and the man says to all of the philosophers and religious leaders, "I am God, bow down to me!"

Everyone in the room hits the floor and bows, pleading to him to be merciful toward them. The only person left standing is an old Jewish janitor of European descent who works for the UN. Despite numerous pleas from all the others, he remains standing and tells this powerful man, "Sir, I have no idea how you did what you did, but God you're not."

How can we understand this janitor's confident refusal to bow down? To answer, let us change the end of the story.

They zoom down from outer space, and the powerful man says, "I am a frog, bow down to me!" Do you think anyone in the room would bow down? Chances are, they would say something similar to what the Jewish janitor said: "Sir, I have no idea how you did what you did, but a frog you're not."

Everyone knows that a human being cannot possibly be a frog, because we all understand what a frog is and what a human being is. The old Jewish janitor has enough understanding of Who Hashem is to know that a human being can never be God, no matter what kind of "miracles" he performs. But if you do not have a clear definition of God, you are liable to jump to false conclusions, especially when "miracles" are involved. You might even believe that acknowledging Christianity was responsible for someone's recovery, when in fact there is no logical correlation between the two.

If you do not have a clear definition of God, you are liable to jump to false conclusions, especially when "miracles" are involved.

So what is the Jewish definition of God?

Creator, Sustainer, and Supervisor

There are three primary axioms that define Hashem, and we are obligated to understand and believe each one as part of the mitzvah to know that God exists:

1. Hashem is the Creator of the universe, Who made the world from nothing.
2. Hashem is the Sustainer Who continually wills every particle in the universe into existence.
3. Hashem is the Supervisor Who orchestrates everything that happens to us.

Each of these axioms carries significant implications for our daily lives.

1. Creator Implies That Hashem Loves Us

   Love is expressed through giving. And the more altruistic the giving, the more it expresses one's love. When a gift is given with an ulterior motive, it is manipulation, not love.

   Since Hashem is infinite and perfect, there is nothing He can receive from His creations. Therefore, His gift of creating life is the purest possible expression of love, and can only be for the benefit of the recipient. We are given the opportunity to develop a personal relationship with the infinite Creator of the Universe, which is the greatest gift possible, and there is absolutely nothing we have done to deserve it. Indeed, as David Hamelech stated, "The world is built on kindness" (*Tehillim* 89:3).

2. Sustainer Implies That There Is No Other Power to Turn to

   The fact that Hashem is the Sustainer means that nothing in the universe exists independently; everything exists only because Hashem wills it into existence. This implies that it is fruitless to rely on any power or person other than Hashem, because ultimately all these other powers are themselves completely dependent on Hashem. They can only help us if Hashem decides to work through them as His messengers.

Therefore, it only makes sense to go to the source; deal with the puppeteer, not his puppets.

3. Supervisor Implies That There Are No Accidents

Hashem, in His role as Supervisor, orchestrates everything that happens to us.[2] Even trivial events happen for a reason, as the Talmud teaches that even the frustration of having to stick your hand into your pocket a second time to retrieve the correct coin is a lesson from the Almighty (See *Berachos* 5a).

There are no accidents; everything that happens to us is a personal message from Hashem. He is constantly talking to us through the events that occur in our daily lives. Pay attention and listen.

The Jewish people survived as a tiny minority in a very hostile world for over 2000 years in exile. We clung to our beliefs despite unremitting persecution because we were supremely confident that our beliefs were true. We understood the intellectual foundation for our core beliefs, and that enabled us to reject all attempts to convert us regardless of the terrible consequences we faced. And it is this clarity of conviction that will enable us to survive the unremitting temptations of secular society, and to give over to our children a rock-solid understanding in the reality of Hashem and His Torah.

---

2. The *Sefer HaChinuch* includes all three aspects in his explanation of the mitzvah to know God exists:

    a. Creator: "To believe that the world has one God Who created everything..."

    b. Sustainer: "...and all that was, is, and will be forever and ever came about from His power and will. . ."

    c. Supervisor: "...and that He took us out of the land of Egypt and gave us the Torah."

Naaseh venishma is stating that we recognize Hashem's perfection and love, and therefore trust Him completely. We have no need to read the fine print.

פרשת משפטים

arashas Mishpatim:

Naaseh Venishma

The end of this *parashah* contains the Jewish people's famous statement of allegiance to the Torah: "Everything that Hashem has said, we will do and we will listen — *naaseh venishma*" (*Shemos* 24:7). In response to this statement, Hashem compared the Jewish people to angels, asking, "Who revealed to My children this secret expression used only by heavenly angels?" (*Shabbos* 88a).

When Hashem offered the Torah to the non-Jewish nations, their response was quite different. The Midrash (*Sifri, Devarim* 343) says:

When Hashem wanted to give the Torah to Israel, He revealed Himself not only to the Jewish people but to all the other nations of the world as well.

First Hashem went to the children of Eisav. He asked them, "Will you accept My Torah?" They said, "What is written in it?" He answered, "You shall not murder." They replied, "Master of the universe, this goes against our very nature. Our father, whose *hands are the hands of Eisav* (*Bereishis* 27:22), led us to rely only on the sword, because his father told him, '*By your sword you shall live*' (ibid. 27:40). Therefore, we cannot accept the Torah."

Then Hashem went to the children of Ammon and Moav and asked them, "Will you accept My Torah?" They said, "What is written in it?" He responded, "You shall not commit adultery." They replied, "Master of the universe, our very origin is from illicit relationships, as it is written, *Thus, Lot's two daughters conceived from their father* (ibid. 19:36). Therefore, we cannot accept the Torah."

Then God went to the children of Yishmael. He asked them, "Will you accept My Torah?" They said, "What is written in it?" He said, "You shall not steal." They replied, "Master of the universe, it is our very nature to live off only what is stolen and acquired through violence, as it is written regarding Yishmael, *And he shall be a wild-ass of a man: his hand shall be against everyone, and everyone's hand against him* (ibid. 16:12). We cannot possibly accept the Torah."

There was no nation that Hashem did not approach, knocking on their door, as it were, and asking them whether they would be willing to accept the Torah. Finally, after being turned down by every nation, Hashem came to the nation of Israel, who said, "*Naaseh venishma* — we will do and we will listen" (*Shemos* 24:7).

Was there something wrong with asking, "What's written in it?" After all, how can you commit to keeping the entire Torah, forever, without knowing what's written in it? Clarifying its contents before accepting it seems like a perfectly reasonable thing to do. But for some reason, asking this question led the non-Jewish nations to reject the Torah.

Furthermore, why did Hashem present each nation with what was for them the most difficult mitzvah of the entire Torah to keep? He could have presented them with mitzvos that would not be particularly challenging for them to keep, such as Shabbos, love your neighbor, and various Yamim Tovim, and then eventually tell them about the more difficult mitzvos. That would have given them a far more objective picture of what the Torah contains. Instead, Hashem specifically picked the one mitzvah that would unquestionably cause them to reject the Torah. What kind of offer is that?

Does It Fit into My Lifestyle?

By asking, "What's written in it?" the non-Jewish nations were in effect saying to Hashem that if the Torah fits into their lifestyle, they would accept it. They each had their own set of ethics and principles that they were comfortable with, and they therefore wanted to see if the Torah fits into their chosen lifestyle. That approach undermines the idea that Torah is from an infinite and perfect Source, and can only enhance, not hamper, our life. The non-Jewish nations viewed Hashem's offer with great suspicion and doubt, thinking that some of the mitzvos of the Torah would impede their pleasure in life. But the Jewish people understood that the Torah is only for our good, and that it is ultimately the only avenue for fulfilling our goals and deepest aspirations.

The non-Jewish nations viewed Hashem's offer with great suspicion and doubt, thinking that some of the mitzvos of the Torah would impede their pleasure in life.

In addition, the Torah is the blueprint of creation. It is eternal and unchangeable, and its reality is not contingent on our liking it. The nations of the world already rejected the Torah by asking, "What's written in it?" and attempting to evaluate the Torah's worthiness based on their preconceived beliefs.

Hashem presented each of the nations with the one mitzvah that they were most loath to accept simply in order to help fulfill their desire to reject the Torah. Their very question was the rejection of the Torah; the rest was just formality and process.

Only the Jewish people understood the one and only way Torah can be accepted: "We will do and we will listen." The reality of Torah does not need our stamp of approval. The Jewish people embraced the Truth embodied in the Torah, and were prepared to forgo everything else, knowing that anything that is contrary to the Torah must be false and empty.

A Leap of Faith?

But isn't *naaseh venishma,* accepting the Torah sight unseen, a blind leap of faith, the type of belief that we previously condemned as spurious (see Parashas Yisro)?

Not at all.

Blind faith is based on an emotional desire for something to be true. It is completely irrational. Chazal call the generation of Jews who stood at Sinai and trekked through the desert the *Dor De'ah,* the generation of knowledge, because they experienced national revelation, which gave them the greatest clarity possible about Hashem's existence. They heard God speak! They were all prophets; there can be no greater knowledge of Hashem than that.

*W*hen a parent gives his child medication, the child does not ask, "Hold it right there! Before I take this I must know exactly what's in it and how it works."

Once you know it is Hashem Himself Who is giving the Torah, then the only rational response is to accept it unconditionally, sight unseen. Hashem is perfect, and everything He does stems from His immense love for us. When a parent gives his child medication, the child does not ask, "Hold it right there! Before I take this I must know exactly what's in it and how it works." Because the child knows that his parents love him dearly, he trusts them and realizes that they are only doing what is best for him.

Naaseh venishma is eminently rational, if — and only if — one knows that the Torah is coming from Hashem, a perfect Being Who loves us. *Naaseh venishma* is stating that we recognize Hashem's perfection and love, and therefore trust Him completely. We have no need to read the fine print.

Yet we can't forget the second part of the phrase: "*venishma* — and we will listen (i.e., understand)." Obeying Hashem's command is not predicated on our understanding the Torah. That would be presumptuous, and would constitute a misunderstanding of Hashem and ultimately a rejection of the entire basis of Torah, similar to the other nations' rejection of it. But we still do need to strive to understand the Torah. As the Rambam explains: "It is appropriate for a person to meditate on the judgments of the holy Torah and know their ultimate purpose according to his capacity" (*Hilchos Me'ilah* 8:8).

We are not meant to be mere robots performing mitzvos by rote. Hashem wants us to delve into Torah, comprehend as much as we can, and absorb His *Toras Chaim*, His instructions for living, into our daily lives. By doing so we will develop a greater appreciation of the power of Torah and increase our motivation to fulfill the mitzvos to the best of our ability.

No matter what our limitations, each of us has the potential to become great in Torah. It is our birthright.

פרשת תרומה

arashas Terumah:

The Crown of Torah

Rabbi Yochanan said: There were three crowns (that adorned the utensils of the *Beis HaMikdash*): the crown of the Golden Altar (the *Mizbeiach HaZahav*), the crown of the Ark (the *Aron*), and the crown of the Table (the *Shulchan*).

The crown of the Altar: Aharon merited and took it. (Rashi: This represents the crown of priesthood, which was given to Aharon and his descendants.)

The crown of the Table: David merited and took it. (Rashi: The Table's abundance and majestic opulence represents the crown of kingship, which was given to David Hamelech.)

But the crown of the Ark (Rashi: which represents the crown of Torah) is still at rest. Anyone who wants to take it may come and take it. Lest you say it is inferior to the other crowns, the Torah states: "Through me, kings will reign (*Mishlei* 8:15)"

(*Yoma* 72b).

The crown of the Ark represents *Keser Torah*, the crown of Torah. The Talmud says that this crown is still available to each and every one of us. How do we attain it? Is it really available to everyone, even if we are not all blessed with the intelligence, diligence, and patience required to become a *talmid chacham*, a Torah scholar?

The Rambam mentions these three crowns given to the Jewish people, and writes, in reference to *Keser Torah*: "The crown of Torah is resting, standing, and ready for each Jew, as it is written: 'The Torah that Moshe commanded us is the inheritance of the Congregation of Yaakov' (*Devarim* 33:4). Whoever wants it may come and take it" (*Hilchos Talmud Torah* 3:1).

The Rambam uses three words to describe *Keser Torah*: "resting," "standing," and "ready." No word of the Rambam is extra; each term comes to teach us something. "Resting" means Torah is waiting here just for you. There are no obstacles to attaining it, and you do not need to fight anything or anyone to get it.

"Standing" means that Torah is not going anywhere. It is not running away, but it will not come to you, either. It will stand still until you come to get it.

"Ready" means that the Torah is custom-made and ready for you. It fits you like a glove, without any adjustment or changes required. It is your inheritance: It is rightfully yours, and your stake of ownership is as valid as any other Jew's.

The Rambam is teaching us that Torah is accessible, attainable, and custom-made for you. There is nothing stopping us from getting it. But there is one caveat, found in the crucial final sentence above: "Whoever wants it may come and take it." The key to attaining the crown of Torah is to genuinely want it. Torah has to be your sole focus, your burning desire, and you have to pursue it passionately, with every fiber of your being. If you want it that badly, then you are guaranteed to get it, regardless of your raw intelligence and capabilities.

> *Torah is accessible, attainable, and custom-made for you.*

Greatness in Torah is almost entirely dependent upon our efforts. If we put in the necessary effort, the resultant understanding is a gift from Hashem. As the Talmud says, "One who says I searched and did not find, do not believe him… and one who says I searched and did find, believe him. This is referring to understanding the words of Torah" (*Megillah* 6b). The Almighty promises that anyone who sincerely puts in the effort to understand Torah is guaranteed to "find" it.

Finding something is not a direct outcome of one's efforts. It implies stumbling across something that appears out of the blue. This is an apt description of learning, since our attaining Torah — and other spiritual accomplishments — is a gift from Hashem. The Almighty gives it to us, but our effort is the means by which we earn this blessing.

If we lack understanding in Torah, it is not because Hashem does not want us to have it. It is because we have not made the right effort to get it.

Yes, acquiring Torah may be a slow process, but if we remain committed, we are guaranteed to succeed. Every drop of effort makes a difference. Torah will eventually change us, even if we do not yet see the impact of the ongoing process.

The Unlikely Gadol Hador: Rabbi Eliezer ben Hyrcanus

Even the least-gifted student in a yeshivah can reach staggering heights, as illustrated by the story of Rabbi Eliezer ben Hyrcanus (*Pirkei d'Rabbi Eliezer* 1).

Eliezer, the son of Hyrcanus, was an unlearned farmhand who worked for his father. One day, while plowing on the mountain, he stopped and began to cry.

Eliezer's father, Hyrcanus, one of the *talmidei chachamim* of his generation, asked his son, "Why are you crying? If it's too hot up on the mountain, I'll move you down to the plain." So Eliezer ben Hyrcanus began to plow in the plain, and soon after began to cry there, too.

"My son, why are you crying?" Hyrcanus asked.

"I want to learn Torah."

"Learn Torah? Come on, son, you are 28 years old! It's time you got married and started a family. Your children can learn Torah."

But Eliezer ben Hyrcanus would not stop crying. He cried until Eliyahu Hanavi came to him and asked, "Eliezer, why are you crying?"

"I want to learn Torah."

"Very well," Eliyahu replied. "Go to Jerusalem and seek out Rabban Yochanan ben Zakkai."

So Eliezer went to Rabban Yochanan ben Zakkai and cried before him.

"Why are you crying?" Rabbi Yochanan ben Zakkai asked.

"I want to learn Torah."

"Did your father not teach you *Krias Shema*, *Birkas Hamazon*, and *tefillah*?"

"No."

"Then come and I will teach you."

And so, Rabban Yochanan ben Zakkai, the *gadol hador*, taught Eliezer *Krias Shema*, *Birkas Hamazon,* and *tefillah*. Then he said, "Very good, Eliezer. We succeeded, and now it's time for you to return home."

Hearing this, Rabbi Eliezer ben Hyrcanus cried again. "Why are you crying?" Rabban Yochanan ben Zakkai asked.

"I want to learn Torah."

"O.K., I will teach you more Torah."

Meanwhile, because his son had refused to work the fields, Hyrcanus cut him out of his inheritance.

Rabban Yochanan ben Zakkai taught Eliezer more Torah — some *Chumash* and *Mishnah*. After this, Rabban Yochanan said, "Eliezer, it is time for you to go."

But Eliezer cried, "I want to learn Torah!"

And so it continued — until one day, when Rabbi Eliezer ben Hyrcanus was sitting and learning in the back of the *beis midrash*, and his father, Hyrcanus, walked in unexpectedly. Rabban Yochanan ben Zakkai told Rabbi Eliezer to move to the front and recite his Torah aloud, and Rabbi Eliezer stood up and taught Torah that had not been heard since Sinai.

When Rabbi Eliezer finished, Hyrcanus was beaming with pride. "Eliezer," he said, "at first I wanted to give my all property to my other sons and not to you, but now I am going to give everything I have to you and you alone!"

"My father," replied Rabbi Eliezer, "if I wanted gold and silver, I would have stayed in the field plowing. All I want is Torah." And

Rabbi Eliezer ben Hyrcanus eventually became the *gadol hador*, and the rebbi of Rabbi Akiva.

This is a powerful story, but one that raises many questions.

1. How could it be that Hyrcanus, himself a *talmid chacham*, did not teach his son the basics of Torah? Even the simplest Jew teaches his son *Krias Shema*, *Birkas Hamazon*, and *tefillah*.

    Furthermore, Hyrcanus was a multimillionaire. He could have hired the best teachers in the world to teach his son!

2. Why did Eliezer ben Hyrcanus cry? He was a grown man. Let him speak up for what he wants!

3. Hyrcanus was very wealthy — why did he care whether his son worked or not?

4. Why did Hyrcanus make his son do the menial labor of plowing? He could have hired 100 workers to plow and had his son do more honorable work, such as that of a foreman.

5. Why did Eliyahu Hanavi tell Eliezer ben Hyrcanus to go to the *gadol hador*, Rabban Yochanan ben Zakkai, to learn *Krias Shema*? Any milkman or *talmid* in the *beis midrash* could have taught him that! This is comparable to sending a recent *baal teshuvah* to Rav Aharon Leib Shteinman, *shlita*, to learn *Alef Beis*!

6. Once Eliezer finally got to Rabban Yochanan ben Zakkai, why did he cry? Speak up!

7. Rabban Yochanan ben Zakkai heard a 28-year-old man say, "I want to learn Torah." Why would he assume that he had not yet learned *Krias Shema*?

8. Why didn't Rabban Yochanan ben Zakkai know why Eliezer was crying after he told him to return home after teaching him *Krias Shema*? Of course he was crying! All he had learned was *Krias Shema*, *Birkas Hamazon*, and *tefillah*!

There is only one answer that can explain all of these difficulties: Eliezer ben Hyrcanus had a head made of straw. He was extremely dim-witted.

Of course Hyrcanus had gotten his son a teacher! He was a *Yarei Shamayim*. He certainly hired the very best teacher there was.

But even the best *melamed* could not get *Krias Shema* into that thick head of Eliezer ben Hyrcanus. So what is a father supposed to do with such a dim-witted son? Make him a foreman? No way. Give him a plow, so that at least he will do something productive.

Eliezer cried. He wanted to learn! But his father told him: "We've tried everything, son. Forget it." The only option left was to approach the *gadol hador*. Only someone with such genius would stand a chance of getting through to Eliezer. That was why Eliyahu Hanavi told him to go to Rabban Yochanan ben Zakkai.

So Rabban Yochanan ben Zakkai struggled to teach Eliezer, and he accomplished what no one else was able to do: He taught Eliezer *Krias Shema*, *Birkas Hamazon*, and *tefillah*.

Great, you've got the basics. Now go home! But when Eliezer cried for more, Rabban Yochanan ben Zakkai decided to take a chance. Since it had worked before, maybe he could teach him more. And this student, who was considered least likely to succeed, went on to become Rabbi Eliezer ben Hyrcanus, the leader of his generation, demonstrating that even the slowest of the slow can become the *gadol hador*.

What was the secret behind his success? He wanted Torah so badly that he was willing to cry for it.

What was the secret behind his success?

He wanted Torah so badly that he was willing to cry for it.

No matter what our limitations, each of us has the potential to become great in Torah. It is our birthright. Our precious inheritance is waiting for us; all we have to do is truly want it.

*Like the incense's sublime power
to reach spiritual heights, the path
of humility enables us to connect
to the soul's yearning for ultimate
meaning.*

פרשת תצוה

*P*arashas Tetzaveh:
The Soul of Incense

arashas Tetzaveh ends with the construction of the Golden
Altar, the *Mizbeiach HaZahav*, upon which *ketores*, incense,
was burnt as an offering every morning and evening. The placement
of this section is striking, for its rightful location seems to be four
chapters earlier, in Parashas Terumah, where the details of all the
other sacred vessels of the Tabernacle are explained. Why does the
Torah leave the *Mizbeiach HaZahav* for the very end of the next
parashah?

The burning of the incense represents the highest level of service
to Hashem; it is the pinnacle that can only come after all else is
in position.[3] The Torah hints to the lofty status of the incense by
describing the Golden Altar as "*kodesh kodashim hu laShem —
holy of holies to Hashem*" (*Shemos* 30:10), whereas the Copper
Altar is referred to only as "holy of holies" (29:37).

---

3. The Abarbanel states that the burning of the incense was the most spiritual and
holy of all the services performed in the Temple.

The exalted status of the incense is reinforced by the fact that the primary sense involved in its burning is the sense of smell, the most spiritual of all the five senses. As the Talmud says, "Rav Zutra bar Toviyah said in the name of Rav: From where is it derived that we recite a blessing over a fragrance? As it is stated: 'Let every soul praise God.' What is something from which the soul derives pleasure but the body does not? You must say that this is the pleasure of smell" (*Berachos* 43b). Smell is the sense of the soul.

The Maharsha explains that smell is more spiritual than our other senses since it was through Adam's nose that Hashem invested mankind with a soul, as it says, "He blew into his nostrils the soul of life; and man became a living being" (*Bereishis* 2:7).

Slaying the Ego

We find a unique halachah regarding the *Mizbeiach HaZahav*: Unlike the other services of the *Beis HaMikdash*, the incense can still be offered even if the altar was uprooted. (See Rambam, *Hilchos Temidim U'Musafim* 3:2, and *Zevachim* 59a.) Therefore, even without the altar, one can still burn it in its place. On a symbolic level, we can still access the power of the incense by applying this sacrifice to our daily lives.

The incense, that sublime spiritual offering, represents transcending one's physical limitations and sense of self. Burning the incense is the ultimate sacrifice because it represents giving up the most important but least tangible part of who you are; namely, your sense of self-importance. It symbolizes transcending your subjective view of what is important and channeling this drive toward doing Hashem's will. It stems from recognizing that the only true meaning in life is attained through sacrificing your personal agenda to become a vehicle to express Hashem's eternal will. All else is really trivial and fleeting. Just as the incense becomes intermingled with the surrounding air, you, too, can become one with the Almighty by transcending your artificial sense of meaning and importance and embracing Hashem's meaning and purpose.

The Way to Get There

The way to reach this sublime level is through humility.

Most people have a mistaken understanding of what humility is. By way of illustration, imagine a person who is the paragon of humility walking into your home. How do you picture him? Meek, slightly hunched over, self-effacing, someone who hides in the back of a room, too shy to engage in conversation. Yet who was the most humble of all people? The Torah tells us, "Now the man Moshe was exceedingly humble, more than any person on the face of the earth" (*Bamidbar* 12:3.) Can you imagine Moshe Rabbeinu walking into your home? The entire house would shake! He was the most powerful, charismatic leader in Jewish history, yet he is the paradigm of humility. Clearly, our concept of humility is wrong.

> An arrogant person has to work hard to keep up the facade that he has everything under control, when deep down he is consumed with doubt and insecurity.

Humility does not mean denigrating your strengths and denying your inner greatness. It means recognizing that your strengths and inner greatness are a gift from Hashem. An arrogant person thinks it is all about him and all because of him. He has to work hard to keep up the facade that he has everything under control, when deep down he is consumed with doubt and insecurity.

In contrast, the humble person realizes it is all about God and all from God. He rises above petty concerns and does not care about gaining people's approval. He cares only about utilizing the gifts Hashem has given him to tackle the world's problems and make a real difference in people's lives. Humility actually generates charisma, because by nullifying your ego you attach yourself to God and become a conduit for His unlimited resources. No problem is unmanageable with God on your side.

You Are a Soul, Not a Body

The *Chovos Halevavos* teaches that the essence of humility is to live with the realization that you are a soul, not a body. The *yetzer hara*, the evil inclination, trips us up by getting us to identify with the physical, animalistic side of us that is a cauldron of raging desires and egotistical self-centeredness. When we live with the awareness that we are a lofty soul that yearns for meaning and connection to the Almighty, we gain the clarity to make the proper choices that create a deeply fulfilling life.

The essence of humility is to live with the realization that you are a soul, not a body.

The battle for life is the battle for sanity. When we follow the dictates of the body we hurt ourselves and create a hollowed-out existence of degradation and shame. When we live as a soul we tap into the power of genuine meaning and pleasure. Every day, identify with the soul, not the body, by remembering that your body is a mass of bones, flesh, and skin that will one day be buried and disintegrate into nothing, whereas your soul is pure and stems from the Infinite Source of existence. It longs to return to its eternal Source. All the pain and aggravation that your body feels, and all the sensations and physical pleasures it experiences, are fleeting and temporal. Your soul is eternal and the spiritual growth it attains in this world will last forever.

Like the incense's sublime power to reach spiritual heights, the path of humility enables us to connect to the soul's yearning for ultimate meaning.

Moshe's cry of "'Whoever is for God, join me!" reverberates throughout the ages. There will inevitably be a time in your life when you will hear that call.

פרשת כי תשא

arashas Ki Sisa:

Mi LaShem Eilai!

After the *cheit ha'eigel*, the sin of the golden calf, Moshe descended Har Sinai and was confronted with the scene of the Jews reveling with their newly formed deity. Moshe's reaction was swift and furious:

> *It happened as he drew near the camp and saw the calf and the dances that Moshe's anger flared up. He threw down the Tablets from his hands and shattered them at the foot of the mountain. He took the calf that they had made and burned it in fire. He ground it to a fine powder and sprinkled it over the water. He made the Children of Israel drink. Moshe said to Aharon: "What did this people do to you that you brought a grievous sin upon it?"*
> *(Shemos 32:19-21).*

Standing at the edge of the camp, Moshe cried out to the Jewish people, "*Mi LaShem eilai!* Whoever is for Hashem, join me!" And who came? The entire tribe of Levi. Together with Moshe they meted out punishment to those who had worshiped the golden calf.

Where was everyone else? Only a tiny percentage of the Jewish people actually worshiped the calf; a total of three thousand people were killed. Why didn't many more people answer Moshe's call? Where were the rest of the Jewish people?

Only Shevet Levi answered his call. They were also the only ones who did not worship idols the entire time the Jewish people were enslaved in Egypt. They clung steadfastly to God because their only interest was doing the *ratzon Hashem,* the will of God; everything else was nonsense. The rest of the people did not answer the call.

When you hear the call "Whoever is for Hashem, join me!" only one thing should be on your mind: standing up for *kevod Shamayim,* the honor of Hashem. In these defining moments nothing else matters: not your family, not your personal ambitions. The only thing you should value is doing Hashem's will. Moshe knew that to set the Jewish people straight, only those whose sole consideration is what God wants could get the job done.

Rav Shimon Schwab (1908-1993), the rabbi of Manhattan's Khal Adas Jeshurun, told me that he went to the Chofetz Chaim for a *berachah* before he left Europe to take his first rabbinic position in America. The Chofetz Chaim, who was a Kohen, spoke to him and asked him where he was going. He then asked Rav Schwab, "Why are you not a Kohen?"

"Rebbe," Ravi Schwab replied, "my father wasn't a Kohen, so I'm not a Kohen."

"No, that's not the answer," the Chofetz Chaim said. "Tell me, why are you not a Kohen?"

Rabbi Schwab, somewhat taken aback, said, "Rebbe, my grandfather wasn't a Kohen, so I'm not a Kohen."

"No, that's still not the answer. I will tell you why I am a Kohen and you are not. Three thousand years ago, when Moshe called out to the Jewish people, 'Whoever is for God, join me!' your great-great-grandfather did not step forward, but my great-great-grandfather rose to the occasion and answered Moshe's call. That is why I am a Kohen and you are not. I am telling you this in order to teach you a crucial lesson. There will be times in life when you will hear the call of 'Whoever is for God, join me!' These moments demand that you stand up and be counted among the defenders of *kevod Shamayim*, and how you respond will have far-reaching consequences. Do not make the same mistake as your great-great-grandfather. This time, answer in the affirmative!"

Moshe's cry of "'Whoever is for God, join me!" reverberates throughout the ages. There will inevitably be a time in your life when you will hear that call. When you do, stand up and seize the challenge. It will transform you and all your descendants after you.

Do Not Wait for the Call

Before Moshe's appeal on behalf of the Jewish people, the Torah describes the following interchange between Hashem and Moshe:

> Hashem spoke to Moshe: "Go, descend — for your people that you brought up from the land of Egypt has become corrupt. They have strayed quickly from the path that I have commanded them. They have made themselves a molten calf, prostrated themselves to it, and sacrificed to it, and they said: 'This is your god, O Israel, which brought you up from the land of Egypt.'" Hashem said to Moshe: "I have seen this people, and behold! It is a stiff-necked people. And now, desist from Me. Let My anger flare up against them and I shall annihilate them; and I shall make you a great nation"
> (ibid. 32:7-10).

The Almighty told Moshe that He is prepared to wipe out the entire Jewish people, and start anew with just Moshe. Through him He will make a great nation.

And Moshe responded by praying and pleading with God: "Relent from Your flaring anger and reconsider regarding the evil against Your people. Remember for the sake of Avraham, Yitzchak, and Yisrael, Your servants..." (ibid. 32:12-13). Hashem accepted this prayer, as the next verse says: "Hashem reconsidered regarding the evil that He declared He would do to His people." But our sages teach us that every time the Jewish people are punished, even to this very day, they are in part being reprimanded for the sin of the golden calf (*Sanhedrin* 102a). Moshe did not completely cancel out the punishment; he merely softened it by stretching its implementation over time.

The Torah clearly says that the Almighty initially wanted to destroy the entire Jewish people. What about the entire tribe of Levi who were always faithful and fully prepared to answer Moshe's plea of "*Mi LaShem eilai*"? Why would Hashem annihilate them as well? Is there something they did wrong in the episode of the golden calf?

Yes, there is. They mistakenly waited for Moshe's call to arms. They should have taken their swords of their own initiative and immediately defended Hashem's honor. What were they waiting for? They waited for someone to lead them, for someone to rally them with the call of "*Mi LaShem eilai*."

> If you see a problem and know what needs to be done, do not wait for orders. Take charge and act!

The Torah is teaching us a very important lesson about taking responsibility. If you see a problem and know what needs to be done, do not wait for orders. Take charge and act! Don't wait for someone to call out "*Mi LaShem eilai*." Don't wait for a leader to show up and tell you what to do. Your responsibility begins the instant you recognize a problem. This was Shevet Levi's mistake.

> Taking responsibility is not just the province of leaders; every one of us is equally responsible to address the problems at hand and do all that we can to solve them.

Leaders certainly have to lead. They need to show the way and inspire others by calling out "*Mi LaShem eilai*." And each and every one of us needs to respond to the call and dedicate our lives to God. But Hashem demands even more than that. Taking responsibility is not just the province of leaders; every one of us is equally responsible to address the problems at hand and do all that we can to solve them. Taking this initiative will cause you, and the generations after you, to merit unimaginable blessing.

Every person has one dominant drive, and identifying that drive is a crucial step in our personal avodas Hashem.

פרשת ויקהל/פקודי
Parashas Vayakhel/Pekudei:
The Three Drives

The purpose of the Mishkan is for Hashem to dwell within us, as the *passuk* says, "They shall make a Sanctuary for Me, so that I may dwell among them" (*Shemos* 25:8). Every detail of the Mishkan teaches us how to build oneself into the type of person who can have a meaningful relationship with Hashem and thereby make Hashem's presence manifest in the world.

> Every detail of the Mishkan teaches us how to build oneself into the type of person who can have a meaningful relationship with Hashem.

Rav Dessler explains that our forefathers, Avraham, Yitzchak, and Yaakov, personify three essential drives that are implanted in every Jew's spiritual DNA (*Michtav M'Eliyahu* vol. 3, p. 211). Each of these traits is symbolized, as well, by one of the main vessels of the Mishkan. Every person has one dominant drive, and identifying that drive is a crucial step in our personal *avodas Hashem*. It is also a valuable gateway to understanding what motivates others.

These three traits are *emes* (truth), *gevurah* (inner strength), and *chessed* (caring about others). These three traits are also reflected in the mishnah in *Pirkei Avos* that states, "The world stands on three things: Torah, *avodah* (service), and *gemilus chassadim* (acts of kindness)." All three are essential to create a stable world; if just one is missing, the world collapses.

Let's define each drive and identify the vessel that represents it in the Mishkan.

Emes/Truth: This trait is the desire to understand Torah, and was the hallmark of Yaakov Avinu, who studied Torah for 14 years without interruption and about whom we say in Minchah of Shabbos, "Give Truth to Yaakov." The trait of seeking Torah is symbolized by the *Aron*, the Ark, which contained the first Tablets that Hashem dictated to Moshe.

Gevurah/Inner Strength: This is the desire to curb your ego and physical desires and do the right thing. It is epitomized by Yitzchak Avinu, who was willing to be sacrificed on the altar even though it seemingly meant the end of the Jewish people. The trait of *gevurah* is represented by the *Mizbeiach*, the sacrificial Altar, which takes a lowly physical animal and dedicates it completely for a higher cause.

Chessed/Caring about Others: This trait was embodied by Avraham Avinu, whose tent was open on all four sides to ensure that he could greet and host everyone who walked by. It is symbolized by the *Shulchan* (Table), which held the *lechem hapanim*, the showbread.

> *Understanding another person's primary drive gives you the ability to tailor your message in a manner that will more likely resonate with and affect that person.*

While everyone possesses elements of all three traits, we each have one dominant drive that serves as the engine through which we operate. Understanding another person's primary drive gives you the ability to tailor your message in a manner that will more likely resonate with and affect that person, since you are "speaking his language." This can be very valuable when introducing people to the depth and meaning of Judaism. To reach them, you must emphasize that aspect of Torah that speaks to the frequency they operate on.

For example, the trait of seeking Torah is fundamentally the desire to attain wisdom and understanding. A person who works on this wavelength will be drawn to opportunities that satisfy his desire to comprehend and make sense of the world. He is a truth seeker. In order to interest this person in Judaism, you must emphasize the comprehensive wisdom and depth of the Torah and our Sages. He will be most interested in the philosophical ideas and profound truths of Torah, and less interested in the halachic intricacies of what makes a lulav kosher. If he perceives that through learning Torah he will gain great understanding of himself and the world around him, he will become motivated to learn.

The second frequency is the trait of *gevurah*, which essentially means desiring responsibility. A person whose primary drive is *gevurah* is motivated by a strong aspiration to fulfill his obligations, do the right thing, and gain the self-respect that comes from being responsible. This personality type cares passionately about justice, fighting evil, and making the world a better place. He will respond to the cause of the Jewish people's mission to perfect the world, and the need for every Jew to live up to his responsibilities and remain loyal to the Jewish people's mission. By emphasizing the impact the Jewish people have made on the world and highlighting the comprehensive system of Jewish law contained in the Torah, you can ignite his desire to investigate and explore his heritage. This approach has the greatest chance to succeed at motivating him to pursue a path of Torah and commit to being a fully observant member of the Jewish people.

The third characteristic is *gemilus chassadim*. A person with this primary drive seeks to experience pleasure through helping others and building relationships. He feels most alive when giving other people pleasure. With his expansive heart, this person loves to experience the joy of life. Since his frequency is pleasure, the most effective way to draw him to Torah is by providing experiences that are enjoyable and fulfilling — an animated Shabbos table, dancing at a wedding, a kumzitz — and by also showing him the Torah's wisdom regarding how to nurture healthy relationships, build vibrant Jewish homes, and connect to the essence of spirituality: *ahavas Hashem,* love of Hashem.

The essence of kiruv is communication, and one of the keys to successful communication is understanding the "language" that best speaks to the individual.

Knowing yourself and the drive that most motivates you will help you recognize the frequency that motivates others, and will allow you to tailor your message to newcomers to Judaism in the most effective way possible. The essence of *kiruv* is communication, and one of the keys to successful communication is understanding the "language" that best speaks to the individual.

ספר ויקרא

Sefer Vayikra

Our job is to foster within ourselves the desire to do Hashem's will. Then Hashem gives us the opportunity and ability to accomplish our goal.

פרשת ויקרא

arashas Vayikra:

The Small Aleph

וַיִּקְרָא אֶל מֹשֶׁה ...
"And Hashem called Moshe..." (Vayikra 1:1).

Rashi explains that the word "*vayikra*" is an expression of affection. Hashem not only spoke to Moshe, He made direct, intimate contact with him. This was in stark contrast to how Hashem spoke to the non-Jewish prophets, where the verb used to describe the communication is "*vayikar.*" *Vayikar,* without the letter *aleph* at the end, implies a chance encounter, a lesser form of communication.

The word "*vayikra*" at the beginning of the *parashah* is written with the letter *aleph* in smaller type. The *Baal Haturim* explains that Moshe wrote it this way due to his humility, for he wanted to downplay the public statement of his preciousness to Hashem implied by the word "*vayikra.*" Making the *aleph* small does not change the meaning of the word, yet at a quick glance the word appears to connote the inferior relationship that *"vayikar"* — without the *aleph* — entails.

Moshe was the greatest prophet in history and also the epitome of humility. He was aware of his own greatness, yet careful not to flaunt it.

The essence of humility is recognizing that all your strengths, your Torah learning, your blessings, and even your efforts, are all a gift from Hashem.

The Strange God Inside of Us

We mistakenly attribute our accomplishments to our own abilities instead of recognizing that they are gifts from Hashem. The Talmud (*Shabbos* 105b) explains that the verse, "There shall be no strange god within you" (*Tehillim* 81:10), refers to the *yetzer hara*, the evil inclination, which constantly tempts us to believe that our powers are the cause of our successes, instead of attributing these successes to Hashem. As the *passuk* says, "And you may say in your heart, 'My strength and the might of my hand made me all this wealth'" (*Devarim* 8:17); in other words, *I* accomplished this. The following joke illustrates this human foible:

A multimillionaire makes a bad investment that wipes out his fortune. He takes his last $10,000, goes to the racetrack, and picks a horse called Dancer that pays 1,000 to 1. He figures that if he wins, he'll be a millionaire again, and if he loses he is already broke — so he has nothing to lose.

The race is about to begin and he starts to pray with fervor. "Almighty, the odds are 1,000 to 1. Please make this horse run!" Off they go, and sure enough his horse is running. "Almighty, please, please move him up in the pack!" The horse moves up in the pack. "Almighty, get him up in front, please, please!" Dancer is ahead by a nose. "Thank You, Almighty, please, keep him in front!" The horse is ahead by a length. "Please, please keep him going!" He's ahead by five lengths and entering the final homestretch. Then he says, "O.K., God, I can take over from here. Come on, Dancer!"

When we are just starting out, overwhelmed by the challenges ahead of us, we naturally turn to Hashem for help and guidance. But once we have succeeded, we all too easily forget Hashem's role in guiding every step we took, until we mistakenly conclude that it was only our abilities and efforts that caused our success.

Nor can we take credit for our spiritual accomplishments, even when they require self-sacrifice. Whatever we accomplish is a gift from Hashem; our efforts and self-sacrifice are what make it possible for Hashem to bless our efforts. As the Talmud teaches, "A person's *yetzer hara* attacks him every day, and wants to kill him. . . and if not for Hashem's help, he would be unable to withstand him" (*Kiddushin* 30b). Even our power to stand up to the *yetzer hara* is a gift from the Almighty. Our value is found in the privilege of Hashem choosing us to fulfill His will.

Believing in Our Own Power Actually Diminishes Us

We take credit for our accomplishments in order to feel important, but instead of empowering us, this actually diminishes us. By way of illustration, if someone were to ask you if you can recite the *Shema* twice a day or say *Birkas Hamazon* after eating bread, you would answer, "Of course I can."

If someone were to ask you if you can know the entire Torah by heart or think about Hashem every second of the day, you would probably answer that you cannot do it.

Which response is more accurate? When you say "I can recite the *Shema*," or when you say "I cannot know the entire Torah by heart"?

The truth is that you cannot learn the entire Torah by heart because the reality is that you cannot even lift a finger without Hashem's help. But that is not the reason why we answer that we cannot do it. If that were the underlying reason then we would have answered that without Hashem's help we cannot say the *Shema* or *Birkas Hamazon* either! We say that we cannot know all of Torah because we think do not have the intelligence and capabilities.

We rely only on our own prowess, believing deep down that it is our power that enables us to accomplish. If we would realize that Hashem is the only power, that in truth we cannot do anything without Him — even say *Shema* — then we would believe that just as Hashem gives us the ability to recite *Shema*, He will give us the ability to learn the entire Torah, if we want it badly enough. If

Hashem wants it to happen because it is consistent with His will, it will indeed happen — if we show him that we are doing all that is required to succeed.

Therefore, taking credit for our accomplishments does not empower us; it ultimately limits what we believe is attainable. Thinking it is all up to us consigns us to the limited and insecure realm of our own resources. But when we realize that everything that happens comes from Hashem, we can transcend our shortcomings and plug ourselves into the Almighty's unlimited power.

Taking credit for our accomplishments does not empower us; it ultimately limits what we believe is attainable.

Saying "I can't" is a form of idol worship because it implies that you are relying on your own power and not Hashem's.

Make the Effort

In describing the building of the Mishkan and its vessels, the *passuk* says, "Moshe summoned Betzalel, Oholiav, and every wise-hearted man whose heart Hashem endowed with wisdom, everyone whose heart inspired him to approach the work, to do it" (*Shemos* 36:2).

The Chofetz Chaim (*Toras Habayis,* Chapter 7) points out that Betzalel's desire to fulfill Hashem's will was the initial catalyst for Hashem's giving him the ability to build the vessels of the Mishkan. This principle applies to all of our undertakings as well. Our job is to foster within ourselves the desire to do Hashem's will. Then Hashem gives us the opportunity and ability to accomplish our goal.

My great-grandfather was the Slonimer Rebbe. After I opened the first yeshivah for *baalei teshuvah*, I met several of my Israeli cousins, Slonimer chassidim, at a *simchah* and they said to me, "The great Rebbes of Europe took such pride in bringing a single Jew back to Torah that they put that accomplishment on their tombstones. Rav Noach, we remember when you first came to Eretz Yisrael and wore a light-colored suit. How is it possible that you have made scores of *baalei teshuvah*?"

I answered them with the following example.

When you walk the streets of Yerushalayim, it is not uncommon to see large cranes lifting many tons of building materials and depositing them in the correct location. There is always one person standing at that location who places his hands under the load to make sure it comes to rest at the right spot. A fool, watching this man, thinks he is stronger than Shimshon, for he is holding tons of weight with his bare hands! But a wise man takes a step back and sees the bigger picture: It is the crane that is carrying the burden; the man below is just guiding it into place.

Similarly, the prophets teach that in the *Ikvesa d'Meshicha*, the End of Days leading up to the arrival of the Mashiach, the Jewish people will do *teshuvah* and come back to Hashem and His Torah (*Amos* 8:11). Hashem is moving the crane and lifting up the burden of the nation. All we need to do is lift our hands and make the slightest effort to guide to the right place those who are returning. When we do, the Almighty credits us with bringing back these souls all by ourselves, as the Mishnah says, "All who exert themselves for the community should exert themselves for the sake of Heaven, for then the merit of the community's forefathers aids them and their righteousness endures forever. Nevertheless, as for you, I [God] will bestow upon you as great a reward as if you had accomplished it on your own" (*Pirkei Avos* 2:2).

> *H*ashem is moving the crane and lifting up the burden of the nation. All we need to do is lift our hands and make the slightest effort to guide to the right place those who are returning.

Greatness in Torah is guaranteed,
as long as you don't stop the water
from dripping — one word at a time.

פרשת צו

*P*arashas Tzav:
The Importance of Consistency

This week's *parashah* continues to discuss the *avodah* in the *Mishkan*, the service of the Kohanim in the Tabernacle. Although the *avodah* involves many details, if we look at the big picture, an important theme emerges that teaches us a crucial lesson about how people grow and change.

The *avodah* in the *Mishkan* — and later in the *Beis HaMikdash* — consisted of a clearly defined, daily routine. For example, each day the service began with the *terumas hadeshen*, the removal of the ash from the previous day's sacrifices. The Kohanim also placed wood on the Altar each day to ensure that the fire burned continuously, and the first and last sacrifice offered daily was the *korban tamid*.

The activities in the *Beis HaMikdash*, the spiritual epicenter of the world, followed a daily schedule that never varied. The Torah is showing us that genuine, sustained growth does not come from sudden bursts of inspiration; it is attained through constant, consistent, and continuous actions that require unwavering commitment and persistence.

How do we make our own actions constant, consistent, and continuous?

1. Constant

Imagine you're stuck in traffic and the driver next to you opens his window and throws out a dollar bill. A minute later, as traffic is inching along, he throws out another dollar bill. You can't believe it! Every minute that you're stuck in traffic another dollar flies out the window!

Crazy, right? You've probably never seen that happen, and you probably never will. But how often do we throw a minute out the window, daydreaming and staring at nothing in particular? And then another minute and another... just killing time. Calculate the number of minutes we throw away any given week and add them all up. We are throwing away time that is worth way more than money.

Life is precious. Use it; don't kill it. Truly living means using your mind constantly. Whatever you are doing at any given moment — watching the news, working on a business deal, talking to a friend, reading this article — give it your full attention. Decide that you are willing to take the pain of thinking, of being aware, all day long.

Life is precious. Use it; don't kill it.

2. Consistent

Consistency is the key to spiritual growth and learning Torah. Just as children crave structure in order to thrive, even though they kick and scream at bedtime, our *yetzer hara* behaves best when you give it structure and a consistent routine. Otherwise it will be throwing a temper tantrum and bouncing off the walls, making it next to impossible for you to focus on the mitzvah at hand.

So select your goal and commit to doing daily activities to reach that goal in the same time, at the same place, and in the same way, as much as reasonably possible.

For example, say your goal is to learn *Shas*, the entire Talmud. Set aside a time to learn, preferably with a *chavrusa*, a study partner, and make that time "holy"; no matter what, rain or shine, sickness or health, you show up and learn at that time. That is the power of commitment. Hammering away day in and day out carves out the path to change.

3. Continuous

Whenever you pursue a specific goal, strive to do it without interruption. It is more effective to study for one hour straight than for two hours with interruptions. Interruptions break your train of thought and limit your ability to retain information. You cannot bring a pot to a boil if you keep taking it off the fire. You have to reheat it all over again.

This razor focus is very difficult for today's attention-deficit, multitasking generation. Concentrating for 20 minutes with no interruptions — no emails, no phone calls, no getting up to get a drink — requires real effort. But it is essential. Try it. Set aside a certain time when you block everything else out, where you will not budge from the activity you're focusing on. You are not endangering your life!

You can practice this while riding on the bus or waiting at the dentist's office. Set yourself a goal of 15 minutes to focus exclusively on one subject. It may be a problem you're having at work, a personal goal, or learning a text. Little by little, increase your time. First 15 minutes, then 30 minutes, then one hour, then two hours. Once you hit four hours, you're sailing.

The Vilna Gaon, the great 18th-century Jewish scholar, said that the first three hours and 59 minutes is stoking the furnace. By the fourth hour, the pot is boiling.

Rabbi Akiva and the Fire of Torah

Aish HaTorah was founded on the concept that lasting change comes through persistent repetition. *Avos DeRabbi Nassan* (6:2) recounts that Rabbi Akiva was a complete ignoramus who did not know the Aleph Beis until the age of 40. What changed Rabbi Akiva and launched him on the path to becoming one of the greatest sages in the history of the Jewish People?

Avos DeRabbi Nassan tells us that Rabbi Akiva bathed by a particular waterfall, and one day he noticed a rock with a hole right through it. He looked to see what caused the hole, and noticed that a steady drip of water was falling exactly where the hole was. Upon seeing this he made the following *kal v'chomer*: If water, which is soft, can make a hole in a rock, which is hard, then all the more so Torah, which is fire, can make a hole in the heart of a man, which is soft. This insight motivated him to learn, until he eventually became the great Rabbi Akiva, teacher of 24,000 students!

What did Rabbi Akiva see in the rock that so dramatically changed the direction of his life?

If you would ask someone watching water drip on a rock if a particular drop of water made any impact, the answer would almost certainly be no, because to the naked eye the impact is not noticeable. But the fact that there is now a hole in the rock means that every single drop counted.

> *T*he rock showed Rabbi Akiva that he was wrong, and that every word of Torah he learned must be affecting him.

Rabbi Akiva, like all of us, yearned for greatness in Torah. But he gave up on becoming great in Torah because he did not see that his learning was changing him. The rock showed him that he was wrong, and that every word of Torah he learned must be affecting him. It just takes time and patience to see the transformation.

Furthermore, the drops of water only made a hole in the rock because they fell in the exact same place over and over again. This point is the basis of all of *Yiddishkeit*. Every day we say the exact same *berachos* and *tefillos*, and we do the same daily mitzvos. It is through persistent repetition that we change and grow, by steadily inculcating the body with the concepts and aspirations of the soul.

> *W*hen we learn Torah we must always remember that it is not possible for the finite heart of man to make contact with the infinite word of God and remain unchanged; it just takes time for that change to become manifest.

When we learn Torah we must always remember that it is not possible for the finite heart of man to make contact with the infinite word of God and remain unchanged; it just takes time for that change to become manifest. Those who take that message to heart will have the ability to sit and learn, because they will know it is worth it; they are changing.

Our generation, more so than any other in Jewish history, is challenged by the problems of impatience and lack of discipline. Why? Because our generation lives in the era of post technology, and technology, despite its achievements, has trained all of us to expect instantaneous results in everything we undertake. Technology has the power to dramatically speed up all physical processes, from food preparation to communicating with our relatives abroad, but spiritual growth, acquisition of Torah, refining our *middos*, and a relationship with Hashem all require patience and discipline.

The above quote from *Avos DeRabbi Nassan*, incidentally, was the inspiration behind the name Aish HaTorah, the Fire of Torah. And the message of this Midrash is the basis of a Torah education, because without understanding the need for persistence and consistency, one can mistakenly give up on becoming great in learning — just as Rabbi Akiva initially did — and remain ignorant of the beauty and depth of Torah forever.

So whenever you see the name Aish HaTorah, remember the message of the rock: Greatness in Torah is guaranteed, as long as you don't stop the water from dripping — one word at a time.

All of us, regardless of our position or stature, are equally responsible to address the problems that we see. When it comes to implementation of solutions, however, we must work under the guidance of the existing leadership.

פרשת שמיני

arashas Shemini:
The Deaths of Nadav and Avihu

For seven days Moshe Rabbeinu constructed and dismantled the Mishkan, and brought all the various offerings to inaugurate the Mishkan. And nothing happened; Hashem did not yet appear.

It was the eighth day and the Jewish people were anxiously awaiting Hashem's appearance. Then finally it happened. Moshe and Aharon blessed the people "and the glory of Hashem appeared to the entire people! A fire went forth from before Hashem and consumed upon the Altar the elevation-offering and the fats; all the people saw and sang glad song and fell upon their faces" (*Vayikra* 9:23-24).

Can you imagine the ecstasy? But then, at the very climax of the Mishkan's inauguration, Nadav and Avihu brought an unauthorized offering and a fire came forth from Hashem and killed them. Immediately after their death, Moshe consoled Aharon by saying, "Of this did Hashem speak, saying: 'I will be sanctified through those who are nearest Me, thus I will be honored before the entire people'; and Aharon was silent" (ibid. 10:3).

According to the Talmud (*Zevachim* 115b), Moshe told Aharon that the Almighty spoke to him in a prophecy and told him that when the Mishkan would be inaugurated, "I shall set My meeting there with the Children of Israel, and it shall be sanctified with My honor (*bichvodi*)" (*Shemos* 29:43). Do not read it "with My honor," says the Talmud, but "through My honorable ones (*b'mechubadai*)." Moshe said, "Aharon, I knew that this House would be sanctified through the death of Hashem's beloved, but I thought it would be through either you or me. Now I see that Nadav and Avihu were greater than you and me!" (*Vayikra Rabbah* 12:2. See also *Midrash Tanchuma, Shemini*.)

> The Almighty does not need blood and death. The presence of His *Shechinah* brings blessing, transcendental pleasure, and healing.

Aharon was silent, indicating that understanding the role their deaths played did indeed console him.

Why would Hashem tell Moshe that the greatest Jews will die on a day of such celebration and joy? The Almighty does not need blood and death. The presence of His *Shechinah* brings blessing, transcendental pleasure, and healing. Why were their deaths necessary?

A Dire Warning

Every prophecy that predicts disaster is only a warning. The Almighty in effect told Moshe, "Watch out. You better take care of this issue; otherwise, when I appear, the greatest of the Jewish people will die." It did not have to happen. Had the Jewish people heeded the warning and taken the necessary steps to avoid making a critical mistake, they could have averted the tragedy. But what mistake was Hashem telling Moshe to correct?

If you pay close attention to how the Jewish people responded when Hashem appeared you will see what they were lacking. "A fire went forth from before Hashem and consumed upon the Altar the elevation-offering and the fats; all the people saw and sang glad song and they fell upon their faces" (*Vayikra* 9:24). What was missing? The Torah does not say that they were afraid. Where was the *yiras Shamayim*, the fear of Heaven?

That lack was corrected through the deaths of Nadav and Avihu. When the fire came down and killed the greatest Jews on the spot, boy, were they afraid. When the Almighty comes, it is not enough to rejoice and be ecstatic. It is not even enough to humble yourself. You need to tremble at the awesomeness of Hashem's presence.

Hashem tried to warn Moshe ahead of time, so that He would not have to bring about such a calamity. Instead, He had to correct the mistake for them, through the deaths of the greatest of the Jews, which restored the proper level of awe.

But why did Hashem bring about this fear specifically through the death of Nadav and Avihu?

Because ultimately they were responsible for this problem not being corrected.

The Talmud (*Sanhedrin* 52a) tells us that Nadav and Avihu were once walking behind Moshe and Aharon, and Nadav said to Avihu, "When will these two elders get out of the way so we can lead the Jewish people?"

The Talmud's characterization of Nadav and Avihu as arrogant upstarts, impatient with the current leadership, is not very flattering. However, the Midrash — cited by Rashi, and mentioned above — describes Nadav and Avihu as being greater than even Moshe and Aharon.

Which is the true depiction of Nadav and Avihu? Were they brash upstarts, or greater than Moshe and Aharon?

Chazal do not contradict themselves. Therefore, these descriptions must be two sides of the same coin.

Nadav and Avihu were in a certain respect greater than Moshe and Aharon, and it was this greatness that caused them to become arrogant and impatient with Moshe and Aharon's leadership. But there is another, more subtle mistake described in the Talmud's narrative, and it is a mistake we all commonly make in relating to the leaders of our generation and their handling of the Jewish people's deficiencies.

Nadav and Avihu thought that you are only responsible to address the problems of the Jewish people once you are appointed to a position of leadership. This is antithetical to the Torah's approach to responsibility, as the Torah says, "The hidden [sins] are for Hashem, our God, but the revealed [sins] are for us and our children forever" (*Devarim* 29:28). The Torah holds each and every one of us accountable to undertake to solve the problems we see the moment we become aware of them.

Taking responsibility for the Jewish people is not just an obligation of those in leadership positions; we are all equally responsible. But how can the Jewish people function if everyone takes responsibility to address the problems they see in the manner they deem fitting? That would create anarchy.

There is a balance between individually taking responsibility and respecting the current leadership. All of us, regardless of our position or stature, are equally responsible to address the problems that we see. There is no hierarchy when it comes to responsibility. When it comes to implementation of solutions, however, we must work under the guidance of the existing leadership to ensure that our proposal is sound and that our problem-solving is conducted properly.

Nadav and Avihu perceived a lack of *yiras Shamayim* in the Jewish people. That was part of their greatness, but because they did not address this problem in their lifetime, Hashem arranged for their death to be the means with which to resolve it. (This is one aspect of the concept that *"misas tzaddikim mechaperes"* — the death of the righteous atones.) Nadav and Avihu mistakenly thought they had to wait until they were appointed leaders to implement a solution to the problem they saw. Instead, they should have gone to Moshe and Aharon, explained the problem they saw to them, and presented their proposed solutions. After receiving the support and backing of Moshe and Aharon, they should have then implemented their strategy. That is the way to address problems constructively.

> We all see problems within the Jewish people, but instead of taking responsibility for them, we tell ourselves that it is our leaders' job to address them.

We often make the same mistake as Nadav and Avihu. We all see problems within the Jewish people, but instead of taking responsibility for them, we tell ourselves that it is our leaders' job to address them. Then, when the leaders are completely overwhelmed by the problems, we criticize them for not acting more boldly and aggressively, and then we become frustrated and even resentful of the lack of progress in these crucial areas.

The proper outlet for our concern is to develop a strategy and discuss it with our leaders, and then implement it with their backing and guidance. This approach ensures that people are empowered to take responsibility and confront the challenges they see without undermining the leadership.

The Greatest Difference

Just after the founding of the State of Israel, there was a bris in Yerushalayim that was attended by many Roshei Yeshivah and Rebbes.

Rav Chatzkel Sarna, the Rosh Yeshivah of Chevron, was asked to speak. Rav Chatzkel was known to be a colorful personality and his words that day did not disappoint.

Rav Chatzkel began as follows:

"I know all of you here think that it was your Zaide that had the greatest impact on *Klal Yisrael* over the last 100 years, but I am here to tell you today that it was none of them."

That certainly raised a few eyebrows.

"Furthermore," Rav Chatzkel continued, "the person who did have the biggest impact on *Klal Yisrael* was not a *talmid chacham* — in fact the person could not read a blatt Gemara." The rabbis asked Rav Chatzkel to change the topic.

Pushing on, Rav Chatzkel said, "When I tell you the person's name all of you will agree with me immediately." Given the people in attendance at the bris, that statement was simply outrageous.

"The person who had the greatest impact on *Klal Yisrael* over the last 100 years," Rav Chatzkel concluded, "was Sarah Schenirer."

Everyone agreed without hesitation.

Without Sarah Schenirer, the Jewish people would have been decimated. While young men were in yeshivah being educated and inspired with Torah and mitzvos, the young women were going to public school and losing their connection to *Yiddishkeit*. Without a generation of religious women, there can be no next generation of the Jewish people. She recognized this problem and created the Bais Yaakov movement of Jewish schools for girls.

What was Sarah Schenirer secret? How did she address a problem of the Jewish people that even great men like the Chofetz Chaim, Rav Chaim Ozer, and the Gerrer Rebbe did not address?

In her diary, she tells her secret. She was a seamstress, and young women would come to her to have clothing made. She would talk to them, and she saw up close how weak these girls were in their commitment to *Yiddishkeit* and understanding of Torah. She writes in her diary that she would cry for them, thinking, *I am sewing beautiful clothing to cover their bodies, but their souls are bare, because they lack mitzvos.*

> *S*arah Schenirer saved the Jewish people because she saw a critical problem, took it to heart, and took action. She did not pass the buck and wait for the leaders of her generation to step in and address the crisis.

Sarah Schenirer saved the Jewish people because she saw a critical problem, took it to heart, and took action. She saw the tragedy unfolding and understood that the entire future of *Klal Yisrael* was at stake. Most importantly, she avoided the mistake of Nadav and Avihu; she did not pass the buck and wait for the leaders of her generation to step in and address the crisis. She took action, working with the blessing of the leading rabbis of her generation, and made the difference that saved the Jewish people.

> *Inner peace is attained only by*
> *identifying with your soul and*
> *disciplining the body to follow*
> *its lead.*

פרשת תזריע/מצורע
Parashas Tazria/Metzora:
Five Stages of Mastering Free Will

We have just finished celebrating Pesach, the holiday of freedom. For a week we abstained from eating *chametz*, symbolizing banishing the *yetzer hara* from our midst. How can we hold on to our newfound sense of freedom while transitioning back into eating bread and going about daily life?

The key is mastering mankind's greatest gift: free will.

Our sages teach us, "Beloved is man, for he was created in God's image; it is indicative of a greater love that it was made known to him that he was created in God's image" (*Pirkei Avos* 3:18).

Unlike all other creations, Hashem gave mankind a unique gift, a Divine spark: free will. This gift gives us the ability to emulate God Himself by making independent choices. Used correctly, it gives us the power to create and change the world. If misused, this awesome power can lead to plundering and destroying the world.

But in order to harness this power, we must be aware that we have it in the first place!

Imagine an incredibly generous benefactor giving one million dollars to a homeless man on skid row. His life is completely transformed! He can live in a comfortable home, buy warm clothes, and purchase healthy food to eat.

But there is only one problem. The benefactor slipped the money into the bottom of the homeless man's bag, and he does not know he has it. He is a rich man shlepping around a million dollars, but he lives in the same state of misery and abject poverty because he doesn't know what he has in his possession.

The gift of free will gives each of us enormous power and potential, but only if we realize that we have it. That is the meaning of the Mishnah's statement: "It is indicative of a greater love that it was made known to him that he was created in God's image."

Free will is badly underutilized. Unfortunately, many of us live like that homeless beggar, unaware of the life-transforming power we carry around with us. Defining free will and recognizing its implications will enable us to begin to tap into the awesome potential within ourselves.

What Is Free Will?

Most people define free will as the choice between good and evil. But the Torah frames free will differently. "See — I have placed before you today the life and the good, and the death and the evil... I have placed life and death before you, blessing and curse; and you shall choose life..." (*Devarim* 30:15, 19).

The Torah does not tell us to choose good or to choose blessing, because everyone naturally wants good and blessing. No one wakes up and says to himself, *Let's see what kind of evil I can do today.* Even the most vile, immoral people rationalize their evil choices as good. The Torah instead defines the essence of free will as a battle between life and death, which is why the Torah exhorts us, "Choose life!"

But who chooses death?

Actually, all of us do, to some degree. Hashem made us a composite of a body and a soul, as the Torah says, "Hashem God formed the man of dust from the ground, and He blew into his nostrils the soul of life; and man became a living being" (*Bereishis* 2:7). Our lofty soul yearns to connect to its Infinite Source, and our lowly body yearns to go back to its source, back into the ground, dead, escaping all pain, effort, and responsibility.

Choosing death means choosing comfort, choosing to sleep. In the words of Shakespeare:

> To be, or not to be, that is the question—
> Whether 'tis nobler in the mind to suffer
> The slings and arrows of outrageous fortune,
> Or to take arms against a sea of troubles...
> To die, to sleep...
>
> (*Hamlet*, Act 3, Scene 1)

Our desire to escape from responsibility and challenge is constant. Suicide is the most extreme expression of this desire, but there are less dramatic forms of suicide as well: running away through drugs and alcohol, for instance. At every moment, we have to struggle to choose life — to accept the pain and embrace challenge and growth, to actualize our potential for greatness and change the world; or to choose death — to distract ourselves and avoid pain, to remain a mediocrity and satiate the *yetzer hara*'s endless desires.

Every one of us has a soul that yearns for greatness. Attaining that greatness is dependent upon how well we use our free will to live, to fight, to accomplish, and that begins by mastering the following five stages of free will.

Stage 1: Self-Awareness

The first step in using free will is to become aware of the choices you are making. Life is an ongoing stream of decisions. Once you become sensitive to the fact that you are constantly making choices, then you can monitor them and start actively flexing your free will muscles.

Don't let decisions just happen. Realize that you can take control of your decision-making and your actions. Ask yourself: Why am I reading this right now? Am I paying attention to what I am reading? Am I critically thinking about it or just mindlessly reading?

Your decisions shape your life and determine your destiny. Take charge. If you don't, you're just a pedestrian watching life pass you by.

Stage 2: Don't Be a Puppet of Society or of Your Past Decisions.

Once you are consciously making decisions, evaluate the assumptions that your decisions are built on. Be sure you are independent and not just a puppet of society and a product of its values. Don't accept society's assumptions as your own until you think them through and agree with them. Live for yourself, not for society.

Furthermore, evaluate your past decisions; don't be stuck by the decisions you made five or ten years ago. Start each day anew. The career you chose years earlier in college may no longer be the best thing for you today. Make sure you are guiding your decisions, and your past decisions are not guiding you.

Stage 3: Be Aware of the Body/Soul Conflict.

The Talmud (*Sanhedrin* 11b) tells us that within each of us, there is a fierce battle constantly raging between what our soul wants and what our body desires. The third stage of free will is becoming aware of this conflict.

The alarm clock rings first thing in the morning and the battle begins: Do you jump out of bed, or reach for the pillow while hitting the snooze button?

Sometimes we can actually hear ourselves fighting it out. Do you remember the first time you went jogging? Your body screams, "Stop! This is going to kill you!" Your soul says, "Keep going. You can do it! This isn't going to kill you. It's good for you!"

The soul wants you to exercise; it's healthy, there's a purpose. The body says, "Leave me alone. I'd rather sleep." The soul says, "Give up smoking; it's bad for you." The body says, "I can't quit. I'd rather smoke than face my frustrations. Besides, what's the big deal if I die a little earlier?"

This is the constant battle we face. The body wants to be comfortable, to sleep, and ultimately to die. The soul wants to strive for meaning, to do what's right, to grow, to live vibrantly with every fiber of its being.

To win the inner battle, you first have to distinguish between the cravings of the body and the aspirations of the soul. What does the body feel like doing, and what does the soul want to accomplish?

Make a list. What does the body want? Comfort. Sleep. Indulgence. Excuses.

What does the soul want? Greatness. Understanding. Meaning.

Once you clearly see the two sides, you are ready to make a decision and choose life over death. Work on becoming adept at sorting out the difference between what your soul wants and what your body feels like doing.

Stage 4: Identify With Your Soul, Not Your Body.

Who is the real you: your body or your soul?

The body says: "I'm hungry."

The soul says: "My body needs some food."

The body says: "I'm tired."

The soul says: "My body needs some sleep."

The Midrash teaches: "The righteous talk to their heart, while evil people let their heart talk to them" (*Esther Rabbah* 10:3). The question is, who's in charge? Who will dictate what you're going to do?

Inner peace is attained only by identifying with your soul and disciplining the body to follow its lead. Use your free will to train the body and coax it to service the needs of the soul: the real you.

Once you realize that you are not your body, you attain some mental distance from the body's incessant drives, and you can begin to deal with them effectively. "My body claims that it's hungry and that if I don't feed it it's going to starve to death. Is that true? When was the last time I ate?"

In order for you to gain control of your body, you have to be clever. For example, what happens when you are dieting and someone offers you a mouth-watering piece of chocolate cake? Your first reaction is, "No, I shouldn't. I'm on a strict diet." But your body tries to persuade you: "A little piece won't hurt you." Or, "This is the last piece of cake you'll have. You'll start the diet tomorrow."

The body doesn't say, "Forget the diet, it's O.K. to be fat." It knows you will reject that argument out of hand. So it seduces you by getting you to give in a tiny bit, and then, once you have tasted the first bit of pleasure and your resolve has weakened, it hits you full force. The *yetzer hara* is relentless. If you give it a finger, it will eventually take the whole hand.

To win the war with your body, utilize the same strategies and beat the *yetzer hara* at its own game. Want to start an exercise routine? Don't tell your body, "From now on, every morning, fifty push-ups." Tell it, "Just for the next five minutes, we'll exercise. And then we'll have a piece of cake." Want to learn something worthwhile instead of killing time in front of the computer? Tell your body, "Let's learn just for ten minutes. Then we'll check our messages." The body will follow, and it may even be convinced to learn for an hour!

The first few times you jog your body will scream bloody murder. But if you keep it up, after two months the body will enjoy it as much as the soul does.

As you gain control over your body, it will become easier and easier to win these battles, and the body will actually learn to appreciate what the soul wants. The first few times you jog your body will scream bloody murder. But if you keep it up, after two months the body will enjoy it as much as the soul does. The exhilaration of a runner's high is the inner peace of the soul and body working together in tandem.

Stage 5: Make Your Will His Will.

The highest stage of free will is when you transcend the battle between your body and your soul and ask yourself only one question: What is God's will?

When you subjugate your will to Hashem's will, that is the highest form of living. You are using your power of choice to merge with the ultimate power in the universe: the Infinite, transcendental Source of existence. Making God's will your will is the truest fulfillment of the Torah's exhortation to "Choose life."

Pesach is over, but the challenge to be truly free is constant. Master the power of your free will. Don't be a zombie; make decisions actively. Don't be a puppet of society or your past decisions. Be aware of the conflict between your body and soul and then identify with your soul. Finally, make God's will your will.

Teshuvah creates forgiveness, wipes away the sin, and can actually turn a transgression into a mitzvah.

פרשת אחרי

arashas Acharei:
Seven Steps Prior to Teshuvah

כִּי בַיוֹם הַזֶּה יְכַפֵּר עֲלֵיכֶם לְטַהֵר אֶתְכֶם מִכֹּל חַטֹּאתֵיכֶם לִפְנֵי ה' תִּטְהָרוּ:

For on this day (Yom Kippur) He shall provide atonement for you to cleanse you; from all your sins before Hashem shall you be cleansed (Vayikra 16:30).

When done correctly, *teshuvah* (repentance) is so powerful, it wipes your slate clean and restores your relationship with Hashem. As the Rambam states, "A *baal teshuvah* should not consider himself distant from the level of the righteous because of the mistakes and transgressions that he committed. This is not true. He is beloved and desirable before the Creator *as if he never transgressed*" (*Hilchos Teshuvah* 7:4).

Hashem relates to him as if he never transgressed. His sin is expunged from his past. How do we attain this incredible change? We have all experienced genuine *charatah*, regret, and the next thing we know we are back making the same mistake, stuck in the same rut as before. How do we attain real, lasting *teshuvah*?

The *Chovos Halevavos* teaches us the method, delineating seven steps one must take prior to doing *teshuvah* (see *Chovos Halevavos, Shaar Hateshuvah*, Chapter Three). Before you go through the actual four steps of *teshuvah* — namely, stopping the transgression, regret, *viduy* (confession), and resolving to never do it again — you must implement these crucial steps to ensure lasting change.

Step 1: Focus on one specific moment when you transgressed.

Let us illustrate with a transgression we are all guilty of: *bittul Torah*, wasting time from Torah learning. Think about all the time you waste in every single day, and how much that adds up to every week, every month. It is mind boggling. But in order to do *teshuvah* for this misdeed, you must get very specific. Thinking about all the time you have wasted is too broad and too overwhelming. It will not mean anything. Focus on one concrete instance, when you sat there talking about nonsense with a friend, killing time. You were shmoozing with Yankel while your *chavrusa* was waiting for you, and you took those five minutes and destroyed them.

Now focus on those specific five minutes of *bittul Torah*.

Step 2: Acknowledge that what you did was unequivocally wrong.

You have no chance of changing unless you stop rationalizing and call a spade a spade: *bittul Torah* is a terrible sin. It is murdering life! You are opting out and quitting, and in the end committing suicide in installments. It is a desecration of life itself. Do not sugarcoat it. You transgressed. Now face it. And what is even worse is that you *knew* you were transgressing. You did it *b'meizid*, willfully. Not only that, you were actually rebellious. Underneath it all you said to yourself, *God, I don't care. I've got to waste some time. What does Hashem expect from me?*

> *You transgressed. Now face it. And what is even worse is that you knew you were transgressing.*

You have to feel the gravity of the transgression; otherwise, you cannot do *teshuvah*.

Step 3: Know that you will be punished for this transgression.

After accepting that you did something wrong, focus on the fact that you are going to get punished for wasting those five minutes; your time in Gehinnom just got longer.

Each transgression has consequences. Face the reality: you are going to be punished for this.

Step 4: The punishment is on its way.

The *Chovos Halevavos* takes it one step further: realize that the punishment is already on its way. The bullet has been fired. There is no escape. The missile has left its silo and it is headed right for you. There is no way you can avoid it. The punishment is not something hanging in balance to be decided about in the future; it is already on the way!

Feel that reality. You cannot escape it.

Step 5: The only way to escape the punishment is by doing teshuvah.

Realize there is only one way to save yourself from punishment, and that is by doing *teshuvah*. You have wasted time — those moments are irrevocably squandered — yet Hashem, in His kindness, is giving you a miraculous way out. You can breathe life back into those moments you killed. Whew! *Teshuvah* creates forgiveness, wipes away the sin, and can actually turn a transgression into a mitzvah. Feel the reality of this amazing *chessed*.

Step 6: Do a cost/benefit analysis of the transgression.

The *Chovos Halevavos* explains that in order to do *teshuvah*, it is necessary to understand why you transgressed. Why did you waste the time? What was the *yetzer hara* promising you that tripped you up? Perhaps he was telling you, "Just squander these five minutes doing absolutely nothing, opting out of life for a few minutes, in order to bounce right back with a surge of life. Stop learning and get that cup of coffee you so desperately need so you can really sit down and learn!"

The *yetzer hara* is a master of seduction, promising us all sorts of dubious benefits. But if you pause for a moment you will see he is a liar. How will talking utter nonsense for five minutes enable you to accomplish as you've never accomplished before?

> The *yetzer hara* is a master of seduction, promising us all sorts of dubious benefits. But if you pause for a moment you will see he is a liar.

What did you think you were going to gain by listening to the *yetzer hara*? He was selling you on getting comfort, a space in the day where there is no pain, no work, no effort or worries, just mindless comfort.

After clarifying the proposed benefits, consider what it cost you. Contrast what you gained with what you actually lost. That *bittul Torah* made it harder for you to learn. You broke your momentum, and now you have to battle to get back into it. So you actually made it harder for yourself in the long run. But worse than that, what you really lost was your self-esteem. Living like a zombie, even for just a short time, chips away at your self-respect. You are squandering your potential and you know it.

Now think about what you would have lost if you had not wasted those five minutes. An illusion of pleasure. And what would you have gained if you had not listened to your *yetzer hara* and wasted that time? Self-respect. The pleasure of exercising your free will and eternally connecting to the Infinite through Torah. You would have gained a sense of invigoration that comes through living meaningfully and plugging into the wisdom of Hashem's Torah.

Step 7: Accept the pain of changing your habits.

Now you have the clarity you need to make the concrete decision to change. You know it is worthwhile. The next time you feel like wasting time, fight that urge. Now you are prepared to stand in front of Hashem and say, "*Ana Hashem, chatasi, avisi, pashati*; I made a mistake. I knew it was wrong. I was rebelling. I wasted fifteen minutes, and much more. I'm sorry; it was so stupid of me. Please forgive me. And I'll never do it again, if You help me."

By using these seven steps you have a chance to transform your Yom Kippur into a real opportunity to make lasting changes.

Love is a decision to focus and appreciate another person's virtues. Therefore, it can be commanded.

פרשת קדושים
arashas Kedoshim:
Love Your Neighbor

לֹא תִקֹּם וְלֹא תִטֹּר אֶת בְּנֵי עַמֶּךָ וְאָהַבְתָּ לְרֵעֲךָ כָּמוֹךָ אֲנִי ה':

You shall not take revenge and you shall not bear a grudge against the members of your people; you shall love your fellow as yourself; I am God (Vayikra 19:18).

Chazal (*Yerushalmi, Nedarim* 9:4) identify one mitzvah as the fundamental principle upon which the entire Torah is based: "You shall love your fellow as yourself."

To properly understand how to fulfill this crucial mitzvah we must answer the following four questions:

1. How can the Torah legislate an emotion and obligate us to love?

2. What is the purpose of the seemingly extra words "as yourself"?

3. Why is this mitzvah preceded with the additional prohibitions of "You shall not take revenge and you shall not bear a grudge"? It is highly unusual to have three separate mitzvos in one *passuk*.

4. Why does the verse conclude with the words "I am God"?

Is It Possible to Obligate Love?

Obligating love strikes us as impossible. Yet it is actually something we all do.

Imagine a son telling his father, "I hate my sister!"

No father is going to respond, "That's fine, it's O.K. if you hate your sister." He is far more likely to say, "Don't talk that way! You *have* to love your sister!" We know our children should love each other, even if one took the other's eraser, or iPod, or sweater without asking. Nothing should get in the way of their filial love.

The father is not merely suggesting that the brother love his sister; he is demanding it. It is not just preferable for children to love one another, just as it is not optional for parents to love their children. But do we actually go about loving a sibling, or a child?

Parents love their children naturally, you'll answer. But what if their child turns out to be an obnoxious brat? "It doesn't matter," you say. "They'll find something to love about him no matter what."

We define love as the emotional pleasure of appreciating the virtues of another person and identifying them with those virtues. With our children, we are naturally committed to focusing on their virtues and minimizing their shortcomings. "My son has a heart of gold. So what if he's a little hyper?" Therefore we love them, no matter what.

The reality is that the emotion of love is a decision: if we choose to focus on other people's virtues, we will love them, but if we choose to focus on their faults, we will be repelled by them.

This understanding of love is the basis of a healthy marriage. When a couple marries, they appreciate each other's virtues and begin to build a loving relationship. Yet today almost 50 percent of all marriages end in divorce, and many of those who stay married are not exactly living in bliss. When they first got married they were madly in love. What went wrong? They stopped focusing on each other's virtues, taking them for granted, and instead focused on their spouse's flaws and the subsequent disappointment they caused.

Every person is a mixture of virtues and faults, but what we choose to focus on and identify the person with is entirely up to us. When the Torah obligates us to love it is instructing us to identify people with their virtues. Consequently, this is something that can indeed be commanded.

Love: Greek Style

The Greek concept of love is symbolized by Cupid, who flits around and shoots an arrow into two unsuspecting people. *Presto!* Bob and Sue are now head over heels in love! The Western view of love, which comes from the Greek concept, sees love as an accident that you "fall" into. It either happens or it doesn't; it's not something you can control.

> If love is not something you can actually choose, then all you can do to stay married is hope that Cupid does not shoot you a second time.

However, be forewarned: as easily as you "fall in love," you can just as easily fall out of love. If Bob's love for Sue is not based on a commitment to appreciate her virtues, then when the stresses of married life grow, the following could easily happen. One day, after taking his wife for granted for years, Cupid might suddenly sneak up behind Bob and without warning shoots another arrow into him. *Boing!* Bob has now fallen in love with Jane.

Bob sheepishly returns home and explains to his wife, "I'm sorry, I fell in love with Jane. But it's not my fault, I wasn't looking for it, it just happened since that rascal Cupid shot me!" Out goes Sue and in comes Jane.

If love is not something you can actually choose, then all you can do to stay married is hope that Cupid does not shoot you a second time. Is it any surprise that the divorce rate is so high?

Contrast this with the relationship between parents and their children. No sane parent ever comes home one day and tells his children, "I've fallen in love with the neighbors' kids. They don't cough at night and they get better math scores. Sorry, but you kids are out. The kids next door are moving in."

*N*o sane parent ever comes home one day and tells his children, "I've fallen in love with the neighbors' kids. They don't cough at night and they get better math scores. Sorry, but you kids are out."

We don't "fall out of love" with our children because we understand that loving them isn't a "happening." We don't stop caring about our children just because they annoy us. We accept the obligation to love them despite the fact that they are often far more aggravating than our spouses!

If we carried this same type of commitment into our marriages, our love would continue to grow and deepen over time, just as it does with our children, enabling our marriage to not only withstand the winds of time, but to thrive.

Don't Take Revenge, Don't Bear a Grudge

Resentment poisons love. Someone wrongs you, and for months you cannot see them without recalling how they hurt you. This grudge colors your perspective and renders you completely incapable of seeing the good in this person. Your resentment brews and your desire to even the score and take revenge grows, preventing you from loving the person.

If you want to love your spouse, your parents, or anyone else for that matter, you have to let go of any resentment you have toward them. This is why these two prohibitions precede the mitzvah of loving our fellow Jews.

Letting go of our resentments is not easy, but if we see the person who hurt us as part of us, our resentment disappears. Imagine accidentally cutting your finger while slicing a carrot. Would you take the knife from your right hand and deliberately slice your left hand in revenge? Of course not, because your other hand is you, and hurting it is only hurting yourself.

Humanity is ultimately one. Taking revenge on someone else is as self-destructive as slicing your other hand with a knife, and that is one reason why the Torah says to love your neighbor "as yourself." Seeing the other person as yourself will remove the resentment that is impeding your love.

Unfortunately we often do not realize how we are all connected on our own, and it often takes an outside force to get us to appreciate that we are indeed one people. For example, the Nazis did not differentiate between different types of Jews. In their eyes we were all one people. When Hamas terrorists murdered three boys learning in Gush Etzion, the entire Jewish world united. It did not matter what type of kippah they wore; everyone felt that these were "our boys." During the times in life when we recognize this as true, hold on to that perception because it is the ultimate cure against the destructive effects of resentment.

> The Nazis did not differentiate between different types of Jews. In their eyes we were all one people.

True Friendship

The Jewish people have a rich repertoire of stories that powerfully inculcate Torah principles in our children. Every Jewish child used to hear the following story that shows us the power of loving another "as yourself."

At the time of the Roman Empire, two Jewish boys had grown up together in Israel and become very close friends. Eventually, they moved far apart: one was living under Roman control, and the other under Syrian control. Yet despite the distance between them, they remained dear friends.

Once, when the fellow from Rome was visiting Syria, he was falsely accused of being a spy. He was brought to the Syrian emperor, and eventually sentenced to death.

While being led out to be executed, the emperor asked him if he had any final requests. "Please," he begged, "let me go back to

Rome to settle my affairs and say goodbye to my family. Then I'll return to be executed."

The emperor laughed. "Are you crazy? What guarantee do I have that you'll come back?"

He answered, "I have a friend living here in Syria who will stand in my place until I return. He will be my guarantor. If I do not come back, you can execute him instead."

The Emperor was intrigued. "This I've got to see. O.K., call your friend."

His friend in Syria was summoned and sure enough, he agreed to stand in his friend's place in prison, and risk being killed if his friend did not return on time.

The emperor was so startled by this arrangement he agreed to let the man from Rome return home. "I'll give you 60 days," the emperor said, "but if you're not back by the dawn of the 60th day, your friend is dead."

The fellow from Rome raced home to say goodbye and put his affairs in order. After a hectic time and a lot of tears, he started back in plenty of time to reach Syria before the 60 days were over. But in those days they sailed galleys, and at times you could sit for days waiting for the right wind to blow. As luck would have it, there was no wind for several days, the boat was delayed, and by the time he arrived back in Syria, dawn of the 60th day was breaking.

As agreed, the jailors took the friend in Syria out to be executed.

Executions were gala affairs, and by early morning the crowds began to swell. Then just as they were about to execute him, the friend from Rome came running in, yelling, "Wait! I'm back. Don't kill him! Kill me!"

But the Syrian friend protested: "You can't kill him. He came too late. I'm the guarantor. You've got to kill me instead!"

Each one was equally adamant. "Kill me!" "No, kill me instead!" The executioner didn't know what to do. The crowd was in an uproar!

Finally, the emperor convened a meeting with them in his private chambers. He turned to the two of them and said, "I'll let both of you go free on one condition: that you make me your third friend!"

This is why the verse "Love your neighbor" concludes with the statement, "I am God." Because when there is unity and friendship between people, it is so precious that God so to speak wants to be part of it. He becomes the third friend.

In summary, love is a decision to focus and appreciate another person's virtues. Therefore, it can be commanded. In order to love, we need to let go of resentment by appreciating that we are all connected. When we unite in love, Hashem Himself joins the union. Drop resentments: "Do not take revenge and do not bear a grudge"; choose to love: "Love your neighbor as yourself"; and Hashem will dwell with you: "I am God."

Reaching out to our lost brothers and sisters involves many Torah obligations. The most far reaching of them all is kiddush Hashem.

פרשת אמור

arashas Emor:

Kiddush Hashem

This week's *parashah* contains the mitzvah of *kiddush Hashem*, sanctifying Hashem's Name. "You shall not desecrate My holy Name, rather I should be sanctified among the Children of Israel; I am Hashem Who sanctifies you" (*Vayikra* 22:32).

The Mishnah says, "All that the Holy One, blessed is He, created in His world, He created solely for His honor, as it is said (*Yeshayahu* 43:7), 'All that is called by My Name, indeed, it is for My honor that I have created it'" (*Pirkei Avos* 6:11).

There is only one point to all of creation: *kevod Shamayim* — giving honor to God.

But *Mesilas Yesharim* seemingly contradicts this statement. He explains that "man was not created except for the sole purpose of rejoicing in God and deriving pleasure from the splendor of His Presence; for this is… the greatest pleasure that can be found." There is nothing we can do for God. All of creation is an expression of His kindness: "*Olam chesed yibaneh* — the world is built on kindness." And the ultimate kindness is the pleasure of forging a relationship with Him. How do we reconcile this explanation of our purpose with "All that the Holy One, blessed is He, created in His world, He created solely for His honor"?

There really is no contradiction; these are two sides of the same coin. The Almighty obviously does not need us to honor Him. By appreciating God's greatness, which is conveyed through every aspect of creation, we experience the ultimate pleasure of *ahavas Hashem*, loving the Almighty. Making the world for God's honor is for us, not God. Everything in the world is a vehicle to honoring Him so we can constantly appreciate His awesomeness, and, by attaching ourselves to His infinite existence, attain the greatest source of meaning and pleasure.

> he Almighty obviously does not need us to honor Him. By appreciating God's greatness, which is conveyed through every aspect of creation, we experience the ultimate pleasure of *ahavas Hashem*, loving the Almighty.

The Rambam writes in *Sefer Hamitzvos,* on the mitzvah of *kiddush Hashem* (Positive Mitzvah 9):

> This mitzvah requires us to publicize the true religion to the masses. This must be done without fear of retribution, to the extent that even if a powerful tyrant tries to force us to deny God, we may not obey him. We must rather unquestioningly submit to death, not even allowing him to think that we have denied God, even if we still maintain belief in Him in our hearts. This is the mitzvah of sanctifying God's Name in which all Jews are obligated.

In the Shemoneh Esrei of Rosh Hashanah that describes the utopian vision that the Jewish people yearns for, we daven, "Let everything that has been made know that You are its Maker… and let everything with a life's breath in its nostrils proclaim, 'Hashem, the God of Israel, is King, and His Kingship rules over everything.'" We are beseeching Hashem to enable all of humanity to recognize God so they, too, can bask in the ultimate pleasure of *ahavas Hashem*.

The Uniqueness of Avraham Avinu

The Mishnah states, "There were ten generations from Adam to Noach — to show the degree of His patience; for all those generations angered Him increasingly, until He brought upon them the waters of the Flood. There were ten generations from Noach to Avraham — to show the degree of His patience; for all those generations angered Him increasingly, until our forefather Avraham came and received the reward of them all" (*Pirkei Avos* 5:2-3).

Why did only Avraham receive the reward of them all? What about Noach, who was an "*ish tzaddik tamim* — a righteous, perfect man"? Furthermore, Shem and Ever lived during this time. They had a great yeshivah; Yaakov Avinu spent 14 years learning there! Why was it only Avraham who saved mankind?

In *Hilchos Avodas Kochavim* (1:2-3), the Rambam describes the world's downward spiral from monotheism to idolatry, starting with Enosh, Adam's grandson, who mistakenly honored Hashem's celestial servants as a way of honoring Hashem. This mistake eventually led the entire world to worship false gods.

The Rambam then describes the reversal of this trend:

> The Eternal Rock was not recognized or known by anyone in the world, with the exception of a few individuals, such as Chanoch, Mesushelach, Noach, Shem, and Ever. The world continued in this fashion until the pillar of the world — the Patriarch Avraham — was born...
>
> [Avraham] knew that the entire world was making a mistake. What caused them to err was their service of the stars and images, which made them lose awareness of the truth.
>
> Abraham was forty years old when he became aware of his Creator. When he recognized and knew Him... he began to call in a loud voice to all people and inform them that there is one God in the entire world and it is proper to serve Him. He would go out and call to the people, gathering them in city after city and country after country, until he came to the land of Canaan — proclaiming [God's existence] — as it states (*Bereishis* 21:33): "And there he proclaimed in the Name of Hashem, God of the universe."

When the people would gather around him and ask him about his statements, he would explain to each one of them according to their understanding, until they turned to the path of truth.

The Rambam explains that after Avraham Avinu discovered God, he undertook the mission of teaching monotheism to the entire world. The Raavad asks: Where were Shem and Ever? They knew the truth; why did they not protest against the rampant idolatry?

The *Kesef Mishneh* answers that of course Shem and Ever were great, righteous men, prophets who taught Torah to their students in their great yeshivah. But they fell short in one crucial area: they did not "call out in the Name of Hashem" — they taught only those students who came to them. They did not proactively undertake to draw people away from idolatry and bring them to turn to the Almighty.

> *I*ndeed, Noach was a *tzaddik* who perfected himself and "found grace in the eyes of God." But he did not take the initiative to teach humanity the ways of Hashem.

This was Noach's failing as well. Indeed, he was a *tzaddik* who perfected himself and "found grace in the eyes of God." But he did not take the initiative to teach humanity the ways of Hashem. Therefore, he managed to save only himself and his immediate family.

Only Avraham Avinu traveled around teaching everyone he encountered about the reality of God's existence. It was Avraham who shattered his father's idols and told their followers, "You are mistaken! There is only one God Who created all mankind. Worshiping rocks and trees is nonsense." Avraham dedicated his life to *kiddush Hashem*, to bringing the reality of Hashem to the world. Therefore, only Avraham received the reward of his predecessors, and, in doing so, merited to become the father of the Jewish people, whose mission is to partner with Hashem in making Him known to the entire world.

Today, the vast majority of the Jewish people are not undertaking the mission of bringing the awareness of God into the world and serving as His ambassadors, for they themselves unfortunately do not understand His existence and the truth of His Torah. Can there be any greater *chillul Hashem* than this? The messenger has forgotten his message.

> *Today, the vast majority of the Jewish people are not undertaking the mission of bringing the awareness of God into the world and serving as His ambassadors, for they themselves unfortunately do not understand His existence and the truth of His Torah.*

Reaching out to our lost brothers and sisters involves many Torah obligations. The most far reaching of them all is *kiddush Hashem* — to fight the desecration and fill this aching vacuum with the recognition of Hashem and His everlasting love for His people — because this is Hashem's purpose in creating the world and our purpose as the Jewish people.

Today there is a terrible famine, as the prophet says, "Behold, days are coming — the word of the Lord Hashem/Elokim, when I will send hunger into the land; not a hunger for bread nor a thirst for water, but to hear the words of Hashem" (*Amos* 8:11). By making the effort to reconnect your fellow Jews to their heritage, you are helping to fulfill the purpose of creation.

Shemittah is the one mitzvah that demonstrates to all future generations that the Torah was indeed given by Hashem at Mount Sinai, for the author of the Torah could only be God, not a human being.

פרשת בהר

*P*arashas Behar:
The Only Possible Author

וַיְדַבֵּר ה' אֶל מֹשֶׁה בְּהַר סִינַי לֵאמֹר: דַּבֵּר אֶל בְּנֵי יִשְׂרָאֵל וְאָמַרְתָּ אֲלֵהֶם כִּי תָבֹאוּ אֶל הָאָרֶץ אֲשֶׁר אֲנִי נֹתֵן לָכֶם וְשָׁבְתָה הָאָרֶץ שַׁבָּת לַה': שֵׁשׁ שָׁנִים תִּזְרַע שָׂדֶךָ וְשֵׁשׁ שָׁנִים תִּזְמֹר כַּרְמֶךָ וְאָסַפְתָּ אֶת תְּבוּאָתָהּ: וּבַשָּׁנָה הַשְּׁבִיעִת שַׁבַּת שַׁבָּתוֹן יִהְיֶה לָאָרֶץ שַׁבָּת לַה' שָׂדְךָ לֹא תִזְרָע וְכַרְמְךָ לֹא תִזְמֹר:

Hashem spoke to Moses on Mount Sinai, saying: Speak to the Children of Israel and say to them: When you come into the land that I give you, the land shall observe a Sabbatical year of rest for Hashem. For six years you may sow your field and for six years you may prune your vineyard; and you may gather in its crop. But the seventh year shall be a complete rest for the land, a Sabbath for Hashem (Vayikra 25:1-4).

When conveying the mitzvah of Shemittah, the Sabbatical year, why does the Torah specify that God is speaking on Mount Sinai?

Rashi answers that the Torah is pointing out that just as all of the laws of the Sabbatical year were taught at Sinai, so, too, all of the Torah's laws, with all their details, were taught at Sinai.

But this begs the question: All the mitzvos of the Torah were taught at Sinai. So why does the Torah teach this lesson specifically through the mitzvah of Shemittah, when any mitzvah could have been chosen?

Shemittah was chosen because it is the one mitzvah that demonstrates to all future generations that the Torah was indeed given by Hashem at Mount Sinai, for the author of the Torah could only be God, not a human being.

Would You Include This Mitzvah?

Let's examine how, in fact, Shemittah demonstrates this.

Let's imagine for a moment that a group of people got together to write the Torah. And let's imagine that we are on this committee. Since our aim is to get as many people as possible to accept our book, we are going to perpetrate a hoax and pass on our religion as if it were given by God, who ostensibly appeared to the Jewish people at Sinai and gave them this Torah.

We are starting from scratch, and we are going to include a truckload of commandments. So what would be a good law to include in our Torah? How about "Thou shalt not steal"? That is necessary for a functioning society. Let's include it.

Thou shalt not murder? O.K., we'll put that in, too.

Shabbos? A day of rest and rejuvenation? Sounds good.

Now I would like to propose the following law: Every seventh year, the entire Jewish people must cease working the fields. They may not plant, plow or harvest for an entire year, once every seven years.

Do you think this is a good law to put in the Torah?

Sure! Crop rotation is an important farming technique. Letting the land lie fallow helps replenish the nutrients, and the land yields better crops than it would if the soil were used without rest year after year. And the respite will give the nation the opportunity to spend more time focusing on learning Torah.

But there is one problem. Remember, we are an agrarian society and live off what we plant and harvest. If we do not plant for an entire year, we will have nothing to eat! How can people learn if they are literally starving to death? That's no small problem.

> *Remember, we are an agrarian society and live off what we plant and harvest. If we do not plant for an entire year, we will have nothing to eat!*

There are a couple of obvious solutions. We can store one-sixth of the harvest during each of the first six years and then eat from that during the Sabbatical year. Alternatively, we can divide the country into seven regions, and each year the people of a different region will let their fields rest and borrow food from all the others. Simple enough.

Suddenly, someone on the committee pipes up with a different, more radical solution. "Forget dividing the land or storing up grain. I have a much better idea. Let's write in the Torah that God promises to deliver a triple crop in the sixth year!"

The committee erupts. "That's absurd! We obviously can't guarantee that the sixth year will miraculously yield a triple crop. We have no control over nature. If we include this insane guarantee, our religion is doomed. We're trying to pass this book off as if it's written by God. If we promise something we can't deliver, we'll be exposed as frauds!"

> *There is no doubt that our imaginary Torah-writing committee would shoot down the ridiculous triple-crop idea and select one of the more sensible solutions.*

"If we include this triple-crop idea," another committee member says, "how long do you think this religion will last? Exactly six years! As soon as the triple crop doesn't come, we're out of business. Everyone will see that the religion is a sham."

There is no doubt that our imaginary Torah-writing committee would shoot down the ridiculous triple-crop idea and select one of the more sensible solutions. It would be completely counterproductive to include a miraculous blessing that you know you cannot deliver and that would undermine the entire enterprise of perpetrating the hoax that this Torah was written by God.

Parashas Behar: The Only Possible Author / 187

Promises, Promises

Yet this promise is exactly what the Torah guarantees:

> *But the seventh year will be a complete rest for the land...*
> *your field you shall not sow, your vineyard you shall not*
> *prune. The aftergrowth of your harvest you shall not reap*
> *and the grapes you had set aside for yourself you shall not*
> *pick; it shall be a year of rest for the land. . .*
> *If you will say: What will we eat in the seventh year? —*
> *behold! We will not sow and not gather in our crops! I will*
> *ordain My blessing for you in the sixth year and it will*
> *yield a crop sufficient for the three-year period*
> *(Vayikra 25:4, 5, 20-21).*

The Torah's solution to procuring food for the Shemittah year is not dividing up the land or storing grain. The Torah makes the incredible promise that the sixth year will produce enough crops for three years.

The Torah could have hedged this promise with a built-in excuse. It could have said: "Keep the Sabbath laws in the seventh year. It's going to be a difficult year; everyone will be hungry. But as a great reward, you will get a triple crop in the eighth year." That would have been smart, because then, when the promised bumper crop does not happen, the excuse could always be, "Well, some people were cheating in the seventh year. So God punished us and didn't give us the triple crop."

There is only one Author Who can indeed guarantee a miraculous triple crop and include this promise in His Torah with complete confidence.

But our Author promises a triple crop in the *sixth* year, before we even observe the laws of Shemittah. Should there fail to be a bumper crop, there is no possible excuse.

Who could have written this and made such a promise? There is only one Author Who can indeed guarantee a miraculous triple crop and include this promise in His Torah with complete confidence — and that Author is the Almighty, Who controls all of nature.

Instead of complaining or questioning God's ways, we need to focus on hearing His message and paying attention to Him.

פרשת בחקתי
arashas Bechukosai:
Hearing God's Messages

This week's *parashah* contains the *Tochachah*, the series of horrific punishments that will befall the Jewish people if they do not listen to Hashem and if they continue to ignore His admonitions. What is the primary cause of the intensification of these punishments?

The Torah says:

> If you behave with Me happenstance (*keri*) and refuse to heed Me, then I shall lay a further blow upon you...
>
> If despite these you will not be chastised toward Me, and you behave with Me happenstance (*keri*), then I, too, will behave toward you happenstance, even I, seven ways for your sins (*Vayikra* 26:21, 23-24).

What does the word "*keri*" mean?

The Rambam defines "*keri*" as denying Hashem's orchestration of events and instead viewing them as random accidents. He writes (*Hilchos Taaniyos* 1:3):

> But if the people do not cry out [to God] and sound the trumpets, and instead say, "What has happened to us is merely a

natural occurrence, and this difficulty is merely by chance," this is a path of cruelty and causes them to continue in their wicked deeds. And this time of distress will lead to further distress.

This is what the Torah says: "If you behave with Me happenstance, I will behave toward you in a fury of happenstance." The implication of the verse is: When I bring difficulties upon you to encourage you to change, if you say it is a chance occurrence, I will add to your [punishment] as an expression of anger for that indifference [to Divine Providence].

The Rambam calls ignoring Divine Providence "a path of cruelty." Why does he call it cruelty when the essential problem with this approach is that it is heresy? The Rambam does not need to tell us that this is heresy; that is obvious. Instead he is focusing on the root cause for the heresy; namely, cruelty, because attributing painful occurrences to random forces positions God as an uncaring, vindictive Father. Only a cruel person could imagine a father actually abandoning his children to the treacherous whims of fate and allowing them to be hurt for no reason.

Furthermore, reducing difficulties to mere accidental occurrences ensures that people will not do *teshuvah*, which causes Hashem to bring upon us even greater difficulties. This is another manifestation of cruelty. It is like taking away a person's life preserver, the one thing that can save him while treading water in the middle of the ocean.

There Are No Accidents

The *parashah's* central message is that there are no accidents. Nothing just happens. God is running the world, and everything that occurs is a Divinely calibrated message from Hashem. He is constantly communicating with us, and we need to stop and ask, "What is the Almighty teaching me?" Something happens in Israel, there is a major economic downturn, someone close to you gets ill — ask yourself: *What am I supposed to learn from this?* Do not think it is an arbitrary occurrence, a chance happening. Realize that Hashem is the ultimate Cause behind everything that happens in the world, and He is very articulate. If we genuinely want to understand His message, we will hear Him and save ourselves a lot of grief.

Instead of complaining or questioning God's ways, we need to focus on hearing His message and paying attention to Him.

A student traveling the world once met me and said, "Rabbi, I don't need a yeshivah! You see, God and I are very close. He does miracles for me."

I eyed him a little suspiciously. "Would you mind describing a miracle or two?"

"Sure," he said. "Recently I was riding my bicycle up a winding mountain road. A Mac truck swerved into my lane, coming straight at me. Having no choice, I drove off the side of the mountain, over a sheer cliff, and fell fifty feet onto jagged rocks. I screamed out, 'God!'

"Rabbi, as I hit the ground I felt God's hand cushioning me. I got up without a scratch! It was a total miracle! So you see, God and I are very close."

Rabbi Weinberg leaned in, looked the fellow in the eye and said, "Tell me, my friend, who do you think pushed you off the cliff?"

The young man was speechless.

Rabbi Weinberg explained, "God isn't Superman, waiting until you stumble off a cliff and then flying in at the last moment to save you. He controls everything in your life: the problems and the solutions. First He sends a truck to force you off the cliff, and *then* He saves you. The question you need to ask is, why would God throw you off a cliff and then catch you? Clearly, He wants to get your attention. What does He want to teach you? You need to work on your relationship with God by going to yeshivah!"

A Sign of Love

When Hashem sends a message to get our attention, it is an expression of His love and concern, even when that wake-up call entails some pain.

Imagine that you are driving your car and suddenly a 7-year-old boy darts into the street chasing his ball. You screech to a halt and just narrowly miss him. Then, you roll down your window and yell at the boy, "Hey, be careful! I almost hit you!" You are about to drive off when you see a man chasing the boy and tackling him to the ground. The man is screaming at him, "Are you crazy!? You almost got yourself killed!" And then he gives the boy a *potch*.

Who is that man who actually chased the boy and was not satisfied with a mere finger-wagging?

It's the boy's father. He loves his son so much, he will not stop until he is sure that the boy gets the message never to run into the street again, even if it means giving him a *potch* to get the point across. It is a sign of his love and concern, not his abandonment.

Hashem is our Father in Heaven, and because He loves us deeply, He won't give up on us. He will send us a wake-up call if necessary, and if He does, we need to remember that it is a sign of His love.

Getting the Message

In order to hear Hashem's message properly we need to first connect to the reality of His love for us and realize that His message is for our good. If one's relationship with God is steeped in mistrust and anger, Hashem's message will get distorted through that subjective lens, since it is the emotional context of a relationship that largely determines how we interpret our interactions.

For example, Rachel has been working for the last four years on completing her Master's degree. Tonight is the graduation. She tells her husband, Michael, "Meet me there at 8 p.m. and please — don't be late."

"Don't worry," he assures her. "I'll be there on time."

"You promise?"

"Promise."

Eight o'clock rolls around and he's not there. Rachel starts getting agitated. It's 10 after 8 and still no show — now she's mad. At 8:30 she can't believe he let her down again. She feels hurt and dejected.

Now let's take a look a second couple, Sarah and David. Sarah is also graduating tonight, and she tells David to be there at 8 and to try not to be late.

"This is such an important evening," he says. "I wouldn't want to miss a minute of it!"

Eight o'clock rolls around and he's not there. What does Sarah think? *Maybe he's stuck in traffic.* Ten after eight. . .she starts to worry. *Maybe something happened.* At 8:30 she leaves the auditorium, in a state of panic, and starts calling the local hospitals.

Same situation, two very different reactions. When the relationship is one of resentment and mistrust, the action is interpreted through that negative lens. When the relationship is one of love and trust, that same action is viewed in an altogether different light.

When we are unaware of God's unwavering love, we will necessarily misinterpret His message. Therefore, the initial challenge is to ensure that our relationship with Him is rooted in trust and love.

> *Hashem does not lash out in anger, inflicting pain because of His own frustration and lack of impulse control. He is not a dysfunctional parent.*

Hashem does not lash out in anger, inflicting pain because of His own frustration and lack of impulse control. He is not a dysfunctional parent. Everything He does stems from His love, which is infinite and boundless, greater than all the love in the world. As the Torah says, "As a parent will chastise his son, so Hashem, your God, chastises you" (*Devarim* 8:5).

But how do we connect to God's love for us and put our relationship with Him into a positive context? By building gratitude.

Gratitude

Acts of kindness build love and trust in a relationship. But in order for the bonds of love to be strengthened, the acts of kindness need to be appreciated and recognized. If the kindness is taken for granted and the recipient is not grateful, then no emotional deposit is made and the two parties will miss out on the opportunity to be drawn closer.

> *Acts of kindness build love and trust in a relationship. But in order for the bonds of love to be strengthened, the acts of kindness need to be appreciated and recognized.*

We are all recipients of an overwhelming abundance of gifts from the Almighty: our life, our eyesight, our legs, our children, our clothing, our homes, our food, *every single breath* — it is really endless. The problem is that we often take God's innumerable blessings for granted and forget that we are the recipients of His myriad precious gifts. In order to feel His love for us, we need to actively pause and appreciate the countless, ongoing demonstrations of that love. By recognizing His unceasing involvement in our lives, both past and present, we can build a loving context for our relationship with God.

This was one of God's essential messages to the Jewish people when He introduced Himself at Mount Sinai. "I am Hashem, your God, Who has taken you out of the land of Egypt, from the house of slavery" (*Shemos* 20:2).

> *God could have introduced Himself by declaring, "I am Hashem, your God, Who created the heavens and the earth." But He wasn't interested in showing off His power.*

God could have introduced Himself by declaring, "I am Hashem, your God, Who created the heavens and the earth." What could be more impressive than that? But He wasn't interested in showing off His power. He wanted to show His fledgling nation that He is there for them, committed, loving, and caring. "Yes, it is I, your God, Who overturned nature to liberate each and every one of you, the One Who saved you and freed you from slavery and chose you to be My people."

The following exercise can help you appreciate God's active, loving role in your personal life. If you take the time to do it, it will transform your relationship with Him.

Write down 50 blessings you have in your life (e.g., your sense of smell, your spouse, your health...).

Now write down 50 more (your morning coffee, your son's smile, your car...).

Every day, write down one new blessing you have received in your life. Do this every day for a month. On Shabbos, ask your family and guests to share one thing for which they are grateful.

By building your gratitude muscles, you will begin to recognize and appreciate Hashem's boundless love for you, which is the essential prerequisite to understanding the messages He is sending you.

ספר במדבר

*S*efer Bamidbar

*By creating the Mishkan first
and placing it in the center of
the Jewish people, Hashem was
giving the Jewish people a tangible
reminder not to be distracted by
the positions and prestige of others,
but to focus on what really counts:
our relationship with Him.*

פרשת במדבר
Parashas Bamidbar:
Know Your Place

This week's *parashah* describes the hierarchy of the Jewish people and the formation in which they traveled. It identifies the *nesi'im,* the leaders of every *shevet* (tribe), and then describes how the twelve *shevatim* are divided into four different camps, consisting of three tribes each, one of which led the camp. Finally, the sons of Levi are assigned their specific responsibilities vis-à-vis the Mishkan (Tabernacle) and its vessels, as well as their place of encampment around the *Ohel Moed,* the Tent of Meeting.

The Jewish people had been in the desert for over a year. Why did Hashem wait until the Mishkan was constructed to delineate the structure and hierarchy of the Jewish people?

When appointing an individual or tribe to a position of leadership and prestige, you run the risk of diminishing those not chosen. Rav Yaakov Kamenetsky explains that Hashem gave instructions regarding the hierarchy of the Jewish people only after the Mishkan was built, in order to mitigate this potential drawback (*Sefer Emes L'Yaakov, Parashas Bamidbar*). The Mishkan, which brought the palpable presence of Hashem to the Jewish people, is the antidote to the jealousy and resentment that is often caused by organizational hierarchies.

> The true measure of a person is not his position, power, or title, but rather the closeness to Hashem he has attained through his own choices.

The true measure of a person is not his position, power, or title, but rather the closeness to Hashem he has attained through his own choices. You can be the king of Israel, the most powerful man in the nation, but still be completely evil, like Yeravam ben Nevat. Conversely, you can occupy the lowly position of woodchopper, like Hillel Hazaken, and be counted among the greatest sages in Jewish history. Each person's desire to grow in his or her relationship with Hashem is completely up to them and cannot be stymied by any other person or external factor. No position, hierarchy, or lack of power can impede your spiritual growth.

By constructing the Mishkan first and placing it in the center of the Jewish people, Hashem was giving the Jewish people a tangible reminder not to be distracted by the positions and prestige of others, but to focus on what really counts: our relationship with Him. To that, we all have equal access. Once that realization is in place, Hashem can implement a hierarchy of positions without impinging on anyone's sense of worth.

Generations and Their Leaders

But the fact that we are all equally obligated to come close to Hashem does not obviate the need for strong, clearly defined leadership that is accepted by all.

Throughout Jewish history, every generation had its leaders. Many were exceptional and led the Jewish people to great heights, while others caused enormous damage to the Jewish people by leading them astray. Leaders are not infallible, but they are necessary, and every generation must appoint a leader, despite the inherent risk that a person of low caliber will take the helm. As the *Sefer HaChinuch* explains (Mitzvah 71), the alternative — having no leader — would be far worse:

> "It is impossible for a community of people to exist and function without making one among them the head over the others, to obey his order and carry out his decrees. For people are divided one from the other in their views, and no one will agree on any one view in order to do any one particular thing. The result will be a total standstill and the death of all activities. For this reason it is necessary to accept the view of one among them, be it good or bad, that they may successfully engage in building the world. Sometimes great benefit will result from his counsel, and sometimes the reverse; but all this is better than dissension, which causes a complete standstill."

Know Your Place

The formation of the Jewish people defined the place of each Jew as the nation traveled through the desert. No one was left guessing where they belonged.

Hamakir es mekomo, knowing your place, is one of the forty-eight ways to acquire Torah (*Pirkei Avos* 6:6). Doing so starts with understanding your personal makeup: your unique traits, talents, abilities, and knowledge, as well as your weaknesses and the limits of your knowledge. Having this requisite self-understanding helps you determine when it is appropriate for you to speak up or take action and when it is appropriate for you to remain silent or let others take the lead.

In order to respond to situations correctly, you need to know your place. Remaining on the sidelines when you are the most fitting person to take charge creates a leadership vacuum that damages the nation. On the other hand, rashly stepping into the fray when others who are more qualified have already taken responsibility is self-centered and can wreak havoc. Today, for instance, the Internet has unleashed a wave of self-proclaimed experts and pundits offering unsound and wrongheaded advice on every topic imaginable, especially when it comes to Israel and the Jewish people.

> *R*emaining on the sidelines when you are the most fitting person to take charge creates a leadership vacuum that damages the nation. On the other hand, rashly stepping into the fray when others who are more qualified have already taken responsibility is self-centered and can wreak havoc.

The trait of recognizing your place is integral to Jewish leadership. When Moshe saw the Egyptian beating the Jewish worker, the Torah tells us that he "turned this way and that and saw that there was no man, so he struck down the Egyptian and hid him in the sand" (*Shemos* 2:12). The next day, Dasan and Aviram answered back to Moshe, saying, "Who appointed you as a dignitary, a ruler, and a judge over us? Do you propose to murder us as you murdered the Egyptian?" Obviously, there were people watching when Moshe killed the Egyptian. What, then, does the *passuk* mean when it says that he looked both ways and saw that there was no man?

The answer is that before Moshe took action he first evaluated if there was anyone else willing and more capable to respond to the outrageous behavior of the Egyptian. Only after he determined that no one was more capable than he to take responsibility did he step in and act.

> *A* leader who always needs to be at the forefront is driven by his ego, not by the cause.

A true leader does not push himself into the limelight in order to gain attention and fame. He takes responsibility when there is a clear and definite need, but he is fully prepared to take the backseat when that is what the situation calls for. A leader who always needs to be at the forefront is driven by his ego, not by the cause. In contrast, a person who knows his place takes action when it is appropriate to do so and allows others to take the lead when that's what's best for the Jewish people.

A person who witnesses the shocking death of a sotah must transform the startling lessons he learned into action.

פרשת נשא
arashas Nasso:
Putting Wisdom into Action

I n this week's *parashah* we find the episode of the *sotah*, the woman suspected of adultery by her husband. She is brought to the *Beis HaMikdash* and given a choice: Admit guilt (if guilty), or drink the "bitter waters," which serve as a miraculous test. If she is guilty she will die on the spot, and if she is innocent she can return to her husband.

What immediately follows is the discussion of the *nazir*, who takes a vow of abstinence that prohibits him from drinking wine, cutting his hair, or coming in contact with the dead for a specified period of time. Chazal explain that the laws of the *nazir* are juxtaposed with the laws of the *sotah* because one who sees a *sotah* in her state of degradation, and perceives firsthand what frivolity and wine can cause, should immediately take a nazirite vow prohibiting him from drinking wine (*Sotah* 2a).

Now, isn't the person who witnessed the ordeal of the *sotah* the last one who needs to become a *nazir*? He has seen upfront the horrific consequences of too much wine. So why does the Torah teach that specifically he who has seen the *sotah* should become a *nazir*?

The Mishnah says, "Anyone whose good deeds exceed his wisdom, his wisdom will endure" (*Pirkei Avos* 3:12). This means that if everything a person understands he immediately puts into action, his wisdom will endure. But if he understands something and does not put it into practice, his wisdom will disappear. As the Mishnah continues, "Anyone whose wisdom exceeds his good deeds, his wisdom will not endure."

> *If one does not translate his new awareness into some concrete action, the inspiration will fade and he will forget the lesson he learned, making himself susceptible to the dangers of intoxication and escapism.*

If you have an insight but don't act on it, you are going to lose that insight. That is the nature of the human condition. Therefore, the person who has seen the *sotah's* degradation must immediately react and do something to fortify himself against similar transgression. That is the only way for him to hold onto his clarity. In contrast, if one does not translate his new awareness into some concrete action, the inspiration will fade and he will forget the lesson he learned, making himself susceptible to the dangers of intoxication and escapism.

A Generation of Ingrates

One of the more problematic areas where a failure to act leads to denial is gratitude. When I started my first yeshivah, Rav Yitzchak Hutner, my rosh yeshivah in Yeshiva Rabbeinu Chaim Berlin, gave me a startling piece of advice. He said, do not expect that your *talmidim* (students) will have any *hakaras hatov*. They will not have any gratitude. It's not in the mindset of this generation.

I was taken aback, but it did not take too long to discover that Rav Hutner, of course, was right. Today, young people do not even think they owe their parents anything. "What do I owe my parents?" they say. "Did I ask to be born?" This lack of gratitude comes from not acting on the realization that they do indeed owe their parents, and it, in turn, leads to the perverse situation of children feeling betrayed by their parents for not giving them what they crave. "What do you mean I can't have the car? You're not even using it!"

In previous generations, even non-Jews understood the Torah principle of honoring your parents. No one's parents owed them anything. They owed their parents. Regardless of what they did to you, they gave you the gift of life and brought you into this world. You didn't expect anything from them because you owed them.

I remember that when I was a child, two brothers stopped talking to each other because one of them convinced their elderly father to move in and stay with him instead of sharing the burden with his brother and having the father move every other week. The brother was upset about losing the opportunity to take care of his father. Today, siblings will fight over whose turn it is to visit their parent in a nursing home. "It's your turn to visit! I can't go." That's what happens when we don't put into action the gratefulness we should have toward our parents. We soon forget we even owe them and then start thinking how much they owe us.

Taking It to Heart

In contrast, let me tell you a story about a remarkable man who took to heart what he understood and completely turned his life around. He was a young, athletic man when he was shot at a university in Chicago and became a quadriplegic. He told me that when he lay in the hospital bed, realizing that he would never move his arms and legs again, what flashed through his mind was: What is life really all about? Is it worth living? If you can't move your hands and feet, if you can't go anywhere, if you can't play sports, what then does it mean to be alive?

He spent an entire hour pondering these questions and thinking about the meaning of accomplishment. *How can I make a difference in life? I'm never going to run a mile; I'm never going to feed myself. So what is life all about? Is it about attaining wisdom and understanding? What is there to understand?*

He was fascinated by these questions, and he spent the next hour thinking about the meaning of life. Then, all of a sudden, something clicked: *If I had never been shot and forced to confront these questions, I never would have stopped to think about the purpose of my existence. I've been running too fast, going nowhere.* With great determination, he decided to go figure out what the true meaning of life is.

He then began to think about what human beings are really seeking. *What do I want? Who am I? What are the genuine pleasures that life has to offer? How can a human being be utterly preoccupied with making money, or jumping from one sensory pleasure to another, or consumed with what people think of him, and ignore his own quest for meaning?* He told me that he realized then how insane we can all be.

Then he had another epiphany. Which is a greater tragedy: not to be able to move your arms and legs for fifty years, or to spend seventy years running around and conquering the world without knowing what life is all about? Which is a greater tragedy: living a full seventy years in possession of all your faculties and not knowing the true meaning of life, or being a quadriplegic and knowing what it is that makes life meaningful?

And then he said, "You know, it's a good thing I was shot."

He told me that the answer was immediately obvious: what a tragedy to spend a lifetime not knowing the purpose of your life.

And then he said, "You know, it's a good thing I was shot." He didn't thank God at that point because he didn't know yet that there is a God. But he appreciated that it was good to be alive, even if you cannot move your arms and legs. He understood that life is precious and meaningful. And he spent the rest of his life pursuing meaning, eventually becoming an observant Jew, immersing himself in Torah study, and making an incredible *kiddush Hashem.* All because he acted on his insight.

Nothing changes if nothing changes.

A person who witnesses the shocking death of a *sotah* must transform the startling lessons he learned into action. He has to take a step and make a change; otherwise, he will have squandered a great opportunity. Nothing changes if nothing changes.

If we lack appreciation for the good that Hashem has lovingly granted us, we are likely to respond with complaints and negativity, even mistakenly concluding that the Almighty has abandoned us.

פרשת בהעלותך
arashas Beha'aloscha:
Complaining

Complaints, complaints! This week's *parashah* is filled with puzzling complaints.

> *The people took to seeking complaints; it was evil in the ears of Hashem… The rabble that was among them cultivated a craving, and the Children of Israel also wept once more, and said, "Who will feed us meat? We remember the fish that we ate in Egypt free of charge; the cucumbers, melons, leeks, onions, and garlic. But now, our life is parched, there is nothing; we have nothing to anticipate but the manna!" (Bamidbar 11:1, 4-6).*

The *erev rav*, the mixed multitude, had an intense craving, and they cried. The Jewish people also cried for meat, and they remembered the free fish they ate as slaves in Egypt, as well as the squash, the watermelon, the onions, and the garlic. Rashi, quoting the Sifri, explains that they mentioned these specific foods because the manna tasted like anything they wanted except these foods, which are injurious to nursing women.

What is going on here? The Jewish people are complaining about a meat shortage? They are longing for fish? They miss the taste of squash? That is what they are complaining about? Remember, we are talking about the *dor dei'ah,* the generation who saw the pillar of fire by night and the Clouds of Glory by day. They lived with miracles and heard God speak at Sinai — and they are asking, "Where's the garlic?"

> **The Jewish people are complaining about a meat shortage? They are longing for fish? They miss the taste of squash?**

How do we understand this? Grown men do not cry over a lack of meat, certainly when they are prophets of God! We have to examine the meaning of their complaining, because it cannot be taken at face value.

The Ultimate Tragedy

Ultimately, there is only one tragedy great people cry about, and that is being distant from the Almighty. For the generation that received the Torah directly from God, closeness to God is the only thing that matters, and a vacuum of this sort is indeed a tragedy.

> **Ultimately, there is only one tragedy great people cry over, and that is being distant from the Almighty.**

The Jewish people are not simply complaining about not having fish; they are reacting to what the lack of fish implies about their relationship with God. They realize that this shortage means that the Almighty has pulled back from them. Even while enslaved in Egypt, Hashem arranged for them to have plentiful free fish from the Nile. They even managed to eat cucumbers and watermelon in Egypt; yet now they are missing these things. This prompts them to think, *If Hashem were truly close to us, then we would have everything we need. Having this deficiency must mean that we have somehow moved away from Him!*

The tragedy is their realization that they are not as close to the Almighty as they used to be. *That* is something truly worth crying about. In fact, it is the most important thing to cry about.

If their crying was warranted, then what did they do wrong? Rashi (11:7) explains, "The Israelites said, 'We have nothing but manna to look at,' whereas the Holy One, blessed is He, inscribed in the Torah, 'The manna was like coriander seed...' as if to say, 'See, all you who inhabit the world, what my children are complaining about — the manna is excellent in so many ways!'" Furthermore, there was a reason why the manna could not taste like those foods they lacked; they are harmful to nursing women (Rashi 7:5). *Bnei Yisrael* erred in not living with the belief that *Kol d'avid Rachmana l'tav avid* — everything Hashem does is for our good (*Berachos* 60b). There were deficiencies, yes, but those were for a reason. The mistake of the Jewish people was interpreting the deficiencies as God's abandonment, instead of viewing them as something a loving Father was doing in order to encourage them to grow.

The root cause of their mistaken conclusion was a lack of *hakaras hatov* (appreciation) for all the good the Almighty had given them. They were embraced by the *Shechinah*, and surrounded by miracles: Clouds of Glory, water from a stone, manna every single morning that tasted like anything they wanted. Although they found good reason to conclude that the Almighty was distant from them, had they been sufficiently grateful for all of Hashem's gifts, they would not have complained. They would have realized that the manna was just what they needed: It was teaching them a lesson in *bitachon*, training them to trust that Hashem would provide their daily sustenance. They would have understood that everything Hashem did was to help them grow, and that a lack is not a sign that He is rejecting them.

Every one of us experiences some type of lack in life, and how we respond to our unique challenges reflects our sense of gratitude. If we lack appreciation for the good that Hashem has lovingly granted us, we are likely to respond with complaints and negativity, even mistakenly concluding that the Almighty has abandoned us. But if we are grateful for everything Hashem does for us and as a result feel His unstinting love, then we can take the lack in stride and focus on what the Almighty is teaching us and how He is pushing us to grow. When we recognize all that Hashem has done for us, our complaints will evaporate.

> When we recognize all that Hashem has done for us, our complaints will evaporate.

Waking up every morning is a perfect time to work on appreciating God's unceasing gifts. When you say *Modeh Ani*, feel that you are in the presence of God and feel His love. He is giving you the gift of another day. And know that everything He is going to do today is also for your good. The Almighty is right here with you, rooting for you and showering you with gifts. So stop complaining and start appreciating, and listen to the messages Hashem is sending you.

One moment, the spies were tzaddikim, and the next moment, they were evil — with no time in between for anything to have caused them to fall so precipitously. What changed?

פרשת שלח
Parashas Shelach:
How the Mighty Fall

This week's *parashah* tells the fateful story of the twelve spies who were sent to spy out the Land

"*Shelach lecha anashim...* Send forth, for yourself, men..." (*Bamidbar* 13:2). Hashem is telling Moshe to send them out "for yourself" — not for Me. I've already told you that it is a good land; there is no need for spies. But if this is what you want, I will not stop you. I will not take away your independence. But be sure to choose "*anashim*" (which Rashi tells us means men of distinction, righteous leaders). It is a dangerous mission; be sure to send the best.

The Torah says, "Moshe sent them forth... by the mouth of Hashem; they were all distinguished men; heads of the Children of Israel" (ibid. 13:3). What does "by the mouth of Hashem" mean? The Midrash (*Bamidbar Rabbah* 16:5) explains that Moshe did not rely on his own judgment in selecting them. He conferred with the Almighty on each one: "Is he up for the task? Is he the strongest leader of this tribe?" And Hashem gave His stamp of approval for each man chosen, testifying that indeed, "*kulam anashim* — they are all distinguished men."

Moshe then sends twelve of the greatest men of the Jewish people to spy out the land. It's a dream team! Yet for some reason Moshe is very concerned that something horrendous is going to happen.

Moshe's fear compels him to change the name of his devoted student: "And Moshe called Hoshea the son of Nun, Yehoshua" (ibid. 13:16), adding a *yud* to signify the prayer, "May God save you from the evil counsel of the spies." He is actually worried that Yehoshua, the future leader of the Jewish people, the one who will lead them into the land of Canaan and wage fierce battles against the thirty-one kings, is going to be convinced to become a traitor. Why was Moshe so concerned?

Moshe was not alone in recognizing the insidious dangers of this mission. The Talmud (*Sotah* 34b) tells us that the only reason Calev ben Yefuneh was able to resist the temptation to join the other spies was that he went to the graves of the patriarchs in Chevron to pray that he be protected from their evil counsel. Why did a great *tzaddik* like Calev feel that he was in such great danger that he needed the Almighty to save him?

But perhaps the most mystifying aspect of this saga is how quickly this illustrious, handpicked group went from being righteous leaders to being disloyal, faithless liars who brought back an evil report that demoralized the entire nation. The *passuk* says, "They went and they came" (ibid. 13:26). But the previous *passuk* already says they returned, so how can the Torah say, "They went"? Rashi explains: "What is meant by 'They went'? To compare their going with their coming. Just as their return was with evil intent, so was their departure with evil intent." The ten spies were infected with evil intent the moment they left, long before they entered the Land and began their mission.

What is happening here? Hashem Himself gives testimony that each of the spies is a righteous, distinguished leader. Yet as soon as they start on the road they already have the appalling intention of undermining Hashem's plan, preventing their generation from entering the Land of Israel and planting the seeds of all future calamities, culminating with the destruction of our two Temples on Tishah b'Av (*Taanis* 29a). One moment, the spies are *tzaddikim*, and the next moment, they are evil — with no time in between for anything to have caused them to fall so precipitously. What changed?

Face the Nation

The only thing that changed was that now they are going to the land with the responsibility of reporting back to the Jewish people. They are going to have to face a fearful nation that is eagerly await-ing their report. A moment before, they were *tzaddikim*, but now they have to stand up to their society and tell the people something they do not want to hear: "Friends, we have to fulfill our mission and invade the land of Canaan! The Almighty is with us, and there's nothing to fear!" Suddenly these courageous, righteous men are thrust into the difficult situation of confronting the people and giving them a report the majority are not interested in hearing. The people do not want reassurance; they want confirmation of their fears.

Right from the start, the pressure to bring back a negative report subtly affected the objectivity of ten out of the twelve spies and caused them to decide not to risk their popularity and stature by pushing an agenda that went against what the Jewish people desired.

We are all creatures of society. We crave approval and validation. We prefer not to take a stand that goes against the grain and makes us vulnerable to criticism or attack. When Yehoshua and Calev got up in front of the nation and told them, "You have nothing to fear. We can go up!" the people called them murderers and wanted to stone them. Who wants to be called a murderer? It is far easier to put on blinders and view the situation through subjective eyes that will appease the people.

> Who wants to be called a murderer? It is far easier to put on blinders and view the situation through subjective eyes that will appease the people.

Society is an incredibly powerful force. If the masses expect you to come back with a report that says they do not have to enter the land, you come back with that report. That type of societal pressure creates a formidable undertow that constantly erodes our understanding of what is true and good. And it is very easy to get caught in this pull.

For example, we know that the crown of Torah is available to each and every Jew, regardless of his level of intelligence (See "Terumah: The Crown of Torah"). As the Rambam authoritatively states, "Whoever wants it may come and take it" (*Hilchos Talmud Torah* 3:1). Chazal say, "One who says I searched and did not find, do not believe him… and one who says I searched and did find, believe him. This is referring to the area of understanding Torah" (*Megillah* 6b). We have a guarantee that anyone who sincerely puts in the effort to understand Torah will attain it. That is a halachah, an indisputable fact.

> We have a guarantee that anyone who sincerely puts in the effort to understand Torah will attain it. But deep down, do we believe it?

No matter who you are, if you make the genuine effort to learn and know Torah, you can attain the crown of Torah. Hashem will help you; He makes that promise.

But deep down, do we believe it? Our society tells us that only the gifted individuals can become towering *talmidei chachamim*, Torah scholars. For the rest of us, it's just not realistic.

We think this way because our society conveys that message, drowning out the reality that is defined only by the Torah. We all get caught in the undertow and lose our bearings, which causes us to give up on the goal.

Realizing how dangerous societal pressure can be, Moshe prayed for Yehoshua. Calev recognized this danger as well, and so he prayed to Hashem to give him the strength to resist the pressure and be able to stand before the people and tell them they are all wrong.

Recognize the Danger

The Rambam says, "It is natural for a man's character and actions to be influenced by his friends and associates and for him to follow the local norms of behavior" (*Hilchos Dei'os* 6:1). This is a reality that every one of us must contend with. It is hard to hold onto your sanity and stand up to society. But the first step in winning this battle is to recognize how powerful the pull of society is. If you do not appreciate the need to struggle, there is no chance you can resist the undertow.

Then you have to work on attaining clarity, to know what is true and what is false as clearly as you know that you have five fingers on each hand. It would be exceedingly difficult for someone to convince you that you have six fingers. Reach that level of clarity with regard to your fundamental convictions, too.

> It would be exceedingly difficult for someone to convince you that you have six fingers on each hand. Reach that level of clarity with regard to your fundamental convictions, too.

And lastly, tap into the power of social pressure and channel it toward good. As the Rambam continues, "Therefore, one should associate with the righteous and be constantly in the company of the wise, so as to learn from their deeds. Conversely, one should keep away from the wicked who walk in darkness, so as not to learn from their deeds." It's a crazy world out there. Surround yourself with role models and a community that embodies Torah values.

If you want to resolve a difference of opinion and show people that they are mistaken, don't challenge them. That just ignites their ego.

פרשת קרח

arashas Korach:
Getting to the Truth

"Any argument that is for the sake of Heaven will have a lasting, constructive outcome, and any argument that is not for the sake of Heaven will not have a lasting, constructive outcome. What sort of dispute was for the sake of Heaven? The dispute of Hillel and Shammai. And which was not for the sake of Heaven? The dispute of Korach and his entire community" (*Pirkei Avos* 5:20).

We would have expected the Mishnah to say, "the dispute of Korach and Moshe," as a parallel example to "the dispute of Hillel and Shammai." Why does the Mishnah omit Moshe, Korach's disputant?

This omission is teaching us what it means to argue *shelo l'shem Shamayim*, not for the sake of Heaven. The argument between Hillel and Shammai was for the sake of Heaven because their only interest was discovering the truth, whatever it may be. They both realized that the best way to discover the truth is by respecting the other side, listening to their perspective, and then hashing it out together. "Come, now, let us reason together, says Hashem" (*Yeshayah* 1:18). When people of good will reason together, putting their egos aside in their quest to find the truth, they will reach a common understanding.

*K*orach and his followers were not interested in the truth; they wanted only to push their personal agendas and win the argument. For them, the other side of the argument was irrelevant.

Korach and his followers were not interested in the truth; they wanted only to push their personal agendas and win the argument. For them, the other side of the argument was irrelevant, and so they were not open to listening to a differing viewpoint. Therefore, in essence there was no other side, which is why the Mishnah does not mention Moshe.

Flower Power

How do you argue with someone who won't hear your side? Let's examine the way Korach's rebellion is brought to a final resolution, conclusively demonstrating whose position is correct.

After Moshe fails to convince Korach and his main followers through dialogue that their position is wrong, he gathers all the people and announces the first part of his two-pronged test to determine who is correct: "Take for yourselves fire-pans — Korach and his entire assembly — and put fire in them and place incense upon them before Hashem tomorrow. Then the man whom Hashem will choose — he is the holy one" (*Bamidbar* 16:6,7). And then Moshe throws down the final gauntlet, audaciously proclaiming the second part of the test, which will remove all doubt: "If these die like the death of all men... then it is not Hashem Who has sent me. But if Hashem will create a phenomenon, and the earth opens its mouth and swallows them and all that is theirs, and they will descend alive into the pit, then you shall know that these men have provoked Hashem!" (ibid. 16:29,30).

As soon as Moshe finishes speaking, Hashem obliges by performing an unprecedented miracle: The earth opens its mouth and swallows Korach and his household alive. This is followed by a fire that comes down and burns the 250 men. One would think that is a very convincing presentation, but the Torah tells us otherwise.

The next day the nation complains to Moshe and Aharon: "You have killed the people of Hashem!" (ibid. 17:6). *Murderers!* The people are not convinced of the truth of Moshe's position, and the fury of Hashem is unleashed, killing 14,000 Jews, until Aharon atones for the people through an incense offering.

What resolves the conflict and finally convinces the Jewish people that Moshe was acting on Hashem's orders, not nepotism, in selecting his brother Aharon as the Kohen Gadol? The final test — ordered by Hashem — is for each tribe to place a stick carrying its leader's name into the *Ohel Moed*. The next day Aharon's stick blossoms. This confirms Aharon's rightful selection as the Kohen Gadol and satisfies the nation.

How is it possible that the incredible miracle of the earth opening up and killing Korach, followed by the miracle of the Heavenly fire that killed the 250 men, did not convince the Jewish people, yet a stick that sprouts a flower overnight does the job? Why does the more powerful demonstration of the veracity of Moshe's argument fail to convince them, while the second, far quieter miracle is compelling enough to settle the matter?

In the first instance, Moshe locks horns with Korach and his followers, along with the nation, and tells them, "You are wrong, and I will prove it to you!" This approach only puts people on the defensive and causes them to become entrenched in their position. No matter how powerful the miracle, they are not willing to listen; the situation has devolved into a test of wills.

> When people are objective and want to know the truth, a little bit of evidence is compelling. A stick blossoming with a flower is sufficient.

If you want to resolve a difference of opinion and show people that they are mistaken, don't challenge them. That just enflames their ego. Instead, invite them to reason together and consider the evidence, without trying to prove them wrong. When people are objective and want to know the truth, a little bit of evidence is compelling. A stick blossoming with a flower is sufficient.

Not only was the argument resolved after that test, everyone went home feeling like a winner. The *passuk* says, "And Moshe brought out all the staffs from before Hashem to all the Children of Israel; they saw and they took, each man his staff" (ibid. 17:24). Every man took his staff back home, even though theirs did not sprout, because they were not bothered that they were not chosen. In fact, they were proud to be part of the process that established Aharon as the Kohen Gadol. There were no losers; each stick signified being part of the greater good and became a precious treasure that represented a moment they would never forget.

When the intent is different,
the results are radically different
as well.

פרשת חקת
arashas Chukas:
For All Intents and Purposes

וַיָּבֹאוּ בְנֵי יִשְׂרָאֵל כָּל הָעֵדָה מִדְבַּר צִן . . . וַתָּמָת שָׁם מִרְיָם וַתִּקָּבֵר
שָׁם: וְלֹא הָיָה מַיִם לָעֵדָה וַיִּקָּהֲלוּ עַל מֹשֶׁה וְעַל אַהֲרֹן:

The Children of Israel, the whole assembly, arrived at the
Wilderness of Zin... Miriam died there and she was buried
there. There was no water for the assembly, and they
gathered against Moshe and Aharon (Bamidbar 20:1-2).

The juxtaposition of Miriam's death and the lack of water is no
accident. The Talmud explains that it teaches us that the Jews
received water during their entire forty years in the desert from a
miraculous well that followed them throughout their journeys, and
this well was in the merit of Miriam (*Taanis* 9a). Therefore, when she
died, the miracle ceased and the well dried up.

What did Miriam do to merit this great miracle? The *Zohar* (*Emor*
103b) says that Miriam's reward came from her standing at the side
of the Nile River to ensure that her baby brother, Moshe, who was
placed in a basket in the river, was saved. "His sister stood from afar,
to know what would be done to him" (*Shemos* 2:4). In the merit of

this one act Hashem miraculously provided the Jewish people water for forty years in the desert.

Miriam can be contrasted with another woman who lived at that time: Basya, the daughter of Pharaoh. Basya was actually the one who saved Moshe from the Nile. She saw the basket among the reeds and, as Rashi says, she stretched out her arm, which miraculously became long enough to reach the basket. Then, she raised Moshe as her own son in the palace of Pharaoh. Basya also merited to name Moshe. The Midrash teaches that Moshe had many names; his father Amram named him, his mother Yocheved gave him a name (*Shemos Rabbah* 40:4). But the name the Torah itself calls him, the name that he is known by for all of history, is the name Basya gave him: Moshe. Because she saved his life, she merited naming him. But that reward pales in comparison to Miriam's reward.

Who did a greater act: Miriam, who waited by the water's edge, or Basya, who plucked Moshe from the water and raised him?

Clearly, saving Moshe's life is a much greater act, with more far-reaching consequences, than merely standing by and waiting to see how he was going to be saved. Why, then, did Miriam's act merit a far-superior reward?

The Torah is showing us that the intention defines the act. Basya saw a child and saved him. She had no inkling who this child was destined to become; all she knew was that she saved a Jewish child from being swept away by the river. That act turned her into Moshe's surrogate mother, and she therefore merited naming him.

Miriam was a prophetess, and she knew that Moshe was destined to be the redeemer who would take the Jewish people out of Egypt. She was not merely waiting by the water. The Talmud says (*Sotah* 13a):

> Miriam prophesied while she was only the sister of Aharon and said, "My mother is destined to give birth to a son who will save the Jewish people." When Moshe was born and the entire house was completely filled with light, her father Amram proceeded to kiss her on her head. He said to her, "My daughter, your prophecy has been fulfilled." But when they cast Moshe into the river, her father proceeded to tap

her on her head. He said to her, "My daughter, where is your prophecy now?" And that is the meaning of that which is written, "His sister stood at a distance to know what would transpire with him." She wanted to know what would transpire with the resolution of her prophecy.

Basya was acting on behalf of one child, but Miriam was acting to ensure the survival of the Jewish people.

Miriam was not merely watching a Jewish child; she was waiting to see what would happen to the future leader of the Jewish people. Basya was acting on behalf of one child, but Miriam was acting to ensure the survival of the entire nation. Miriam's intention transformed her deed into a greater act than Basya's, and that is why the nation was supplied with water in her merit.

Transform Your Actions

We need to examine the intent underlying our actions, because our intent defines the action. This is especially relevant in the realm of prayer.

When you pray, instead of praying only for yourself, broaden your vision and have in mind the entire Jewish people. Pray for everyone you know, for every Jew across the globe. Pray that Hashem give us understanding, return us to His Torah, and forgive us. When we have other people in mind and think about the whole Jewish people, it is a very different quality of prayer. In fact, Chazal built that focus into our prayers by formulating the requests of the *Shemoneh Esrei* in the plural. But it is our intent that defines our prayers. We can limit our prayers to ourselves, or we can use the same words with a more expansive intent and pray for all Jews.

When we have other people in mind and think about the whole Jewish people, it is a very different quality of prayer.

Our intent can also transform the way we learn Torah. The Mishnah says, "Rabbi Yishmael bar Rabbi Yose said: One who studies Torah in order to teach is granted the ability to study and to teach. One who studies in order to do is granted the ability to study, to teach, to observe, and to do" (*Pirkei Avos* 4:6). If your intent in learning is to also teach, you have a different *siyatta d'Shmaya* (Heavenly assistance) than one who learns solely in order to learn. One who learns in order to teach is guaranteed by the Almighty that he will know what he has learned and merit to teach it. And one who learns Torah in order to fulfill it is promised much more. But the one who learns just in order to learn merits none of this. The intent makes it a completely different kind of learning.

One who learns Torah *lishmah*, for its own sake, is guaranteed even more. As the Mishnah says, "Rabbi Meir said: Whoever engages in Torah study for its own sake merits many things; furthermore, the creation of the world is worthwhile for his sake alone. He is called 'friend, beloved'... [the Torah] clothes him in humility and fear of God; it makes him fit to be righteous, devout, fair, and faithful. It moves him away from sin and draws him near to merit... the secrets of Torah are revealed to him" (*Pirkei Avos* 6:1). He gets it all! He can be learning the same Torah as the person beside him, but because his intent is different, the results are radically different as well.

> *You are putting the time into learning anyway. It pays to figure out how to optimize it.*

If you are putting in the many hours of learning Torah already, examine your intent and make sure you are learning Torah *lishmah,* to know God and be close to Him. You are putting the time into learning anyway. It pays to figure out how to optimize it. The Almighty guarantees tremendous blessing, but it all depends on your intention.

*Bilaam was given the sam chaim,
the elixir of life, the ultimate gift
of connecting with the Almighty.
Despite receiving this gift, he
decided not to partner with God
and His people.*

פרשת בלק

Parashas Balak:
Choosing a Non-Jewish Prophet

And there was no other prophet who arose **in Israel** like Moshe, whom Hashem knew face to face (*Devarim* 34:10).

In Israel no one arose like Moshe, but among the nations there did arise a prophet like Moshe. Who was that? Bilaam (*Sifri, Devarim* 357).

In this week's *parashah* we meet Bilaam, the non-Jewish prophet, who was hired by Balak to curse the Jewish people. But Hashem thwarted his plan, and despite all his efforts, his curses were transformed into great blessings.

Despite his status as a prophet, Bilaam was no *tzaddik*. The Mishnah casts him as the polar opposite of Avraham Avinu: "Whoever has three particular traits is counted among the students of Avraham Avinu, and whoever has three other traits is among the students of the wicked Bilaam. He who has a good eye, humility, and contentedness is a student of Avraham Avinu, while he who has an evil eye, arrogance, and greed is a student of the wicked Bilaam"

(*Pirkei Avos* 5:22). Bilaam also advised Balak to use the women of Moav and Midian to entice the Jewish people to worship idols (*Sanhedrin* 106a).

Chazal ask: "Why did God bestow His *Shechinah* on such a wicked non-Jew? The answer is so that the nations of the world would not say, 'Had we had prophets we would have repented.' So He assigned them prophets. . ." (*Bamidbar Rabbah* 20:1). If not for Bilaam, the nations of the world would have had a legitimate complaint. "It's not fair," they would have said. "You sent the Jewish people a prophet like Moshe, who guided them and taught them. If you would have sent us a prophet like Moshe, we would have been just as good!"

Therefore, the Almighty sent them Bilaam, who prophesied on the same level as Moshe. And what happened? Moshe led the Jewish people to God, while Bilaam tried to curse the Jewish people, and in doing so destroyed his own people. This was God's answer to the nations: "See what happens when I give you a prophet! So stop your excuses."

You sent the Jewish people Moshe Rabbeinu, an incredible tzaddik who was a humble yet powerful leader. But for us you selected someone like Bilaam?

But that wouldn't put an end to the discussion, for the non-Jews could retort and say, "You sent the Jewish people Moshe Rabbeinu, an incredible *tzaddik* who was a humble yet powerful leader. But for us you selected someone like Bilaam? Is that fair? Hashem, couldn't you have found someone better than the evil Bilaam? Why not someone like Iyov, who, according to some opinions, was a righteous non-Jew?" (*Bava Basra* 15b).

In choosing a prophet for the nations, the Almighty had one crucial condition. Even though this prophet would be given Moshe Rabbeinu's level of prophecy — the ultimate, transcendental clarity of knowing God — he must still choose to remain a non-Jew and not join the ranks of the Jewish people. If he were to convert and become a Jew, that would undermine the entire goal of giving the nations a prophet.

So the Almighty searched high and low and found Bilaam, a non-

Jew who, while having the ultimate knowledge of the awesome, loving Creator of the universe, would still refuse to merge with Him by becoming a Jew. This refusal would eventually cause him to attack the Jewish people and destroy himself.

We can understand why Bilaam couldn't have converted. But why did he have to be so evil? Couldn't he have remained neutral?

Elixir of Life, Potion of Death

There is no neutral when it comes to Torah. Chazal teach, "If a person is worthy, the Torah is an elixir of life (*sam chaim*), and if not, it is a death potion (*sam hamaves*)" (*Yoma* 72b). The Almighty's Torah is the path to full clarity, the repository of the deepest wisdom in the universe. If you learn it and apply it, it gives you strength and meaning. If you don't, those same words of Hashem can destroy you.

> *I*f you learn Torah and apply it, it gives you strength and meaning. If you don't, those same words of Hashem can destroy you.

How do we understand this? Bilaam was given the *sam chaim*, the elixir of life, the ultimate gift of connecting with the Almighty. Despite receiving this gift, he refused to make a covenant with Hashem, deciding not to partner with God and His people. That decision itself was a rebellion, and in order to justify his choice, Bilaam had to denigrate the Jewish people and become an enemy of the good they represented. He had to actively oppose them, even seek to destroy them, in order to remain resolute in his decision to reject God and walk away from the ultimate truth. That is why Bilaam became a *rasha*, an evil person, despite being a prophet.

This type of rebellion is not to be confused with a typical *baal teshuvah* who, at the beginning of his process of *teshuvah*, is still committing numerous transgressions while taking on the performance of some mitzvos. The inconsistent, imperfect level of observance of a *baal teshuvah* does not signify a Bilaam-style refusal to follow the path of God. The *baal teshuvah* says, "Yes, the Torah is true and I want to observe it, but I'm weak, I'm not ready to give up my Saturdays and lobster. I wish I had the strength to do it all."

The *baal teshuvah* has discovered the *sam chaim*, the gift of life, and is growing step-by-step. The Torah was not given to angels; it takes time. He has a long way to go, but over time he will get there. He is not saying, "I cannot accept the reality of Shabbos. I refuse to keep kosher. This is something I do not want to do." He is just struggling with the Torah's sudden demands. Eventually, his Torah learning will give him greater clarity and empower him to change. And the Almighty has an infinite amount of patience for him.

Good people not only can fall, they will fall, but the key is that they strive to get up and keep growing.

"For the righteous one will fall seven times and arise, but the wicked will stumble into evil" (*Mishlei* 24:16). Good people not only can fall, they *will* fall, but the key is that they strive to get up and keep growing. They are on the path, despite the inevitable setbacks. But the *rasha*, the evil man like Bilaam, is down for the count. He has decided not to get up, but to remain firmly entrenched in his detachment from God.

We are all weak and imperfect, but what differentiates us from Bilaam is that we are working toward success. The righteous man can fall seven times — he is depressed, he quits, he is frustrated and angry — but he gets up! You want to climb that mountain and reach the pinnacle, without compromising. Be careful not to put up a wall or filter that shields you from any aspect of the truth, like Bilaam, because that will only lead to self-destruction.

Clarity or death. Life is a difficult trip; we have our weaknesses. But as long as we remain honest and strive to grow we will never become an enemy of good, for we will be attached to the *sam chaim*, the elixir of life.

To save the Jewish people, you can count on a miracle.

פרשת פינחס
arashas Pinchas:
Relying on Miracles

וַיְדַבֵּר ה׳ אֶל מֹשֶׁה לֵּאמֹר: פִּינְחָס בֶּן אֶלְעָזָר בֶּן אַהֲרֹן הַכֹּהֵן הֵשִׁיב אֶת חֲמָתִי מֵעַל בְּנֵי יִשְׂרָאֵל בְּקַנְאוֹ אֶת קִנְאָתִי בְּתוֹכָם וְלֹא כִלִּיתִי אֶת בְּנֵי יִשְׂרָאֵל בְּקִנְאָתִי:

Hashem spoke to Moshe, saying: "Pinchas son of Elazar son of Aharon the Kohen turned back My wrath from upon the Children of Israel, when he zealously avenged My vengeance among them, so I did not consume the Children of Israel in My vengeance"
(Bamidbar 25:10-11).

This week's *parashah* describes how Pinchas merited a covenant of peace with God in reward for being a *kana'i*. The Hebrew term *kana'i* is often mistranslated as fanatic or extremist. But the true definition of *kana'i* is someone who passionately cares about doing the right thing, regardless of its consequences. His personal well-being takes a back seat to the will of Hashem and the needs of the Jewish people. He firmly believes that if he does what is right, the Almighty will take care of him.

he Hebrew term kana'i is often mistranslated as fanatic or extremist. But the true definition of a kana'i is someone who passionately cares about doing the right thing, regardless of its consequences.

Pinchas was a true *kana'i* for the Almighty. He saw the terrible desecration of God's Name wrought by Zimri, who brazenly took a Midianite princess named Kozbi into his tent before the entire nation. Pinchas risked his life to kill the two of them, which ended the devastating plague that destroyed 24,000 Jews who had been seduced into idolatry by the Midianite women.

The Midrash (*Tanchuma*, Parashas Balak 21) says that for Pinchas to succeed in his mission, twelve miracles had to occur. Among the miracles listed: An angel shut Zimri and Kozbi's mouths so they could not scream; the blade of his sword miraculously extended long enough to pierce both of their bodies simultaneously; Pinchas was given exceptional strength that enabled him to lift their bodies while impaled on his spear; the handle of his spear did not break under the weight of the bodies. The final miracle was that the attempt of Zimri's supporters to kill Pinchas was thwarted by an angel.

What was Pinchas thinking? How could he have undertaken this mission? The Talmud states that you are not allowed to rely on a miracle: "A person should never place himself in danger and expect a miracle to happen, because perhaps the miracle will not take place, and if it does it will diminish his merit" (*Shabbos* 32a). Hashem put us in a world that operates according to certain rules, and we need to act responsibly by making a reasonable *hishtadlus*, effort, based on the circumstances we face. We cannot count on miracles.

Even our patriarchs did not rely on miracles. When Avraham Avinu went to fight the four kings to redeem his nephew Lot, the Midrash says he went with the intent to die *al kiddush Hashem* (*Bereishis Rabbah* 43:2). He figured he was going to die. He had also been prepared to die several years earlier, when placed in Nimrod's fiery furnace, rather than worship idolatry.

Pinchas was different. He did *not* assume that he was going to die *al kiddush Hashem;* he relied on a miracle. How do we know? The Talmud teaches that Pinchas deceived the tribe of Shimon — the supporters of Zimri, their prince — by pretending that he wanted to join Zimri and partake in the depravity. They allowed him entry, saying, "Even the *perushim* [ascetics] have permitted this act!" (*Sanhedrin* 82b). If Pinchas had been killed, it would have caused an even greater *chillul Hashem*, because the Jewish people would have mistakenly thought that Pinchas had become an active participant in this brazen sin! Therefore, Pinchas must have thought that the Almighty would miraculously save him, in order to avert the potential *chillul Hashem*.

But what about the principle of *"Ein somchin al hanes"* (we may not rely on a miracle)? How could Pinchas put himself into danger and assume that a miracle would take place?

Miracles and the Jewish People

There is one exception to the rule of *"Ein somchin al haneis,"* and that is when someone undertakes to save the Jewish people. As the Alshich writes, "One cannot rely on a miracle and say, 'I will learn Torah for the sake of Heaven and God will provide for me.' That is concerning an individual. But one who tends to the needs of the nation should not be afraid that any obstacle will stop him. Rather, since he is tending to their needs for the sake of Heaven and placing his trust in God, Hashem will act on his behalf" (Alshich, *Vayikra* 13, Parashas Tazria).

Hashem promises that the Jewish people will survive for eternity. If the only way to save them requires a miracle, as was the case for Pinchas, then one can count on that miraculous strategy to get the job done.

At the same time, Pinchas had to make the effort to implement the best strategy he could come up with. He pretended to be joining Zimri's ranks; he concealed his spear by turning it into a walking staff, and then he relied on the Almighty for a miracle. He knew Hashem was going to enable him to succeed because he was acting solely to save *Am Yisrael*.

During the economic downturn at the beginning of the twenty-first century, a nurse specializing in pain management came to treat me. "Rabbi," she asked, "what do you hope to achieve with my help?" I told her that I wanted to be strong enough to go fundraising in America.

The nurse was taken aback. "Don't you realize that America is going through one of the worst economic periods in recent history? How can you raise money in such a climate?"

I answered her, "It all depends what I'm raising money for. If I'm raising funds for my private yeshivah, then the downturn in the economy will affect me, but if I'm raising money to save the Jewish people, then I don't have to worry about the limitations created by a bad economy." To save the Jewish people, you can count on a miracle.

> If I'm raising funds for my private yeshivah, then the downturn in the economy will affect me, but if I'm raising money to save the Jewish people, then I don't have to worry about the limitations created by a bad economy.

Miracles Today

To those of us living in Israel, it is obvious that the Jews here are relying on miracles. There is no other way to explain our survival and our commitment to remain here while surrounded and outnumbered by a vicious enemy who wants to destroy us. Neighboring countries are determined to build weapons to wipe us off the face of the earth, while at the same time, the rest of the world is becoming more and more anti-Semitic. We cannot rely on them to protect us.

> To those of us living in Israel, it is obvious that the Jews here are relying on miracles. There is no other way to explain our survival.

But more than six million Jews do live in Israel, without looking to flee the country. Israel consistently ranks in the top fifteen countries in the world-happiness index. Tourism is booming. Ultimately, the reason we feel safe and secure despite our precarious situation is because we are relying on a miracle. We believe Hashem will take care of us.

As individuals we cannot rely on a miracle, but as a nation we can bank on it.

Today, because the Jewish people are disunited and assimilating, we need a miracle perhaps more than ever before. Millions of our brethren are on the brink of being lost to their people forever. We need miracles: to bridge the gap, to understand each other, to reach out to our brothers and sisters and bring them back to their Father in Heaven.

We can count on Hashem to do miracles if we dedicate ourselves to creating a renaissance to bring back our people. We just need a few good men, *kana'im* like Pinchas — not fanatics, but serious people who are not self-absorbed and who passionately care about doing the will of God, regardless of the consequences.

Klal Yisrael needs you! Make the commitment, and remember: When working on behalf of the Jewish people you can rely on miracles. If we are true *kana'im*, the Almighty will empower us to do the seemingly impossible.

*If he is Amish, then his traditional
garb and customs are perfectly
O.K. But if he is a Jew respecting
his tradition and observing the
commandments, that is unacceptable.*

פרשת מטות

Parashas Mattos:
The Root of Anti-Semitism

וַיְדַבֵּר ה' אֶל מֹשֶׁה לֵּאמֹר: נְקֹם נִקְמַת בְּנֵי יִשְׂרָאֵל מֵאֵת הַמִּדְיָנִים
אַחַר תֵּאָסֵף אֶל עַמֶּיךָ: וַיְדַבֵּר מֹשֶׁה אֶל הָעָם לֵאמֹר הֵחָלְצוּ
מֵאִתְּכֶם אֲנָשִׁים לַצָּבָא וְיִהְיוּ עַל מִדְיָן לָתֵת נִקְמַת ה' בְּמִדְיָן:

*Hashem spoke to Moshe, saying, "Take vengeance **for
the Children of Israel** against the Midianites; afterward
you will be gathered unto your people." Moshe spoke to
the people saying, "Arm men from among yourselves for
the legion that they may be against Midian to inflict the
vengeance **of Hashem** against Midian" (Bamidbar 31:1-3).*

After 24,000 Jews died in the plague that resulted from the
Midianites' ensnaring the Jewish people in the sins of immo-
rality and idolatry, it was time for retribution. Hashem refers to it as
nikmas Bnei Yisrael, vengeance for the Jewish people. Yet Moshe
changes the language and summons the people to take *nikmas
Hashem*, revenge for the Almighty against Midian.

Rashi, noting the discrepancy, explains that if someone attacks the Jewish people it is as if he is attacking the Almighty Himself. The Midrash (*Bamidbar Rabbah* 22:2) elaborates:

> Moshe said, "Master of the universe, if we were just like any other nation they would not hate us and they would not come after us. It is only on account of the Torah and mitzvos that You gave us that they come to destroy us. Therefore, the vengeance is for You." Accordingly, Moshe instructed the Jewish people "to inflict the vengeance of Hashem against Midian."

Moshe is saying that if we were Amish or Shiites, no one would care what we do, and they would not harm or kill us. The only reason they seek to destroy us is because Hashem gave us the Torah and mitzvos. The nations of the world hate and attack the Jewish people because deep down, they wish to attack the Creator of the universe, Who gave His Torah and mitzvos to the Jewish people. In doing so, He attached Himself to them: *Yisrael v'Oraysa v'Kudesha Berich Hu, chad hu* — the Jewish people, the Torah, and the Holy One, blessed is He, are one (*Zohar, Parashas Acharei Mos* 73a).

Torah is the expression of Hashem's will. When you learn Torah you are connecting to Hashem, and when you perform mitzvos, you are drawing closer to God, because you are becoming like Him. Torah and God are inextricably linked.

The Jewish people are the manifestation of God's will in this world. We have a *bris,* a covenant, with the Almighty that began with Avraham Avinu and transformed the Jews into God's chosen people. We are the nation responsible to reveal His reality to the world, to be *mekadesh Shem Shamayim* and teach the world how to live with God. That covenant bonds us to Hashem, making us one.

Hating Jews, Hating God

Why do they hate the Jews? Theories abound to explain anti-Semitism. But the Talmud (*Shabbos* 89b) gives the true explanation: The moment Hashem gave the Torah at Mount Sinai, the hatred of the non-Jews toward the Jewish people was ignited. At Sinai (which is related to *sinah,* hatred) the Jewish people became the bearers of God's absolute standard of morality for all of humanity. Consequently, if someone wants to liberate himself from the all-encompassing moral demands and obligations delineated by the Torah, they attack the messenger — the Jews — who represent this Divine standard of morality in this world. The physical target may be the Jews, but they believe the real enemy is God.

Our archenemy, Adolf Hitler, may his name be obliterated, openly acknowledged the uniqueness of the Jews as a people. We were his mortal enemy because we represented Hashem's morality as embodied in the Torah. Hitler viewed National Socialism as a new world order, a way to create mankind anew.

Hitler said, "They refer to me as an uneducated barbarian. Yes, we are barbarians. We want to be barbarians; it is an honored title to us. We shall rejuvenate the world. This world is near its end." (Hermann Rauschning, *Hitler Speaks* p. 87).

He recognized that the Jewish people — who introduced to the world the concepts of monotheism, love your neighbor, help the poor and the infirm — were his primary obstacle in achieving his world vision. Hitler declared: "The struggle for world domination will be fought entirely between us — between Germans and Jews. All else is facade and illusion. Behind England stands Israel, and behind France, and behind the United States. Even when we have driven the Jew out of Germany, he remains our world enemy" (ibid., p. 242).

He told his people: "Providence has ordained that I should be the greatest liberator of humanity. I am freeing man from the restraints of an intelligence that has taken charge, from the dirty and degrading self-mortifications of a false vision known as conscience and morality, and from the demands of a freedom and personal independence which only a very few can bear" (ibid., p. 222).

And Hitler understood full well the source of this conscience and morality. He said: "The Ten Commandments have lost their validity. Conscience is a Jewish invention; it is a blemish, like circumcision" (ibid., p. 220).

Who was Hitler's real enemy? Was it the Jewish people who placed shackles on humanity? No, it was the Almighty Himself.

Who was Hitler's real enemy? Was it the Jewish people who placed shackles on humanity? No, it was the Almighty Himself. Hashem obligates us to care for each other, not to murder, not to be immoral. The moral conscience that we have "inflicted" on humanity is from God. Hitler was obsessed with eradicating the Jews because he hated the God Whom we, as His people, represented in this world.

Self-Hating Jews

It is not only non-Jews who can harbor anti-Semitic sentiments; Jews can, too, and for the same underlying reason: They resent the Almighty. This is not the only reason for internecine hatred, but it is definitely a common one.

> *It is not only non-Jews who can harbor anti-Semitic sentiments; Jews can, too.*

Rabbi Michel Twerski relates that he was once on a plane, wearing his usual Chassidic *bekeshe* and round black hat. A Jewish woman sitting near him turned to him and said, "You are an embarrassment to the Jewish people, a disgrace. It is people like you who think they are still living in the Middle Ages that cause all of the anger and anti-Semitism toward us."

Rabbi Twerski was astounded to be attacked this way, and by a Jewish woman no less, but he did not miss a beat. In his customary calm demeanor, he said to her, "Pardon me, ma'am, but I'm Amish."

"Oh! I'm terribly sorry!" she said. "I hope I didn't hurt your feelings. Of course I respect people who respect their heritage. Please forgive me!"

If he is Amish, then his traditional garb and customs are perfectly okay. But if he is a Jew respecting his tradition and observing the commandments, that is unacceptable, because people intuitively understand that he represents the Master of the universe, Who has given us the Torah and mitzvos. This non-observant woman viewed the Torah's commandments as a burden, a threat to her sense of freedom; Rabbi Twerski's presence therefore made her defensive and antagonistic.

> *Someone who appreciates the Jewish people and the Torah they represent is someone who loves God.*

The opposite is also true. Someone who appreciates the Jewish people and the Torah they represent is someone who loves God.

And someone who loves God and His Torah will go out of the way to love his fellow Jew. Indeed, the Jewish people, the Torah, and God are one.

The reason the daughters of Tzelafchad saw what Moshe Rabbeinu did not see was not because they were smart. That would not have sufficed. The reason they saw what he did not was because they loved the land.

פרשת מסעי

Parashas Masei:
For the Love of Israel

At the end of *Sefer Bamidbar* the *parashah* revisits the five daughters of Tzelafchad, who were instructed by Hashem to marry within their tribe of Menashe in order to ensure that their father's ancestral inheritance would remain within the tribe. Let's review how they inherited their father's land in the first place.

The daughters of Tzelafchad, son of Chepher, son of Gilead, son of Machir, son of Menashe, of the families of Menashe son of Yosef drew near... and they stood before Moshe, before Elazar the Kohen, and before the leaders and the entire assembly at the entrance to the Tent of Meeting, saying: "Our father died in the desert, but he was not among the assembly that was gathering against Hashem in the assembly of Korach, but he died of his own sin; and he had no sons. Why should the name of our father be omitted from among his family because he had no son? Give us a portion among our father's brothers" (Bamidbar 27:1-4).

The daughters of Tzelafchad petition Moshe, Elazar, and the Sanhedrin that they should be the heirs of their father's land because he died without leaving any sons. Moshe does not know the answer and consults with Hashem, Who replies, "The daughters of Tzelafchad speak properly." They are right.

Rashi says that they saw with their eyes what Moshe Rabbeinu could not see. They understood what Moshe Rabbeinu and the Sanhedrin did not understand.

When they presented their argument they said, "Our father did not have a son." Rashi explains: "But if he had had a son, they would have made no claim at all. This teaches us that they were smart women." These were not simple women; they were learned and intelligent. But why does the Torah need to go out of its way to tell us that they were smart women? Of course they were smart! They saw what Moshe himself could not see!

There is another difficulty in the first Rashi on this chapter, where he explains why the Torah traces the lineage of Tzelafchad's daughters all the way back to Yosef. Rashi says this teaches that just as Yosef cherished Eretz Yisrael — as demonstrated by his commanding his children to bring up his bones from Egypt for burial in Israel, 210 years after his death — so, too, the daughters of Tzelafchad cherished Eretz Yisrael, as the Torah says, "*Tenu lanu achuzah* — Give us a portion" (v. 4).

> *I*f someone told you that you have an inheritance in Nebraska, wouldn't you ask for it? You may never want to step foot in it, but you will certainly take ownership of your rightful property.

How do these words prove that they loved the land? If someone told you that you have an inheritance in Nebraska, wouldn't you ask for it? You may never want to step foot in it, but you will certainly take ownership of your rightful property and profit from it. So why does the daughters' asking for a portion show they loved the land of Israel?

The answer is that the reason the daughters of Tzelafchad saw what Moshe Rabbeinu did not see was not because they were smart. That would not have sufficed. The reason they saw what he did not was because they loved the land. They happen to have been learned, so the Torah tells us that, but it was not their brilliance that empowered them to make their argument; it was only their love of Eretz Yisrael. They saw what Moshe did not see because they so badly wanted a portion in the land. They dug deeper and persisted until the right argument came to them.

Passion Is the Engine

The secret to excelling in anything is to be passionate about what you are doing. If you want to succeed in learning Torah, you must cherish the Torah. If you want to bring back *Am Yisrael* and connect them to the beauty and meaning of our heritage, you must passionately love your fellow Jew. If you love them you will find a way to reach them.

I once met a man who owned a nursing home in Baltimore. He was familiar with my efforts in *kiruv*, and he said to me, "I really admire your accomplishments. You know, I also made someone into a *baal teshuvah*."

"That's terrific," I replied. "Who is this person?"

"She is a 95-year-old woman whom I convinced to stop eating *tereifah* food."

"A 95-year-old woman!" I exclaimed. "My friend, you are the expert, and I am the student at your feet. Teach me, how in the world were you able to reach her? Most elderly people — certainly those in their 90's — are not open to changing their lives. What is your secret?"

"I'll tell you," the man answered. "I own a nursing home outside of Baltimore. The clientele is almost entirely non-Jewish. Of the 300 residents, I had three Jews. I fed the non-Jews non-kosher food, since it's much cheaper than kosher food. But I couldn't feed the three Jews food I knew was *tereifah,* so I brought them catered kosher meals. Every day they got special meals wrapped in containers. It cost me an arm and a leg, but I had no choice.

"Everything was fine, until one day an inspector came from the State of Maryland. I showed them all our records on the patients, and thank God the inspectors were very pleased. They were about to leave, when this 95-year-old Jewish woman approaches one of them and says she has a complaint. 'What's your complaint?' the inspector asks. She says, 'He gives me different food. I want to eat like everybody else. He's discriminating against me.'

"The inspector comes over to me and asks, 'What's going on? You know you're not allowed to discriminate.' I try to explain to the inspector that I'm a religious Jew, and I can't feed a Jewish patient non-kosher food. Even though it costs me a fortune, I give her kosher food.

"The inspector says, 'Listen, buddy, you can't force your religion on anyone else. This is America. Either you feed her like everybody else, or I will be forced to shut you down.' So I go over to this 95-year-old woman and tell her, 'The *tereifah* food is very cheap. The kosher food I'm getting you costs almost ten times more!'

" 'Save your money,' she says, 'I want to eat like everybody else.'

" 'Ma'am, everyone knows that kosher food is tastier. It's prepared with greater care.'

" 'I'm 95 years old! You think I can taste anything? I just want to eat like everybody else.'

" 'Ma'am, everyone knows that kosher food is healthier. This *tereifah* food is bad for you. Kosher food is healthy, and it's government inspected.'

" 'I'm 95 years old. The sooner I go, the better. I want to eat what everybody else eats.'"

*I*ch hub gehat a breirah? I had no choice! The inspector was going to shut me down. I don't know what I said, all I know is that now she says *Modeh Ani* and makes *berachos*.

The man from Baltimore turned to me and said, "Now, she washes her hands before she eats. She gets up in the morning and says *Modeh Ani*. She recites *Tehillim*, lights candles Friday night, and she's *shomer Shabbos*. She does everything!"

"That's fantastic," I responded. "But tell me, what did you say to her?"

"I already told you," he says.

"No, you didn't."

"I told you that the inspector said he would shut me down. *Ich hub gehat a breirah?* I had no choice! The inspector was going to shut me down. I don't know what I said, all I know is that now she says *Modeh Ani* and makes *berachos.*"

I spent my life reaching out to Jews of all backgrounds and was never successful in reaching a nonagenarian, yet this inexperienced fellow from Baltimore succeeded in reaching a 95-year-old.

Because he simply had to find a way to reach her, this nursing home owner became a master at *kiruv.* I spent my life reaching out to Jews of all backgrounds and was never successful in reaching a nonagenarian, yet this inexperienced fellow from Baltimore succeeded in reaching a 95-year-old.

Our mistake is that we think we have a choice. If we really want to, we can do it. If we love the Land of Israel the way the daughters of Tzelafchad did, we will see things that even Moshe could not see. We just have to want it badly enough.

ספר דברים

*S*efer Devarim

A leader needs to pick his battles wisely, in order to preserve the respect of the people and safeguard his role as their leader.

פרשת דברים

arashas Devarim:
Effective Leadership

A t the beginning of *Sefer Devarim*, Moshe begins his parting words to the Jewish people by rebuking them for their mistakes throughout their forty years in the desert. In order not to embarrass them, Moshe veils his rebuke by alluding to their transgressions through names of places. "In the desert" refers to when the Jewish people complained to God about the lack of food in the desert, saying, "If only we had died by the hand of Hashem in the land of Egypt" (*Shemos* 16:3). "Di-zahav," which literally means "enough gold" is a reference to the sin of the Golden Calf (Rashi ad loc.).

Moshe also recounts the implementation of Yisro's advice to create a judicial system. "Provide for yourself distinguished men, who are wise, understanding, and well known to your tribes, and I will appoint them as your heads. You answered me and said, 'The thing that you have proposed to do is good'" (*Devarim* 1:13-14).

Rashi explains that this is not a digression from his rebuke; rather, Moshe is criticizing the Jewish people for accepting Yisro's idea. "You should have replied, 'Our teacher, Moshe! From whom is it proper to learn, from you or from your disciple? Is it not better to learn from you, who has taken such pains about them?' However, I knew your thoughts; you were saying to yourselves, "Many judges will now be appointed over us; if one does not know us, we shall bring him a gift, and he will show us favor."

But why did Moshe rebuke them only now for the transgressions they committed nearly forty years earlier? The Torah obligation to rebuke someone begins as soon as we see they are making a mistake. Waiting to rebuke them and allowing them to continue in their mistake is damaging to all. The Rambam writes:

> It is a mitzvah for a person who sees that his fellow Jew has transgressed or is following an improper path to rebuke him for his behavior and to inform him that he is causing himself a loss through his evil deeds, as the Torah says: "You shall surely admonish your fellow" (Vayikra 19:17). . . Whoever has the ability to rebuke and fails to do so is considered responsible for those people's sin, for he had the opportunity to rebuke them (Hilchos Dei'os 6:7).

Delaying to give rebuke, for decades no less, is playing with fire. You risk becoming accountable for the people's transgression by not trying to stop their errant behavior. So how is it possible that Moshe waited so many years and did not rebuke the Jewish people immediately?

Moshe was not the only major figure in Jewish history to delay giving rebuke. Rashi (1:3) says that Moshe waited until a short while before his death to give rebuke, drawing on the example of Yaakov Avinu, who reproached his sons just before he died. Yehoshua, Shmuel Hanavi, and David Hamelech also waited until they were on their deathbed to rebuke their children and followers. How could they all delay in fulfilling such a consequential mitzvah?

Leaders Must Pick Their Battles

When it comes to giving rebuke, there is a crucial difference between the responsibilities of an individual and a leader. Concerning the individual, the halachah is very clear: Provided our words will be heard, we are obligated to rebuke someone immediately. If we do not, we share in their transgression. But a leader is different. He cannot admonish the people for every mistake he sees, even if in the short run he will be listened to, because this will ultimately undermine his effectiveness as a leader and cause even greater damage. He needs to weigh his words carefully and ensure that his reprimands do not become nothing more than a broken record. A leader needs to pick his battles wisely, in order to preserve the respect of the people and safeguard his role as their leader.

When someone is on his deathbed, it is the most opportune time to offer words of criticism. In this situation people are listening intently, because they realize that whatever the person is saying at this critical time must be of utmost importance. Under these circumstances, there is no concern that the person's voice will be ignored. The words he offers at this crucial moment will stay with their listeners forever.

Parents and Children

This approach to giving rebuke is true not only for leaders like Moshe, Yehoshua, Shmuel Hanavi, and David Hamelech, it also applies to anyone in a leadership capacity, including parents, managers, and employers. One of the greatest curses that can happen to parents is having their children simply ignore them. Nothing they say registers, because their children have grown tired of their constant barrage of criticism. In order to prevent this from happening, parents must be very discerning regarding how and when they criticize their children. Criticism needs to be done sparingly and when truly necessary, in a way that does not destroy the love and trust between parent and child. This same dynamic applies to bosses and their relationships with their employees as well.

For words of rebuke to be effective, they must emanate from a warm, loving place of concern. The Rambam writes: "A person who rebukes a colleague... should speak to him patiently and gently, informing him that he is making these statements only for his colleague's own welfare..." (*Hilchos Dei'os* 6:7). If a person feels that you genuinely have his best interests at heart, and that you are speaking not as a ploy to manipulate, but because you truly care about him, he will listen and be more open to accepting your criticism. One suggested formula is to give ten portions of love for every portion of criticism. Express your love before, during, and after criticism. Reassure the person that you are on his side.

If a person feels that you genuinely have his best interests at heart, and that you are speaking not as a ploy to manipulate, but because you truly care about him, he will listen and be more open to accepting your criticism.

This principle cannot be overstated when it comes to parents and children. Parents often make the mistake of criticizing their children too often and without emphasizing how much they love them. Like Moshe Rabbeinu, put the overall relationship first. Focus on being effective, not just right. Evaluate your words and ensure that they promote a loving, trusting relationship, because in the long run, that connection and trust will prove to be most effective vehicle for communicating with your children.

Prayer is an avodah; it requires getting into your bones that the Almighty is your Father in Heaven Who loves you.

פרשת ואתחנן

arashas Va'eschanan:
Getting Your Prayers Answered

In the beginning of this week's *parashah* the Torah describes how Moshe prayed to Hashem to let him enter Eretz Yisrael, using the Hebrew verb "*va'eschanan.*" Rashi explains the meaning of this word: "The word *chinun* is an expression of requesting an unwarranted gift, a *matnas chinam*. Even though the righteous could base their request on the merit of their good deeds, they request a free gift from the Omnipresent."

Moshe realized that despite his accomplishments and steadfast commitment to Hashem, it is always better to appeal to Hashem's *chessed*, rather than request something on the basis of one's own merit. If this is true for a spiritual giant like Moshe, then it is certainly true for us. Hashem wants only our good. Praying to God with the knowledge that He is our Father in Heaven Who loves us unconditionally is such a powerful activity that Hashem had to ask Moshe to stop praying. Had Moshe continued to beseech Hashem, He could not have avoided answering his prayer and allowing him entry to the Land.

Answered Prayers

Have you ever had a prayer answered? Stop for a moment and consider the implications.

You live in a small town in the Midwest. There is an extremely large and unsightly pothole in front of your house. For the last four months the local municipality has ignored your persistent requests to have it fixed. Finally, in an act of frustration, you call the White House and ask for the president. (Hey, it's worth a try.)

To your utter amazement, the president himself gets on the phone. You quickly explain your problem. The president listens for a minute, takes down your address, and then hangs up. You don't really expect anything to be done about it.

The next morning you look out your window and, lo and behold, an army corps of engineers is busy at work fixing your road. The president of the United States took your request seriously and sent in the troops to fix the pothole.

This is what it means to get your prayer answered.

Now, we all know this isn't happening to a regular Joe. But who is the one person who can always get through to the president?

His child, of course.

God is our Father and each one of us is His child. Just as a parent fulfills a child's request, so, too, God answers our prayers. But in order to have God answer your prayer, you need to know He is willing and able to do so. And you have to be honest, sincere and responsible about what you pray for, as David Hamelech wrote, "Hashem is close to all those who call upon Him, to all who call upon Him sincerely" (*Tehillim* 145:18). Prayer requires accessing your inner core and being real with God. Where are you, and what do you really want? It means dropping all pretenses and communicating your genuine thoughts and needs, in the reality of God's presence.

Why Do We Need to Pray?

God already knows our needs. He certainly does not need us to remind Him of them. So why do we need to pray? Why doesn't God just give us what we need without our having to ask?

God does not need our prayers; we do. Prayer is a reflection of our desires and an extension of our power of free choice. It helps us refine and affirm what it is we want out of life. If a billionaire father handed his child unlimited cash on a silver platter, the child would grow up terribly spoiled and irresponsible. Similarly, if God gave us everything automatically, we would never be forced to figure out what it is we really want in life. Life would be comfortable, but we would remain shallow and undeveloped. It is through the challenges we face and the efforts we make as a result of those challenges that we learn to appreciate the value of what we want.

God does not need our prayers; we do.

God has our best interests at heart. He wants us to earn our growth because that is how we retain our independence and become real about what it is we want to accomplish.

Five Aspects to Being Real with Prayer

#1: Get Clear on Your Bottom Line: Is What You Want Good for You?

To have our prayers answered, we have to know that what we seek is in our best interests. Will the fulfillment of this request bring us closer to God or push us further away? We can only expect God to answer our prayer if its attainment will bring us closer to reality, not escapism.

When I was 8 years old, the World's Fair came to New York. My entire class decided to play hooky one day and go to the World's Fair. But there was one condition: Everyone had to bring a dollar. If you did not have a dollar, you could not come.

When I was a child the only way I could get a dollar from my father was to learn a chapter of Mishnah by heart. But there was no way I could memorize a whole chapter on such short notice. So I figured I might as well go to school that day. I would be the only one there: a hero!

I started walking to school when it suddenly occurred to me: Keep your eyes on the pavement, Noach, maybe you'll find a dollar!

I started looking. One block. No dollar. Two blocks. No dollar. I started to pray, "Hashem, a dollar bill. . . You have them lying around the street sometimes. Just this one time, let me find a dollar bill."

Two more blocks, no dollar. I thought maybe God wants something from me. So I started making all kinds of promises. "Hashem, I'll take out the garbage. And I won't fight with my sister."

Still no dollar.

I upped the ante. "Hashem, if You give me a dollar, I'll learn a chapter of Mishnah and I *won't* take the dollar from my father. You can trust me. It's a loan. O.K.?"

No dollar.

Finally, I rounded the corner and the school was in sight. It was time to pull out all the stops. "Hashem, give me one dollar, and I'll never do anything wrong again for the rest of my life!"

And then I caught myself. *Noach, who are you kidding? If you find the dollar, you're going to play hooky!*

We cannot expect Hashem to give us a dollar so that we can do the wrong thing. To avoid this mistake, we need to do the work of clarifying our desires. We need to ask ourselves: *Why do we want this? Does the Almighty want us to have this?* God's answer — whether yes or no — always tells us something important about ourselves or will likely give us insight into the validity of what we are seeking.

Before you ask, make sure what you are praying for is good for you.

#2: Be Responsible, Make an Effort

Prayer is not an escape from personal effort and responsibility. It is a tool to help us refine our understanding of what we want and to realize that God is the true Source of all that we accomplish.

Prayer focuses us on reality. If we are serious about what we are praying for, then we first need to be responsible and put in our best efforts to make it happen. Prayer is not a wish; it is predicated on working hard and taking responsibility.

Ask yourself: *Do I really want to accomplish this? Am I willing to take responsibility to do what I can to attain it? How much am I prepared to sacrifice for it?*

#3: Expect the Good

Being real about prayer means we realize we are praying to our Father in Heaven Who wants only our good and has the power to do anything. Therefore, we should anticipate that God wants to help us. Anything we ask for is infinitesimally less than what Hashem has already given to us.

If we do not expect that God will answer our prayer, God will not invade our space and shock us with success. He wants us to earn the realization that He is our Father in Heaven and that we can always count on Him.

By turning our prayer down, God is telling us that we have a problem that needs addressing; we need to realign.

To illustrate, imagine a 22-year-old driving through Manhattan during rush hour in the middle of July. Red lights, gridlock, honking, summer heat. . . *aggravation.*

If his father was in charge of all the traffic lights in New York City and was able to track his location at any given time, he'd have it made. His father would arrange one green light after another, all the way across town!

The Almighty can arrange it for him. He created the universe. Traffic in Manhattan is not overly taxing for Him.

So here goes our driver. Green light, green light, green light, green light. He says to himself, *This is too good to be true. I don't deserve this.*

Red light.

If you don't anticipate God's help, then you have lost sight of God as your Father. So God breaks the flow in order to realign your focus.

Focus on the fact that the Almighty wants everything to be good for you. When you do that, He'll move mountains to answer a prayer that is good for you.

#4: Be Shocked if You Don't Get It

Nothing God does is an accident. If things do not go smoothly for you, your first reaction should be one of shock. "What's going on? Why is God doing this? What message does He want me to get?"[1]

An uncle wrote letters to his nephew at college to find out how he was doing and keep up the relationship. After six months and numerous letters, the nephew hadn't written back once.

The next time, the uncle wrote his standard letter, but this time, he added a P.S.: "I've enclosed a hundred dollar check for you." Then he deliberately mailed the letter without the check.

The nephew received the letter and could not find the check. As expected, the uncle immediately got a letter in return: "College is great. . . I like my dorm room. . . I'm taking physics. By the way, you forgot to enclose the check. Love, your favorite nephew."

> *he Almighty knows how to get our attention. When we forget that He loves us, He sends a red light to refocus us.*

The Almighty knows how to get our attention. When we forget that He loves us, He sends a red light to refocus us.

But there's one big difference between the uncle and God: God is not hurt when we ignore Him. We are. God has no needs and doesn't need a relationship with us. It is we who need a relationship with Him. Our greatest pleasure is being in touch with God. That's why He arranges small mishaps to get our attention. It is all for our own benefit.

#5: Listen to God's Lessons

If you are serious about a relationship with God, then you understand that God is always teaching you, even when He does not answer your prayer in the affirmative.

When life is suddenly full of inconveniences, stop and ask: *Why is He trying to get my attention?* In some ways this is the most

---

1. The Gemara (*Berachos* 34a) explains that the structure of *Shemoneh Esrei* mirrors a servant's interaction with his master. The servant first praises the master, then asks the master for what he needs, and finally thanks the master for fulfilling his requests (Maharsha ad loc.). The implication is that immediately after asking Hashem for our needs, we are so confident that they are "in the bag," we can already thank Him for fulfilling them (cf. *Beis Elokim Tefillah* 2, s.v. *U'kemo, Vezehu*).

demanding aspect, because it requires us to hold onto the perception that God is our Father in Heaven and that everything He does is for our good, even when we are feeling pain. Saying with clarity and conviction, *"Gam zu l'tovah*, this too is for the good," with no resentment and bitterness, demonstrates the deepest realization that God is our loving Father.

*I*f we are unable to say *"Gam zu l'tovah"* with a full heart, then it is almost impossible for us to properly hear what God is saying to us.

If we are unable to say *"Gam zu l'tovah"* with a full heart, then it is almost impossible for us to properly hear what God is saying to us. God is very articulate, but if we lose sight of the fact that He is our Father in Heaven, then our relationship is off kilter and any lesson we derive will necessarily be distorted. With the awareness that Hashem loves us, we can take stock of this area of our life and try to understand what the Almighty is telling us. (See essay on Parashas Bechukosai for a more in-depth discussion of this point.)

In Summary

The mitzvah to pray is referred to by Chazal as *"avodah shebelev"* — service of the heart. (See Rambam, *Hilchos Tefillah* 1:1.) Prayer is an *avodah*; it takes real work. It requires getting into your bones that the Almighty is your Father in Heaven Who loves you.

Know what you want and why you want it, and ensure that what you are seeking is in fact good for you. Take responsibility and put in your effort. Expect the good and be shocked if things do not go smoothly. Ask yourself: *Why is the Almighty trying to get my attention?* And lastly, strive to understand the lesson the Almighty is sending you. Ask yourself: *What is He teaching me?*

Applying these tools to the daily prayers will transform your relationship with Hashem.

Only yiras Shamayim comes with an ironclad guarantee that one who truly wants it will successfully attain it.

פרשת עקב

arashas Eikev:
Wanting Fear of Heaven

וְעַתָּה יִשְׂרָאֵל מָה ה׳ אֱלֹהֶיךָ שֹׁאֵל מֵעִמָּךְ כִּי אִם לְיִרְאָה אֶת ה׳
אֱלֹהֶיךָ . . .

Now, O Israel, what does Hashem, your God, ask of you?
Only to fear Hashem, your God. . .
(Devarim 10:12).

The Talmud derives from this *passuk* that everything is in the hands of Heaven except fear of Heaven (*Berachos* 33b). Since fear of Heaven is the only thing completely in our power, it is the only thing Hashem can ask of us.

However, every *Shabbos Mevarchim*, the Shabbos before the new month, we pray to Hashem to give us fear of Heaven: "and grant us long life… a life that has within it fear of Heaven and fear of transgression…." Why do we pray for fear of Heaven if it is entirely in our hands, not Hashem's?

In truth, everything is a gift from Hashem, including fear of Heaven. We cannot even lift a finger without the Almighty enabling us to do so. However, before fulfilling our requests, Hashem evaluates what the impact of granting our wishes will be. Will it draw us closer to Him or push us further away? If what we seek is truly good for us and consistent with Hashem's plan, then there is no reason for Hashem not to grant it to us. But if that which we covet will cause us to escape reality and distance ourselves from Hashem, then He will likely be disinclined to give it to us.

Even spiritual goals require this assessment, because they, too, can cause us to move further away from Hashem. For example, if learning a lot of Torah causes a person to become complacent or arrogant, it distances him from Hashem and is therefore bad for him.

The only desire that does not need this evaluation is *yiras Shamayim*, fear of Heaven. By definition, *yiras Shamayim* plants us firmly into reality and brings us closer to Hashem. A person cannot be awake and asleep simultaneously. Similarly, if we are fearing Hashem, we cannot be escaping reality and ignoring Him.

"Everything is in the hands of Heaven except for fear of Heaven" means that only *yiras Shamayim* comes with an ironclad guarantee that one who truly wants it will successfully attain it. There are no obstacles to getting it; it is completely in our hands, because it is the only accomplishment that can never be counterproductive.

The Torah describes fear of Heaven as a small thing. "Now, Israel, what does Hashem, your God, ask of you? *Only* to fear Hashem, your God. . . ." No big deal! That's all God wants from us. But attaining *yiras Shamayim* is not so easy. "Is it just a small matter?" the Talmud asks incredulously (*Berachos* 33b).

True, *yiras Shamayim* is not simple to attain, but it is eminently doable. Nothing is stopping you from attaining it. All that is required is for you to truly desire it. In this respect, fearing Hashem is a small thing.

Why Fear Hashem?

Fear gives us clarity. At the moment when someone jumps out of an airplane or is hurtling at 100 miles an hour into a hairpin curve, he is not thinking about the mortgage or the leaky faucet. The danger he experiences makes him forget about all his petty concerns and awakens him to the exquisite beauty and thrill of being alive. Through the risk of death he touches the sheer joy and meaning that life has to offer.

> **At the moment when someone jumps out of an airplane or is hurtling at 100 miles an hour into a hairpin curve, he is not thinking about the mortgage or the leaky faucet.**

Fear brings into sharp focus the very real consequences at stake in life, infusing every moment with great meaning. Fear of punishment means living with the clarity of the profound consequences that are inevitable if we transgress. It is comparable to the fear one would feel when crossing the Grand Canyon on a tightrope. Each step is taken with great caution and trepidation, because one misstep spells the difference between life and death.

Yiras Shamayim also entails the fear of losing the eternal reward that comes as a result of performing even the simplest mitzvah. The fear of squandering this priceless opportunity is comparable to the desperation of a person who searches frantically for the winning lottery ticket he accidentally threw out.

The last minute of a championship basketball game is always the most exciting because that's when every single second counts. Every shot could be the winning basket. Living with the awareness of life's profound consequences gives us direct access to the pleasure of living a meaningful life.

Stop Sign Against Transgression

Fear of Hashem protects us from transgressing because it makes us aware that we are under constant surveillance, as the Mishnah says, "Look at three things and you will not come to transgress: Know what is above you — an Eye that sees and an Ear that hears, and all your deeds are written in a Book" (*Pirkei Avos* 2:1).

How do you feel when you see a police car with flashing lights in your rearview mirror bearing down on you? You immediately start to worry: What am I doing wrong? Am I speeding? Talking on my cell phone? Am I wearing my seatbelt? Did I pay the insurance? Even if the police are just driving by, their presence makes us check and recheck ourselves.

We would refrain from transgressing if we knew that our every thought and deed is being filmed by the Creator of the universe, and will be broadcast for eternity.

On the first halachah in the *Shulchan Aruch*, the Rema writes, "*Shivisi Hashem lenegdi samid* — I place God before me always — this is the major principle of the Torah." That's because living with the awareness that we are in the presence of the Almighty transforms the way we act and speak. We would refrain from transgressing if we knew that our every thought and deed is being filmed by the Creator of the universe, and will be broadcast for eternity.

He's Watching

There is a famous story told about the Chofetz Chaim, who was once traveling in a wagon when the driver saw an orchard full of ripe, tempting fruit, by the side of the road.

"Wait here for a minute," the driver said, jumping out of the coach. "I'm going to pick some fruit. You keep watch and tell me if you see anyone coming."

The driver was about to enter the orchard when the Chofetz Chaim shouted, "He's watching! He's watching!"

Terrified, the wagon driver ran back to the coach as fast as he could. Out of breath, he looked all around him, afraid of being spotted by the observer. But there was not a soul in sight.

"You lied to me!" he yelled at the Chofetz Chaim. "There's no one here!"

"Of course there is," he replied. "Hashem is always watching. He sees everything."

An Absolute Necessity

The greatest enemy we all face is our own *yetzer hara*, who never lets up until the day we die. *Chovos Halevavos* writes: "[The *yetzer hara*] lies in wait to entice you at your every step. You are unaware of it, but it is aware of you; you are unmindful of it, but it is mindful of you... it will not let you alone until it has destroyed you... Therefore, let no other struggle divert you from your struggle with it" (*Shaar Yichud HaMa'aseh*, Chapter 5).

The *yetzer hara* is constantly confusing us and tempting us to transgress, and what makes matters worse is that we do not even realize that we are under attack. It can defeat us before we realize we are in the midst of a struggle. Without fear of Hashem we do not stand a chance of defeating him.

This is another reason why fear of Hashem is so critical. It puts us on high alert and wakes us up to the insidious dangers of the *yetzer hara*, enabling us to fend off his attack and defeat him. The moment we let our guard down, the *yetzer hara* is infiltrating and ready to pounce.

Particularly in today's world, when our computers and smartphones position us one click away from the *yetzer hara's* nuclear arsenal, it is patently clear that living with *yiras Shamayim* is a matter of life and death. We cannot survive spiritually without it.

Not the Ideal

Serving Hashem out of fear is not the ideal, however. The appropriate motivation for serving Hashem is that it is our honor and privilege to do the will of God, as the Rambam writes (*Hilchos Teshuvah* 10:1):

> A person should not say: "I will fulfill the mitzvos of the Torah and occupy myself with its wisdom in order to receive all the blessings contained within it, or in order to merit the life of the World to Come. Similarly, I will separate myself from all the sins against which the Torah warned so that I will be saved from all the curses contained in the Torah, or so that I will not be cut off from the life of the World to Come."
>
> It is not fitting to serve God in this manner, for a person whose service is motivated by these factors is considered one who serves out of fear. He is not on the level of the prophets or of the wise.

Serving Hashem out of fear is inadequate, because it means we do not really understand the meaning and benefit of doing Hashem's will for its own sake. It makes us mercenaries, focusing more on the payoff we will receive than on doing the right thing.

But fear is an absolute prerequisite to serving Hashem through love, as the *Orchos Tzaddikim* writes (in *Shaar Ha'ahavah*), "It is impossible for a person to reach [love of Hashem] until his awe and his fear are of Hashem. Therefore, fear always precedes love."

Our goal is to serve Hashem out of love, but the starting point must be fear.

Without first fearing God we will be enslaved by the desires of our body, caught in the vise of the *yetzer hara*. Fear ensures that we stay out of the quicksand, and liberates us to develop a relationship with Hashem that is built on appreciating His awesomeness. Our goal is to serve Hashem out of love, but the starting point must be fear.

Hashem expects us to make that first step. After all, it is the one thing that is in our hands.

The meisis, in trying to lead Jews away from Hashem, is destroying the world. One who tries to bring the Jewish people back to Hashem is building the world.

פרשת ראה
arashas Re'eh:
Bringing Jews Back

This week's *parashah* singles out the *meisis* — someone who entices a Jew to worship idols — with the harshest treatment of any transgressor in the Torah. The *passuk* says: "You shall not accede to him [the missionary] and not hearken to him; your eye shall not take pity on him, you shall not be compassionate nor conceal him. Rather, you shall surely kill him" (*Devarim* 13:9,10).

These highly unusual directives comprise five distinct negative commandments, which the Rambam (*Hilchos Sanhedrin* 11:5) summarizes as follows:

> The laws that pertain to a *meisis*, a person who entices others to serve false gods, differ from those pertaining to others liable for capital punishment.
>
> 1) We conceal witnesses in order to observe his act.
>
> 2) Unlike others who are liable to be executed, he does not need a warning.

3) If he departed from the court after being acquitted, and someone said, "I know of a rationale that will lead to his conviction," he is returned and retried.

4) If he was sentenced to death and someone said, "I know of a rationale that will lead to his release," he is not retried.

5) The court does not advance arguments in defense of a *meisis*. An elderly person, a eunuch, and a person who does not have children are placed on the court that judges him, so that they will not have mercy on him. For cruelty to those who sway the people after emptiness brings mercy to the world, as the Torah says, "So that Hashem will turn back from His burning wrath; and He will give you mercy" (*Devarim* 13:18).

The same Torah whose fundamental principle is "Love your fellow as yourself" obligates us to show no mercy toward the *meisis* and to aggressively seek his conviction and execution.

Rav Aharon Kotler, in *Mishnas Rav Aharon* (vol. 1, p. 254), derives the following insight from the unique laws regarding a *meisis*.

Our sages teach us that Hashem's desire to bestow reward is 500 times greater than His desire to punish. This is derived from the *passuk* in *Shemos* (34:7, see Rashi there) that says that punishment can be extended only to the fourth generation, while reward can be extended for 2000 generations.

Consequently, explains Rav Aharon, if a *meisis* is considered the worst transgressor of all and as a result is treated more severely than even an idolater or murderer, the opposite of a *meisis* — namely, a *mekarev*, one who brings Jews back to Torah — must be the most righteous person of all, and will be rewarded 500 times more than the *meisis* is punished.

It is important to note how stringent the Torah's criteria for a *meisis* are. If someone would tell the *gadol hador*, "Bow down to a telephone poll because it will answer your prayers," and the *gadol* would dismiss him outright, saying, "You're a *meshuganer*, get out of here!" the person is considered a *meisis*, even though his words had no impact. The mere attempt to draw a person away from Torah categorizes someone as a *meisis*.

Many people who dedicate their lives to *kiruv* mistakenly believe that their efforts on behalf of their fellow Jews are significant only if the person they are working with becomes *shomer Shabbos*. That is certainly a great achievement, but it's not what confers upon a person the lofty and cherished status of a *mekarev*. If a person is considered a *meisis* just by virtue of his attempt to draw someone away from *Yiddishkeit*, then a person who attempts to draw someone *to Yiddishkeit* must be considered a *mekarev* by virtue of the undertaking alone.

> *M*any people who dedicate their lives to *kiruv* mistakenly believe that their efforts on behalf of their fellow Jews are significant only if the person they are working with becomes *shomer Shabbos.*

Just taking the initiative to try and reconnect a fellow Jew to *Yiddishkeit* is deemed by Hashem to be the greatest good, and worthy of the greatest reward. The actual impact we have on another Jew is secondary.

Someone who tries to lead one Jew astray is attempting to move the world further away from Hashem; he is creating a *chillul Hashem*. This is in contradistinction to someone who tries to bring one Jew closer to his Father in Heaven. The latter is attempting to increase the awareness of God in the world, and just making the effort creates a *kiddush Hashem*. If he actually succeeds, then how much greater is his achievement. This is true for reaching just one Jew; how much more does it apply to someone who is making a genuine effort to impact all of *Klal Yisrael*, to reach the entire Jewish people!

Unparalleled Merit

The *Chovos Halevavos* writes something incredible:

> *A person's good deeds alone do not make him suitable for the reward of the World to Come. God considers him suitable only because of two other factors in addition to*

his good deeds. The first is that he teaches others about the service of God and guides them in doing good... The second is God's kindness and beneficence (Shaar Habitachon, Chapter 4).

A person can serve God with all his heart and raise himself to the level of angels — he can be an angel in his spiritual understanding, an angel in his business dealings, an angel in his relationships with other people — yet the *Chovos Halevavos* states that he cannot enter *Olam Haba* unless he is involved in teaching other people about God.

> **I**f you are not actively trying to bring Jews back to Hashem and His Torah, you do not really love Hashem and His children.

Why is this so? Because if you are not actively trying to bring Jews back to Hashem and His Torah, you do not really love Hashem and His children. As the Rambam writes in *Sefer HaMitzvos* (positive commandment 3), on the mitzvah to love Hashem:

> Our Sages said that this mitzvah includes calling out to all mankind to serve God, exalted be He, and to believe in Him. This is because when you love someone, you turn your attention to him and praise him and call out to others to love him. So, too, if you truly love God — through your understanding and realization of His true existence — you will certainly spread this true knowledge that you know to the deniers and the foolish.
>
> Thus, the Sifri says: "'You shall love Hashem' — that is, make Him beloved among people, as your father Avraham did, as it says, 'The souls that he made in Charan' (*Bereishis* 12:5)."
>
> The Sifri means to tell us that Avraham, as a result of his deep understanding of God, acquired love for God, as the verse testifies, "Avraham, who loved Me" (*Yeshayahu* 41:8). This powerful love spurred him to call out to all mankind to believe in God. So, too, you shall love Him to the extent that you draw others to Him.

People naturally share the things they love. What will compel us to reach out to our fellow Jews is our genuine love, excitement, and appreciation for the Almighty and the wisdom of his Torah. To the extent that we love Hashem and Torah, we will be driven to share this love.

Furthermore, *kiruv* and learning Torah are inextricably linked. The Talmud (*Avodah Zarah* 9a) teaches that the world is destined to exist for 6,000 years, which are divided into three eras: 2000 years of desolation, 2000 years of Torah, and 2000 years of the days of Mashiach. When did the 2000-year era of Torah begin? The Talmud calculates that it was when Avraham was 52 years old, when he and his wife Sarah started the first *kiruv* movement and began to reach out to the masses and bring Torah values to the world.

> The goal of Torah is not only self-perfection, it is to perfect the entire world.

The era of Torah did not begin with Adam Harishon, nor with Shem and Eiver, who had their own yeshivah. It began the moment Avraham realized that the reality of God must be shared with the world. That is because the goal of Torah is not only self-perfection, it is to perfect the entire world. The *meisis*, in trying to lead Jews away from Hashem, is destroying the world. One who tries to bring the Jewish people back to Hashem is building the world.

> *Subjugating your da'as does not mean you do not have a viewpoint. It means you are choosing to be mevatel it, because you recognize that you are not an expert.*

פרשת שופטים
arashas Shoftim:
Knowing Your Right from Your Left

*P*irkei Avos begins by summarizing Judaism's educational philosophy with the statement: "Stand up many students." The mishnah does not say "teach" or "inspire"; it says "stand up," emphasizing that our primary goal in educating our students and our children is to make them independent. Our role as parents and teachers is to raise young people who can think for themselves.

Chazal tell us that Rabbah, when testing Abaye, would purposely impart something incorrect or illogical to ensure he did not just accept what he taught him without first critically examining it (*Berachos* 33b).

> *The mishnah does not say "teach" or "inspire"; it says "stand up," emphasizing that our primary goal in educating our students and our children is to make them independent.*

If we do not think for ourselves, we will remain a passive blank slate conditioned by society, and our values and convictions will be a mere accident of birth. Using our mind to assess and think critically is an essential part of individuation. It is the engine that creates the true, unique self.

Rabbi Kalonymus Kalman Shapira, the Piaseczna Rebbe, who perished in the Holocaust, described it this way in his personal diary, *To Heal the Soul*: "There must be a person who can stand by himself, who can decide what he wants for himself. But if there is no such person, just a crowd, there can be no free choice or personal will. Because who will choose, if aside from the herd there is no one there at all?

If we do not think for ourselves, we will remain a passive blank slate conditioned by society, and our values and convictions will be a mere accident of birth.

"Are you a person who can stand by himself, or are you just a member of the human species? Man cannot remain imprisoned by social rules, cultural customs, or accepted thought without the ability to see beyond them; he must have a mind of his own. Without this, not only is he not a Jew, he is not even a person."

Yet this week's *parashah* seems to contradict the value of being an independent thinker. The *passuk* says, "According to the teaching that they will teach you and according to the judgment that they will say to you, shall you do; you shall not deviate from the word that they will tell you, right or left" (*Devarim* 17:11).

Rashi (ibid. 17:24), citing Sifri, explains, "Even if this judge tells you that right is left, and that left is right. How much more so, if he tells you that right is right, and left is left!" Chazal seem to be instructing us to ignore our own opinion and accept the viewpoint of the rav, even if it seems completely illogical. What happened to the importance of thinking independently?

To complicate matters, the Talmud (*Horayos* 2b) discusses a case where an individual sage is expected to oppose what he considers a mistaken ruling of the Sanhedrin HaGadol and stay resolute in his viewpoint. The case involves a piece of *cheilev*, forbidden fat, that the Sanhedrin HaGadol mistakes for *shuman*, permissible fat. If a member of that very Sanhedrin eats the fat, knowing that his colleagues ruled incorrectly, he is obligated to bring an offering for inadvertently transgressing by eating the non-kosher fat.

The question is, why is his action viewed as inadvertent, when he knew he was eating non-kosher fat?

The Gemara answers that it is because he erroneously thought that the obligation of "According to the teaching that they will teach you... shall you do" applies even in such a case. It does not. The individual sage who recognizes that the Sanhedrin HaGadol is making a mistake is required to stick to his guns and not follow their ruling.

This Gemara seems to be at odds with the statement of Chazal on our *parashah* concerning the obligation to obey our leaders even if they tell us "that right is left, and that left is right." How do we reconcile these two sources?

Fact vs. Judgment

The resolution lies in the different nature of the rulings involved.

Our *parashah* is referring to decisions based on a judgment call or *sevarah*. In cases that require logical deliberation and reasoning, we need to defer to our sages, who are far more educated in these matters and whose perspective and judgment are far more aligned with Torah than ours. This is hinted to by the fact that Chazal illustrate the need to accept their ruling with the example of calling your right hand your left hand and vice versa, because whether something is on the right or on the left is really a question of perspective.

In contrast, the Gemara's case involving the kosher and non-kosher fat is a matter of determining objective fact. In such a situation, we can know the facts even though we are less educated than our sages. Therefore, we are obligated to stick to what we know, even if it contradicts the opinion of our rav.[1]

Rabbi Weinberg's rosh yeshivah in Yeshivas Chaim Berlin, Rav Yitzchak Hutner, was reluctant to answer a student's question unless the student offered his own approach first. Rav Hutner was instilling a powerful lesson about the importance of developing intellectual independence. He trained his *talmidim* to first put in the hard work to think through the issue and arrive at their own conclusions. Only then would he impart his precious words of Torah. Rabbi Weinberg embraced this approach with his own *talmidim*, as well.

You are responsible to have a *dei'ah*, an educated opinion, and you also need to have the humility to defer to those whose understanding is far greater than yours. However, subjugating your *da'as* does not mean you do not have a viewpoint. It means you are choosing to be *mevatel* (forfeit) it because you recognize that you are not an expert in this area and that your perspective is not nearly as pure and Torah based as the nuanced opinion of a *talmid chacham*.

Striking this balance ensures that there is leadership, that there is proper deference for *talmidei chachamim*, and that each individual is encouraged to develop his independence and uniqueness.

---

1. See *Kesubos* 57a, Rashi s.v. *Ha ka mashma lan*, where he explains that in disputes that involve reasoning we can apply the maxim, "These and those are the words of the living God," meaning that both viewpoints express the truth even though they conflict, since different logical arguments may be appropriate at different times. But in matters of fact, in a dispute one side must be wrong. See also the *Be'er Sheva* on *Horayos* 2b, who gives a similar answer.

*Everything that happens to us
in this world is for one reason and
one reason alone: to get closer to
the Almighty, to feel that I am for
my Beloved and my Beloved
is for me.*

פרשת כי תצא

arashas Ki Seitzei:
At War During Elul

כִּי תֵצֵא לַמִּלְחָמָה עַל אֹיְבֶיךָ . . .

When you will go out to war against your enemies...
(Devarim 21:10).

We are all at war with a ferocious enemy. The *Chovos Halevavos* (*Shaar Yichud Hamaaseh*, Chapter 5) describes this battle through the following story. A pious man encountered a group of triumphant soldiers coming back from a fierce battle, flushed with victory.

"You have returned victorious from a minor struggle," he said to them. "Now get ready for the major battle."

"And what is that major battle?" they asked.

"The war within us, against the evil inclination. That is the great war. You just came back from three weeks of intense fighting, and now the enemy has been vanquished. But fighting the insanity of the *yetzer hara* never ends. Even after 100 defeats, he will never leave you alone. The battle is constant. He will not rest until he kills you. The moment you let your guard down, he will pounce and attempt to utterly destroy you.

"In a typical war there is a front line. Sometimes you are surrounded, but at least you know where the enemy lies. The *yetzer hara*, however, is a master of disguise. He knows how to mask illusions as reality, how to rationalize evil as good. He is so devious, he knows how to get you to harm yourself and your loved ones without your even realizing it."

We are in the middle of Elul, and it is time to intensify the battle against the *yetzer hara* and restock our supply of weapons.

The enemy's first plan of attack is to knock out your sense of personal responsibility and get you to hand it over to someone else.

Let my teachers inspire me, you think. Or, *Let my rabbi tell me what I have to work on.*

Stop waiting for someone to tell you what to change during Elul. You are responsible for yourself. You must do the necessary introspection, get in contact with yourself, and determine what you need to work on. As the Mishnah says, "*Im ein ani li, mi li?* — If I am not for myself, who will be for me?" (*Pirkei Avos* 1:14). No one can help you grow unless you take responsibility for yourself. Your teachers can give you the greatest tools in the world for self-transformation, but you will leave those tools on the bench if you don't take responsibility for your own life.

You need to get clarity about what life means to you. What do you want to accomplish this coming year? What are you committed to tackling? If you don't make these decisions, you might easily delude yourself into thinking that you are preparing adequately for Rosh Hashanah by listening to some inspiring *mussar* shmoozes and hoping that somehow these great rabbis will make you great.

No one can make you great. No one can turn you into a *lamdan* (an analytical Torah scholar), or into someone who knows *Shas*. There are no shortcuts; you are solely responsible for your own growth and learning. Toughen up and stop relying on others. No one can do this for you.

Judgment and Love

The month of Elul seems to be paradoxical. On the one hand it is the time for *"Ani l'dodi v'dodi li,* I am for my Beloved and my Beloved is for me" — an acronym for "Elul." It is a time when we feel Hashem's intense love and closeness. Yet Elul is also the time to prepare for Rosh Hashanah, when the Book of Life and the Book of Death are open and the King of the universe sits in judgment, deciding who will live and who will die, who will have cancer and who will be cured, who will be crushed in an accident and who will survive. There seems to be a contradiction between *Ani l'dodi v'dodi li* and the Day of Judgment. How are the two related?

The Ramchal encapsulates in one paragraph the whole point of our existence, and in doing so gives us an answer. In *Derech Hashem* (1:4:6) he writes, "The root purpose of the service of God is for the human being to constantly turn to his Creator, to realize that he was created for the sole purpose of being drawn close to his Creator...." Everything that happens to us in this world is for one reason and one reason alone: to get closer to the Almighty, to feel that I am for my Beloved and my Beloved is for me. The Jew understands that everything Hashem does is for our good; it is an expression of His love. Every judgment He renders — whether a windfall or a bankruptcy — is exactly what we need to grow closer to Him. *Ani l'dodi,* if you love the Almighty and appreciate that He is your Father, then *v'dodi li,* you will see that the Almighty loves you and that everything He does is for your good. But if you don't appreciate what Hashem has done for you and instead you have complaints, you will mistakenly think He does not love you.

The Ramchal describes the objective of the war against the *yetzer hara*: "Man was placed in this world only to overcome his evil inclination and subjugate himself to His Creator through the power of his intellect. He must overcome his physical desire and tendencies, and direct all of his activities toward attaining this purpose [of coming close to God]" (ibid.). It is up to us to choose to cling to Hashem by vanquishing our *yetzer hara* and rising above the vanities and confusion of the world.

Learning Torah

The Ramchal then identifies the primary weapon Hashem gave us to fight the *yetzer hara* and achieve our purpose: "God gave us one means that is greater than anything else in bringing man close to God, and that is Torah study" (1:4:9). There is nothing more powerful than learning Hashem's instructions for living. These are the actual words of our Creator.

Our motivation to get close to God cannot be mixed with the desire for approval or the need to conform to societal pressure.

But the Ramchal sets conditions: "For the person who reads them in holiness and purity, with the proper intent of fulfilling God's will, these words have the unique property of causing the one who reads them to incorporate in himself excellence and the greatest perfection." We need to learn Torah with holiness and purity, which means that our learning has to be *lishmah*, unadulterated, for the sake of Heaven. Our motivation to get close to God cannot be mixed with the desire for approval or the need to conform to societal pressure.

Elul is the time to examine your goals and drives. Why are you learning Torah? Make sure it is for the right reasons. Keep it pure.

And lastly, learn Torah with the intent to fulfill God's will. As we say in our daily prayers, in the second blessing before *krias Shema:* "Instill in our hearts to understand and elucidate, to listen, learn, teach, safeguard, perform, and fulfill all the words of your Torah's teaching with love." Torah study is not just for intellectual stimulation. The goal is for you to absorb it in your bones and live it. Torah learning has to change you and bring you closer to the Almighty. If your intent is not to fulfill what you are learning, you may know an incredible amount of Torah, but you are just a donkey carrying books. Your knowledge has not penetrated into the fiber of your being.

The shofar is blowing; you are moving closer to Yom HaDin. You are at war. The enemy is at the gate.

The shofar is blowing; you are moving closer to *Yom HaDin,* the Day of Judgment. You are at war. The enemy is at the gate. Now is the time to strengthen your resolve to fight the great battle against the *yetzer hara.* It is time to take responsibility for every aspect of your life, to reconnect to Hashem's constant love, and to intensify your determination to learn Torah with purity, in order to fulfill the will of Hashem. No one can do it for you.

Life, Torah, mitzvos — it's all for our benefit. Gratitude and joy are the name of the game.

פרשת כי תבוא

arashas Ki Savo:

Ani L'Dodi

We are in the month of Elul, which is an acronym for *Ani l'dodi v'dodi li* — I am for my Beloved and my Beloved is for me.

But would it not have been more appropriate to call the month *Dalul*, for *Dodi li v'ani l'dodi* — my Beloved is for me and I am for my Beloved? This would seem to be a more accurate description, since Hashem, our Beloved, is the One Who initiated the relationship with us, the Jewish people.

The reason why it is named Elul — *Ani l'dodi v'dodi li* — is because the way we relate to Hashem defines how we perceive the way He is relating to us. Relationships are reciprocal, as Shlomo Hamelech teaches,

> When we love someone, we feel that they love us in return, and likewise, when we resent someone, we feel that they resent us.

"*Kamayim hapanim lapanim ken lev ha'adam la'adam* — As water reflects a face back to a face, so one's heart is reflected back to him by another" (*Mishlei* 27:19). When we love someone, we feel that they love us in return, and likewise, when we resent someone, we feel that they resent us.

This principle applies to our relationship with Hashem as well. *Ani l'dodi,* if you love the Almighty, *v'dodi li,* then you'll see that the Almighty loves you. But if you have resentment — Hashem, You didn't treat me right, You don't appreciate what I've done for You, You are making my life so difficult — then you will think Hashem does not love you.

The spies are an example of this dynamic. After the spies returned from scouting the Land of Israel and gave their evil report, they complained bitterly, as the *passuk* says, "You slandered in your tents and said, 'Because of Hashem's hatred for us did He take us out of the land of Egypt, to deliver us into the hand of the Amorite to destroy us" (*Devarim* 1:27). On the words, "*Besinas Hashem osanu* — Because of Hashem's hatred for us," Rashi comments: "In reality He loves you, but *you* hate Him. As is commonly said, 'What is in your own heart about your friend, you project what is in his heart about you.'"

What you feel about your friend is what you imagine he feels toward you. The same principle applies to God. If you hate Hashem, then you think He hates you. And likewise, if you love Hashem, you will feel that He loves you. That is the meaning of *Ani l'dodi v'dodi li.* Therefore, one of the main areas to work on during the month of Elul is loving Hashem, and in turn feeling His love for you. And this week's *parashah* gives us a powerful tool to accomplish that: gratitude.

Bikkurim — The First Fruits

The beginning of the *parashah* introduces the mitzvah of *bikkurim,* bringing the first fruits of the seven species for which the Land of Israel is praised to the *Beis Hamikdash.* "You shall come to whoever will be the Kohen in those days, and you shall say to him, 'I declare today to Hashem, your God, that I have come to the Land that Hashem swore to our forefathers to give us'" (ibid. 26:3). "Hashem," you proclaim, "I came to recognize that You gave me this Land and the gift of all these abundant fruits." But that's not all you say. On the words, "*ve'amarta eilav* — and you shall say to him," Rashi explains that when you bring *bikkurim*, you should actually inform the Kohen that you are not a *kafui tovah*, an ingrate.

Why do you have to tell that to the Kohen? Isn't it enough not to *be* a *kafui tovah?* No, you must articulate it and say it out loud. Speech is a bridge from the internal to the external. Saying it out loud concretizes your thoughts and makes them real. Therefore, you have to say in the *Beis HaMikdash* — in the presence of the Almighty, to a Kohen who lives with the reality of Hashem — that the Almighty has given you gifts with no strings attached. You have to look the Kohen in the eye and convince him that you have genuine gratitude. He can tell if you mean it or not, if you are full of joy and think life is gorgeous — or not. And saying it out loud enables you to see where you are really holding, as well. There are no more pretenses.

> An essential part of a Jew's *hakaras hatov* is giving thanks to Hashem for being part of the Jewish people, the one nation that is charged with the mission of bringing morality and wisdom to the world.

After you state that you are not an ingrate, and you thank Hashem for bringing you to the Land of Israel, the Kohen takes your basket of fruit and puts it on the altar. Then, you say out loud for everybody to hear, "*Arami oved avi,* an Aramean tried to destroy my forefather..." (ibid. 26:5) — the famous section that forms the backbone of the Pesach Haggadah, and describes how Hashem took the Jewish people out of Egypt and brought them to Israel. An essential part of a Jew's *hakaras hatov*, appreciation, is giving thanks to Hashem for being part of the Jewish people, the one nation that is charged with the mission of bringing morality and wisdom to the world. "You shall rejoice with all the goodness that Hashem, your God, has given you" (ibid. 26:11) — including the privilege of being part of this great nation.

Gratitude is the foundation for every loving relationship, including our relationship with Hashem, and it is the first step to tapping into Elul's power of *Ani l'dodi v'dodi li*.

Why Curses

The *parashah* also contains the list of blessings that the Jewish people will receive if they fulfill the mitzvos, as well as the *Tochachah*, the litany of curses that describe the horrific consequences that will befall the Jewish people if they reject God and His Torah. The custom is for the *baal korei* in shul to read the *Tochachah* quietly. That forces us to wake up, pay attention, and really listen. If we listen to the Almighty, we will merit all the *berachos*.

In the midst of threatening the Jewish people with terrifying misfortunes, the Almighty says, "They will be a sign and a wonder, in you and in your offspring, forever, because you did not serve Hashem, your God, amid gladness and goodness of heart, when everything was abundant" (ibid. 28:46-47). The Torah is stating the reason for all these terrible tribulations: because you did not serve the Almighty with joy.

The Rambam (*Hilchos Succah* 8:15) explains that even if you fulfilled all the mitzvos, learned Torah day and night, and worked hard on your service of God, if you did not do it with joy, you are worthy of retribution and deserve all these curses. To some people, this may seem like a shocking statement. Hashem, what do you want? I did all Your mitzvos; I worked diligently for you. Where is the justice? All this work, and this is what I get, just because I did not do it with joy?

It is critical to remember: Hashem does not need our mitzvos. He is infinite, perfect, and there is nothing we can do for Him. He created us to give us the greatest pleasure and meaning possible. He gave us His Torah and mitzvos for our enjoyment and benefit. We mistakenly think that we are somehow helping God, doing Him a favor, by keeping kosher and observing Shabbos. And we wonder, *Where is God's gratitude?* We are like the ungrateful child who complains that he has to hold the ice cream.

> We mistakenly think that we are somehow helping God, doing Him a favor, by keeping kosher and observing Shabbos. And we wonder, *Where is God's gratitude?*

Life, Torah, mitzvos — it's all for our benefit. Gratitude and joy are the name of the game. If we complain and kvetch, if we think we are doing God a favor, we are missing the entire point of existence. *Ani l'dodi v'dodi li.* We have a Creator Who loves us, Who made us and sustains us every instant. It is essential to remember that the Almighty loves us.

You wake up in the morning and the first thing you say is, "*Modeh Ani* — Thank God I am alive." Do you mean it? Tell it to the Kohen. Speak to the Almighty, not to the wall. Don't just recite it as a formula. Recognize that life is gorgeous — and then thank the Almighty! Don't be a *kafui tovah.* Look what He gave you: He gave you life, He gave you a Torah to teach you how to maximize life, and He charged you with a unique mission in the world. And He made you part of the Jewish people, who bring meaning, wisdom, and values to the world

Ani l'dodi v'dodi li. Appreciate how wonderful it is to be alive, how wonderful it is to have a relationship with God, and how wonderful it is to have a Torah. That is real *teshuvah.* Live with gratitude and joy, and you will receive all the *berachos.*

The shofar is blowing. It says: Wake up and be real; don't do things as a robot sleepwalking through mitzvos. Feel how gorgeous life is. For the remainder of Elul, when you wake up in the morning, say *Modeh Ani* with real intent. Convince the Kohen that you mean it. Thank the Almighty for giving you the opportunity to serve Him. Connect to His love and be grateful for all the good He has given you. Say it, mean it, and it will change your life. *Ani l'dodi v'dodi li.*

If you are prepared to take the
pain, you can make the difficult
choice to overcome the yetzer hara
and the Almighty will help.

פרשת נצבים/וילך
arashas Nitzavim/Vayeilech:
Choose Life!

הַעִדֹתִי בָכֶם הַיּוֹם אֶת הַשָּׁמַיִם וְאֶת הָאָרֶץ הַחַיִּים וְהַמָּוֶת נָתַתִּי
לְפָנֶיךָ הַבְּרָכָה וְהַקְּלָלָה וּבָחַרְתָּ בַּחַיִּים לְמַעַן תִּחְיֶה ...

I call heaven and earth today to bear witness against you:
I have placed life and death before you, blessing and
curse; and you shall choose life (uvacharta bachaim),
so that you will live... (Devarim 30:19).

Choosing life is what Rosh Hashanah is all about. *Zachreinu l'chaim,* remember us for life! *Melech chafetz bachaim,* the King Who wants us to live. But it's not just Hashem Who chooses life for us on Rosh Hashanah. We have to make the choice, too.

A new year is upon us and it is time to make a reckoning. What happened this year? Although we may feel we have another 100,000 years to go, life is a finite number of years, and we need to take stock and do a *cheshbon hanefesh,* a spiritual accounting. It's time to wake up and choose life.

The first aspect of waking up is simple: Stop doing what you know the Almighty considers wrong. Are you wasting time? Are you standing in front of the Almighty in prayer without even knowing what you're asking for, without even believing He will answer you? Are you frequently losing your temper? Forgetting your learning? Are you going to continue doing these things for rest of your life?

There are so many obvious things that we know we are doing wrong. Taking stock of these things is a simple reckoning, but it requires the courage and honesty to confront ourselves and eliminate the excuses. Now that you see these mistakes, what are you going to do about them?

A second aspect of preparing for the new year is to ask yourself: What is the breakthrough I know I can achieve if I would just put my heart and soul to it? What are the next significant rungs on my ladder of growth that I should reach for? Deep down, what am I yearning to accomplish this coming year? Is it learning a *seder* of *mishnayos* by heart? Mastering a complete tractate of the Talmud? Is it getting in shape by losing 15 pounds? What goal do I want to conquer?

Don't let another year go by where you let your dreams slip away. *Uvacharta bachaim* — choose life.

Life and Death Choices

The *passuk* says, "I have placed life and death before you... choose life!" The Torah frames the essential choice of man as a choice between life and death. Why? And why does Hashem bother to instruct us to choose life? Isn't it obvious that everyone wants to live?

To answer these questions, let us take a look at the creation of man. The Torah says, "And Hashem, God, formed the man of dust from the ground, and He blew into his nostrils the soul of life; and man became a living being" (*Bereishis* 2:7). Man is a composite of a physical body and lofty spiritual soul. Both yearn to go back to their source. The body wants to escape from all pain and challenge, to experience nothing but comfort and the all-too-easy fix that comes through instant gratification. The soul yearns to grow, to reach its potential and cling to the Almighty. It craves the meaning and fulfillment that come through toil and exertion.

These two forces are waging a constant internal battle. The alarm clock rings in the morning. The soul wants to declare "*Modeh ani lefanecha*" — another day of spiritual growth and challenge. Let's seize the day! But the body says to hit the snooze button, hug the pillow, and go back to sleep. Your soul wants life; your body wants death.

Why death?

To understand the death wish that exists inside each of us, it is necessary to define the opposite of pain.

Most people answer, "Pleasure," and in doing so they are making a fundamental mistake that has serious ramifications. The opposite of pain is *not* pleasure; it is no pain. No pain equals comfort, not pleasure. Do not confuse comfort with pleasure. Comfort is the absence of pain, the numbing sensation of falling asleep. The ultimate experience of feeling no pain is death. Pleasure, on the other hand, requires pain. "*Lefum tza'ara agra* — according to the effort is the reward" (*Pirkei Avos* 5:26). Real pleasure and fulfillment come through pushing ourselves and tackling challenge. If we mistake pleasure for comfort, we will choose the pillow every time and avoid putting in the effort that will help us accomplish and actualize our potential in life.

The Talmud teaches, "R' Shimon ben Levi said: A person's evil inclination threatens to overpower him every day and seeks to kill him, as it is stated, 'The wicked one watches for the righteous and seeks to kill him' (*Tehillim* 37:32). And if not that the Holy One, blessed is He, helps the person, he would be unable to prevail against him; as it is stated: 'Hashem will not forsake him to his hand'" (ibid. v. 33) (*Kiddushin* 30b).

This is a frightening passage. The Talmud is telling us that we have a death wish, an evil inclination that seeks to kill us, and without Hashem's help we would not stand a chance. But *baruch Hashem*, God has our back. He is supporting us; we can count on Him. And no matter what rut we feel we are in, no matter what habit we feel is straitjacketing us, Hashem gives us the power to choose life. There is no such thing as the excuse, "I can't, I'm stuck." If you are prepared to take the pain, you can make the difficult choice to overcome the *yetzer hara* and the Almighty will help. *Uvacharta bachaim.*

> No matter what rut we feel we are in, no matter what habit we feel is straitjacketing us, Hashem gives us the power to choose life.

Sometimes we feel that doing *teshuvah* and fulfilling the Torah is just too hard; it does not seem attainable. But this is a trap that the *yetzer hara* throws in our path. In this week's *parashah*, the Torah directly addresses this trap: "For this commandment that I command you today — it is not hidden from you and it is not distant. It is not in heaven, for you to say, 'Who can ascend to the heaven for us and take it for us, so that we can listen to it and perform it?' Nor is it across the sea, for you to say, 'Who can cross to the other side of the sea for us and take it for us, so that we can listen to it and perform it?' Rather, the matter is very near to you — in your mouth, and in your heart — to perform it" (*Devarim* 30:11-14).

Do not let the *yetzer hara* defeat you, the Torah is saying. You have the power in your hands to choose life. It is exceedingly near to you. How near? It's right here; you don't have to go anywhere. It is "in your mouth and your heart to perform it." You have everything you need. Just hold on to that clarity, understand the difference between the trap of comfort and the exhilaration of real pleasure, and choose life.

When I was a young *yeshivah bachur*, I had a job in the summers. One summer day, when I returned from my job, my rosh yeshivah, Rav Yaakov Yitzchak Ruderman zt"l of Ner Israel, asked me, "Noach, how are you going to learn this *zman*?"

I said, "Rebbi, *im yirtzeh Hashem*, if the Almighty wills it, I'm going to accomplish great things, I'm going to learn really well."

He bent over and said to me with quiet confidence, "Noach, I arranged it already. The Almighty wants it."

My friends, it has been arranged. The Almighty wants it and is waiting for you. Wake up and live. Choose life.

The strategy for mastering Torah is to use simanim, general principles that amalgamate reams of details into an interconnected, orderly system.

פרשת האזינו

arashas Ha'azinu:

Retaining Torah

This week's *parashah* contains Moshe's enigmatic song. Chazal learn two different — but related — teachings on how to learn Torah properly, from the following *passuk:* "May my teaching drip down like the rain, may my utterance flow like the dew; like storm winds upon vegetation and like raindrops upon blades of grass" (*Devarim* 32:2).

The Talmud derives from this *passuk* that if one is not careful, Torah learning can actually kill him:

> R' Benayah said: Whoever studies Torah for its own sake, his Torah becomes an elixir of life to him.... But whoever studies Torah not for its own sake, his Torah becomes a deadly poison to him, as it says, "May my teaching drip down like the rain," and "*arifah*" [whose form "*ya'arof*" is used in this verse to mean "drip down"] means nothing other than "killing," as it says, "And they shall axe the back of the heifer's neck ['*ve'arfu*'] in the valley" (*Devarim* 21:4) (*Taanis* 7a).

Understand the power of Torah. When learned with the proper motivation, it is a *sam chaim*, an elixir of life. But if learned *lo lishmah*, not for its own sake, that same Torah will become a *sam maves*, a deadly poison. If a person's intent in learning Torah is to use it for his own selfish interests, or to sharpen his intellectual acumen to tear others down, he transforms the essence of Torah — which is *Toras Chaim*, the source of life — into a deadly toxin that drives him away from the Almighty.

> When learned with the proper motivation, the Torah is a *sam chaim*, an elixir of life. But if learned *lo lishmah*, not for its own sake, that same Torah will become a *sam maves*, a deadly poison.

Drawing on this *passuk,* Chazal shed light on a different aspect of how Torah, when not learned properly, can cause damage.

> A person should always assemble his Torah learning into general principles and extract their details, for if one leaves his learning as a collection of details, they will make him weary and he will not know what to do, as it is written, "May my teaching drip down like the rain." The word "*lekach* — teaching" refers to Torah, as it says, "For I have given you a good teaching (*lekach*), do not forsake My Torah" (*Mishlei* 4:2), and the word "*arifah* — drip down" means to gather in (*Torah Temimah, Devarim* 32:2, citing *Sifri*).

The Sifri gives a metaphor to illustrate the point. A traveler does not take his money with him in small denominations, because that would be burdensome and impractical. Rather, he changes his money into large bills, which are easily transportable and can be exchanged for smaller bills when necessary.

The Sifri is teaching a crucial lesson about how to retain your Torah effectively. The Torah is a compilation of thousands of details. If you try to store your learning as minutiae, it will become too burdensome to maintain, and exceedingly difficult to access. This will result in your forgetting much of what you have learned, which Chazal liken to a woman giving birth and burying her child (*Sanhedrin* 99a). Learning Torah will become a very painful endeavor.

What is the solution? You need to collect the myriad details into organized, summarized *klalim*: fundamental, overarching principles. This technique enables you to hold on to enormous amounts of material, and instead of it being a crushing burden, it will be a well-organized and accessible summary of any aspect of Torah you learn.

This is why our Sages teach that the strategy for mastering Torah is to use *simanim*, symbols, general principles that amalgamate reams of details into an interconnected, orderly system, as the Talmud states, "Rav Chisda said: The only way to acquire Torah is through *simanim*, as the Torah says, '*simah befihem* — place it in their mouth' (*Devarim* 31:19). Do not read it as '*simah*' [place it], but rather as '*simanah*' [its symbol]" (*Eruvin* 54b).

Pleasure Through Organization

The Ramchal, in his introduction to *Derech Hashem*, describes the power of organization and the pleasure it gives to one who learns Torah this way. It is worth reading his explanation in his own words:

> When one knows a number of things and understands how they are categorized and systematically interrelated, then he has a great advantage over one who has the same knowledge without such distinction. It is very much like the difference between looking at a well-planned garden, arranged in rows and patterns, and seeing a wild thicket or forest growing in disarray.
>
> When an individual is confronted by many details and does not know how they relate to one another or their true place in a general system, then his inquisitive intellect is given nothing more than a difficult, unsatisfying burden. He may struggle with it, but he will tire and grow weary long before he attains any gratification. Each detail will arouse his curiosity, but not having access to the concept as a whole, he will remain frustrated.

If one wishes to understand something, therefore, it is very important that he be aware of other things associated with it, as well as its place among them. Without this, one's longing for truth will be frustrated and he will be pained by his unsatisfied desire.

The opposite is true when one knows something in relation to its context. Since he sees it within its framework, he can go on to grasp other concepts associated with it, and his success will bring him pleasure and elation.

Organizing your Torah knowledge into general, interrelated principles makes long-term retention a real possibility, and causes your Torah learning to become a source of deep pleasure and gratification.

Organizing your Torah knowledge into general, interrelated principles makes long-term retention a real possibility, and causes your Torah learning to become a source of deep pleasure and gratification.

Learn the Rambam

When Rav Weinberg was an 18-year-old *yeshivah bachur*, he asked Rav Ruderman, the venerated rosh yeshivah of Baltimore's Ner Israel, how he had mastered all of *Shas*, the entire Talmud. Rav Ruderman told him that in Poland he could not learn Torah at night, by candlelight, due to his poor eyesight. Instead he would take long walks in the Polish forest and review pages of Gemara that he had memorized. That is how he mastered the Talmud.

Rav Ruderman was a *yeshivah bachur* in a *shtetl* in prewar Poland. Rav Noach was a *yeshivah bachur* in America in the 1950s. How could he possibly employ the same strategy as Rav Ruderman? His frustration drove him to seek a solution, until he stumbled upon the above Sifri about the importance of structuring Torah learning into *simanim*. Rav Weinberg realized then that the Rambam's *Mishnah Torah* is a comprehensive, highly organized structure of all of *Torah Shebe'al Peh*, the Oral Law, and by mastering it and memorizing *simanim* — one-word summaries that encapsulate the subject matter — for each of its 1000 chapters, a student could realistically attain proficiency in all of its fundamental principles.

This is why Rabbi Weinberg always encouraged his students to learn the entire *Mishnah Torah* and memorize its 1000 *simanim*. It is the difference between experiencing pain, frustration, and forgetfulness in learning versus deep-seated satisfaction, pleasure, and success in retaining one's Torah learning. Rabbi Weinberg believed that after mastering the Rambam, one could learn all of *Shas*, because he now had a platform that made it accessible.

By leaving the palace, Moshe pushed himself beyond his comfort zone. He transcended the familiar and had the courage and grit to wade into unknown territory.

פרשת וזאת הברכה
arashas Vezos Haberachah: Moshe's Leadership

With the kiss of God, Moshe Rabbeinu, the greatest Jewish leader in history, leaves this world, and the Chumash comes to an end. As a tribute to the person who brought us the Torah, let us take a closer look at what made Moshe a great leader and try to apply those timeless principles to our own lives.

To understand Moshe's ascent to greatness, we need to refer back to Parashas Shemos: "It happened in those days that Moshe grew up, and he went out to his brothers and observed their burdens; and he saw an Egyptian man striking a Hebrew man, of his brethren. He turned this way and that and saw that there was no man, so he struck down the Egyptian and hid him in the sand" (*Shemos* 2:11-12).

Since the previous verse (v. 10) already informs us that "the boy grew up," these two *pesukim* must be describing Moshe's spiritual growth, with each phrase conveying additional insights into his trajectory.

"Vayeitzei — and he went out"

Moshe grew up in the palace of Pharaoh, in the lap of luxury and royalty. By leaving the palace, Moshe pushed himself beyond his comfort zone. He transcended the familiar and had the courage and grit to wade into unknown territory that was replete with risks and challenges. It is never comfortable to be a leader, and if you do not consciously decide to forgo a life of comfort you will resent the burdens that leadership entails.

"El echav — to his brothers"

Moshe was raised as Pharaoh's adopted grandson, yet he cast his lot with the downtrodden nation Pharaoh was enslaving. His ability to embrace these battered slaves as "his brothers" represents an enormous spiritual journey on his part, one that involved recasting his entire identity and transforming his vision of the world. Leaders need to be fiercely independent, to think out of the box, and to provide a compelling vision that will galvanize the nation and inspire change.

"Vayar besivlosam — and he observed their burdens"

Rashi explains that Moshe directed his eyes and his heart to feel distress over the Jewish people. It is an active choice to fight your natural self-centeredness and genuinely feel another person's pain. And feeling that pain is the linchpin that motivates you to act.

As an illustration, imagine it is 1941 and you find out that thousands of Jews are being herded onto trains and transported to a concentration camp. Would you drop everything you are doing and try to save some Jewish lives?

When this scenario is presented to an audience, invariably only a smattering of people raise their hands. The vast majority would do nothing.

Now change the scenario slightly: Imagine it is 1941 and you are from a small town in Eastern Europe. Your parents have sent you to North America to study or work and you discover that your entire hometown — your parents, grandparents, siblings, neighbors — are all being herded onto a train headed toward a concentration camp. Would you drop everything you are doing and try to save their lives?

No question, of course you would.

What is the difference between the two scenarios? Objectively speaking, does it make any difference if the woman sitting on that train is your mother or some other Jew's mother? Jewish people are heading toward a concentration camp! The reality is exactly the same in both scenarios. The only difference is that when it is your family on the train, you feel the pain, and you lose sleep at night. The reality of the situation compels you to take responsibility and act.

If people do not put in the effort to transcend their self-absorption and feel the pain of others, they would, in all likelihood, turn their heads away from a holocaust and not do anything to help.

The ramifications of this are sobering. If people do not put in the effort to transcend their self-absorption and feel the pain of others, they would, in all likelihood, turn their heads away from a holocaust and not do anything to help. They would just go about their lives, oblivious to reality.

In order to properly structure our priorities and accurately perceive reality, we must feel the pain of our brethren and truly care about their well-being, both physical and spiritual. Imagine it was your brother or sister engaged to a non-Jew; there is no question you would be motivated to act. Feeling another's pain is the key to leadership, because it means you have no agenda other than what is good for the people. This selflessness builds trust between you and others and determines the degree to which they will follow your lead.

"Vayifen koh vachoh — he looked this way and that and saw that there was no man"

Before taking decisive action, Moshe first looked to see if there was anyone else tackling the job. He was prepared to move aside if someone was already on the scene, since he was not asserting himself out of a need to boost his own ego. His sole concern was ensuring that the problem at hand be dealt with effectively; his personal role was irrelevant. (See essay on Parashas Tetzaveh.)

Humility is the essence of being an effective leader, because it allows you to rise above your self-interest and do what Hashem demands from you. Since a person driven by ego is more concerned with his quest for power than with the well-being of the people he is ostensibly leading, it is only a matter of time before he loses the respect of the people.

The humble leader has the courage to tackle daunting challenges because he knows that ultimately, the outcome of his efforts hinges not on his power, but on Hashem's.

Humility also enables a leader to tap into a power far greater than his own. The humble leader has the courage to tackle daunting challenges because he knows that ultimately, the outcome of his efforts hinges not on his power, but on Hashem's. And that courage, in turn, engenders charisma.

Many people entertain the misconception that humility means being meek and self-effacing. Imagine the most humble person in the world walking into the room. In your mind's eye, whom do you picture? Chances are it is a timid, anxious person that no one really notices. Yet the Torah tells us, "Now the man Moshe was exceedingly humble, more than any person on the face of the earth" (*Bamidbar* 12:3). Imagine Moshe Rabbeinu walking into the room. His incredibly powerful presence would cause every head to turn. It is no accident that the most humble of all people was also the greatest leader. When the ego is out of the way, a person can become a conduit for Hashem's power.

"Vayach es hamitzri — so he struck down the Egyptian"

Moshe took responsibility and acted boldly and decisively. He understood the true meaning of the Talmudic principle that each person must say, "*Bishvili nivra ha'olam* — the world was created for me" (*Sanhedrin* 37a). Each of us is responsible for the entire world; we are Hashem's caretakers. If we see a problem, we cannot pass the buck. Leaders know that greatness comes through shouldering responsibility. As the cycle of reading the Torah comes to an end and we begin *Bereishis* anew, let us turn our hearts and minds to the great challenges and opportunities Hashem has placed squarely upon each of us: "The hidden are for Hashem, our God, but the revealed are for us and our children forever, to carry out all the words of this Torah" (*Devarim* 29:28).

> Each of us is responsible for the entire world; we are Hashem's caretakers. If we see a problem, we cannot pass the buck.